THIS IS REAL

Alex could hear faint talking, and the footsteps growing nearer. His heart beat wildly with each wet scrape of shoe on gravel. It beat so fast there was ringing in his ears. With each footstep, Alex grew more excited. He held the rope taut between his hands, his muscles fully flexed. *This is real. . . This is real.*

The footsteps came closer and closer until Alex could see two shadowy figures in front of him.

David stopped and glanced quickly toward Alex. Adrenaline surging, Alex leaped from the bushes. Kim jumped back and turned to see who it was, recognizing Alex in the shadows.

"You scared me," she said, annoyed. And in a moment she started up the path again.

This time she walked alone.

David cut Alex a look of intense anticipation. *You gotta do it*, Alex told himself. *You've gotta kill this person. No matter what, do whatever Dave says.*

DEADLY SECRETS

FROM HIGH SCHOOL TO HIGH CRIME—THE TRUE STORY OF TWO TEEN KILLERS

PUTSATA REANG

AVON BOOKS

An Imprint of HarperCollinsPublishers

DEADLY SECRETS is a journalistic account of the actual murder investigations of David Anderson and Alex Baranyi for the 1997 killings of Bill, Rose, Kim, and Julia Wilson in Bellevue, Washington. The personalities, events, actions, and conversations portrayed in this book have been reconstructed by the author using court records, personal interviews, newspaper reports, and Alex Baranyi's own recollections.

AVON BOOKS
An Imprint of HarperCollins*Publishers*
10 East 53rd Street
New York, New York 10022-5299

Copyright © 2001 by Putsata Reang
ISBN: 0-380-80087-X
www.avonbooks.com

First Avon Books paperback printing: March 2001

Avon Trademark Reg. U.S. Pat. Off. and in Other Countries, Marca Registrada, Hecho en U.S.A.
HarperCollins® is a trademark of HarperCollins Publishers Inc.

Printed in the U.S.A.

10 9 8 7 6 5 4 3 2 1

To the Wilsons

Acknowledgments

No one ever accomplishes anything alone. There were many people who helped in so many ways with this project. I would first like to thank my agents, Mary Alice Kier and Anna Cottle, for believing in me and this project enough to secure my first book contract. I would also like to thank my original editor, Stephen Power, a meticulous line editor who guided me through the book's earliest and roughest drafts, and Sarah Durand at HarperCollins, for her encouragement and enthusiasm as she shepherded this project through its final stages.

Jan Johnson, my lifelong mentor, provided early insight and feedback before the first chapters were ever written, and I cannot thank her enough for that. I want to thank Keiko Morris, Mary Rothschild, Ian Ith, and John Deleon at the *Seattle Times*, my parents Khen and Sam-Ou Reang, and my sister Sinaro Reang for their unyielding support and encouragement. Thanks also to King County Superior Court Judge Jeffrey Ramsdell, Emelyn and Rick Rodriguez, Barbara Dunshee, Tyrone Beason, Peter Aronson, Elliott Almond, Reva Kindser, Duff Wilson, Paula Bock, Justino Aguila, Meg Heffernan, Judith and Glenn Mason, and Dan and Elsa Distelhorst. I am forever grateful to Penny De Los Santos for her help and friendship.

Finally, I could not have written this book without the generous support and cooperation of Bellevue Police Detectives Jeff Gomes, Bob Thompson, and Jerry Johnson, and King County Prosecutors Patricia Eakes and Jeff Baird. Thanks to Jacquie and Jerry Mahoney, who have suffered an unimaginable loss, and who allowed me to procure photographs for this book.

   A special thank-you to my sister Chanira Reang for carrying me through the tumult of recent years.

Author's Note

When adults kill, motives are often traditional and tangible: jealousy, greed, revenge. But when kids kill, motives can be less obvious, and warning signs are often overlooked.

David Anderson and Alex Baranyi, the teenagers involved in this case, did not have criminal records and did not come from single-parent homes or inner-city neighborhoods—common indicators of a troubled youth's background. Instead, they grew up in a privileged, family-focused suburb and attended good schools. One went to church and played on a city league baseball team, and the other had an above-average IQ and was a gifted artist. These are things which make their crime, and the motives behind it, all the more complex.

As an experienced newspaper reporter, I've covered a wide range of crimes and violence, but nothing as brutal and senseless as the murders detailed in this book. While working for newspapers in Oregon and Washington, I reported on stabbings, shootings, and beatings by teenagers barely on the verge of adulthood. At the *Seattle Times*, I became part of a team of reporters who covered the Wilson family homicide case, and was the only one to follow the story through the trials of David Anderson and Alex Baranyi.

We may never know or begin to understand what moti-vated these two seventeen-year-olds to plan and carry out the murders of four innocent people. But while covering this case and other murder cases, I learned that it is possible to find clues by digging deep into the lives of the individuals involved.

To do that, I interviewed friends and classmates of David and Alex, and immersed myself into the late-night Gothic scene at Denny's, where teenagers like them gathered to kill time by drinking coffee and chain-smoking as they talked until the early-morning hours. I also conducted extensive in-terviews with Alex Baranyi in jail in the months before and after his murder trial. From behind a glass partition in a vis-itor's booth, he spoke candidly of the crime, his life, and his intense relationship with his best friend, David Anderson.

From a combination of court records, personal interviews, newspaper reports, and Alex's own recollections, I have carefully pieced together an account of this quadruple mur-der case as accurately and fairly as possible.

Prologue

Sunlight, on the fourth of January 1997, broke over the Washington suburb of Bellevue like a flood lamp suddenly switched on, shattering the oppressive dark of winter. For weeks, the Northwest had been drenched in depressing grays and blacks; there was no telling dusk from day. The ground was covered with rotting remains—leaves, mostly, and flowers, grass, anything that, months prior, had been sun-dusted, vibrant. A crisp chill hung in the air. But everyone in Bellevue—and in nearby Seattle, for that matter—was used to the damp days that smeared across so much of the calendar year.

The sun was a welcoming break. It was still cold outside, but there was light, and that was good enough for two boys winding their way through a Saturday and a labyrinth of trails in Water Tower Park.

The park—a small tract of trees and trails—was anchored almost precisely in the middle of Bellevue's Woodridge Hill neighborhood. Its giant blue-green water tank served as a beacon of sorts, hovering over the 1,000 residents of this sheltered community. Hemmed in by Interstate 405 to the west, Interstate 90 to the south, and a stack of hills to the north and east, Woodridge was a self-enclosed island of hills whose highest structure was the water tower. It stood directly across the street from Woodridge Elementary School, where clutches of energetic children zipped up in multicolored winter coats burst out of minivans each morning in an explosion of youthful energy. Their laughter cut through the air, silenced only by the piercing blare of the school bell.

The neighborhood had always been this way—full of families. Full of life. Children on bikes and skateboards rode wide circles around their block all day, every day, even in the rain. Mothers hired nannies to help dress their kids and sweep the front porch, and on weekends, gardeners planted bulbs and trimmed hedges. A former enclave for the rich, Woodridge is now tattered and aging, home to a mix of upper-middle- and middle-class families. The less affluent families have snatched up starter homes at the base of the hill, while the well-to-do still perch at the top, where they enjoy panoramic views of downtown Bellevue and, farther west, Seattle's skyline. Many homes near the bottom of the hill have been left in varying states of decay by owners who are too busy with work and raising families. Uncut lawns crawl out into the streets, paint has faded to many shades lighter, and gardens are overrun with hungry weeds. Yet Woodridge has always been a desirable place in which to live. The neighborhood's two primary real estate agents kept long lists of families who waited patiently for retired Boeing engineers and Microsoft computer analysts to die so they could move in. For the most part, that was the only way to acquire a home there.

Just about everyone who grew up in Woodridge had, at one time or another, played at Water Tower Park. It was considered everyone's second backyard. By day, the park was populated by grade school kids and stay-at-home parents who strolled along the trails with their dogs. But at night, the park swirled with currents of activity generated by the neighborhood's teenage population. It filled with the beady eyes and nervous whispers of adolescents who gathered there to gossip, smoke pot, drink, and make out. Bellevue's teenage population had long complained that there was nothing to do in their suburban town; there was nowhere for them to go at night. They groused about boredom, that sort of youthful malaise that brought droves of teens to the malls and parks where they lingered long after closing hours. To escape the prying eyes of adults and the claws of authority, they went out into the darkness, to places like Water Tower Park.

It was at night that the park took on a sinister sheen. Wind hissed cold secrets through the feathery cedar branches, and shadows folded into each other along the darkened lawns. Every now and then, the shriek of a cat penetrated the cool night air.

On that Saturday, January 4, the park released its first secret.

Nathan Richard Keech, a skinny, dark-haired twelve-year-old, and three of his friends, Robbie, Travis, and Yuri, were taking advantage of the sun-bleached morning, ambling along the trails that cut through the park.

Nathan lived just a block away. He played there often, wearing down the various paths that braided through it. On that day, like many others, the kids were using the park as a shortcut to Robbie's house.

The boys walked in a crooked line as they made their way south along the western side of the park. Nathan was the last in line. The trail descended a slight hill and led to a gravel parking lot—the main entrance to Water Tower Park. As the boys tramped along, the wet gravel crunched under their feet. Everything else was silent.

About midway through the park, past a grove of rhododendron bushes thick with leaves, they came to a short flight of steps. Robbie, Travis, and Yuri had already bounded down the steps when Nathan suddenly noticed a patch of blue. The color was out of place amid all the green shrubbery. Curious, Nathan stopped on the last step and glanced toward a leafy cedar tree. He could see a little more clearly now. The blue thing was lying about five feet off the trail. It didn't look like much. Just a pile of clothes. Or maybe someone sleeping, though it was a strange place to nap in the dead of winter.

"Hey, guys, there's something over there," Nathan said.

The boys stopped and doubled back toward him.

"Over there, see it?" Nathan pointed in the direction of the trees.

"Yeah, what is it?" the boys asked.

Unsure of what he had found, Nathan sensed that he should stop and make sure everything was fine.

"Are you okay?" he shouted, remaining about ten feet from the object.

The thing didn't respond.

"Hey, are you okay?" Nathan called out, a little louder this time.

Still, no response.

"It's probably just a mannequin," one of the boys said. "Let's go."

Nathan was still staring hard at the object, but agreed with his friends that it probably wasn't anything to get too worked up over. The boys turned away and trudged back onto the trail and out of the park.

The next morning—on Sunday—Nathan and Yuri went back to the park to see if the thing had moved.

Stopping again at the bottom of the steps, the boys looked to their left. How strange, they thought, that the mannequin was still there. No one had come by to remove it. The boys stepped slowly off the trail, moving in to get a better look. Suddenly, they saw what looked like a human hand.

The boys carefully pushed aside a few tree branches and crouched down. The closer they got—this time stopping about a yard away from the object—the clearer it became. The object on the ground wasn't a bundle of clothes or a mannequin; it was a person.

Nathan and Yuri turned and looked at each other, their eyes wide with fear.

"What should we do?" Nathan asked, his voice spiked with panic.

"Don't know." Yuri got up, his eyes fixed on the body.

"Get a stick. Let's see if it moves," Nathan suggested.

The boys backed away from it and found a stick a few feet off. Nathan whacked the tree and ground with the stick, hoping the noise would rouse the figure. Both boys kept a safe distance in case the person was still alive.

"Are you okay!" Nathan shouted as he slammed the stick against the ground.

Nathan couldn't tell for sure whether the person was a man or a woman. It had on baggy blue jeans, a sweatshirt, and boots, and to him, these looked like something a man would wear.

Nathan poked the left arm. If the thing were really a mannequin, the limb would be hard. But when Nathan prodded the object, the tip of the stick pushed gently inward. The skin yielded.

The person, whoever it was, did not respond or twitch a hand. The boys listened for breathing, but all they heard was the nervous pitter-patter of their own hearts.

Scared and confused, they dashed out of the park and raced home to Nathan's mom.

During the week, Susan Matney, a petite woman with long auburn hair, worked as a technical editor for a Bellevue computer company. But right now, she was doing laundry and cleaning the house when the front door was flung open and her son, Nathan, ran inside, followed closely by their neighbors' son, Yuri.

"Mom! Mom! There's a man at the park!" Nathan

shouted, words firing out of his mouth as he tried to catch his breath. "I think he fell or something. He's lying on the ground."

"Okay. Just calm down," Susan said.

Susan had never seen her son so anxious. Whatever he had found had clearly frightened him.

She, too, was very familiar with the park, as was her older child, Naomi. She was aware that it was a popular hangout for teenagers who wanted to smoke and drink. She heard the partying late at night, and on occasion her neighbors had called the cops to complain about the noise. She figured it was only a matter of time before someone got hurt there.

"Where did you see him?" Susan asked.

"Under a tree," Nathan gasped. He explained how he had seen the man in the same spot the day before while walking through the park.

Susan got dressed and followed her son and Yuri out to the park in order to see for herself what the boys were so upset about.

Within a few minutes, Susan was standing at the top of the steps along the trail where Nathan and Yuri had found the man on the ground.

"You guys stay right here, okay?" She instructed the boys.

Susan had a difficult time finding the person lying hidden in a thick wall of shrubbery. But as she moved off the trail and into the cedar grove, she got a perfect view.

She could just make out a figure, but from where she was standing, it was hard for her to see much else. The person was lying facedown with its back toward the trail. The left arm was twisted behind its back.

Susan walked cautiously up the hill and into the bushes.

"Are you okay? Are you okay?" she shouted, but each time there was no response, not even the slightest movement.

Inching her way closer, Susan stopped just near enough to reach for the person's wrist to take a pulse. There was none.

She felt a catch in her breath. The man was dead.

She shuddered and frantically went out to search for her son.

"Nathan, go home and tell Naomi to call nine-one-one," Susan yelled, retreating from under the tree. "Tell her someone died in the park. We need some help."

As she heard the footsteps of her son and his friend slowly fade, Susan wondered what to do next.

Just to be sure the person was not alive, Susan went back up the slope to check one more time. The figure was dressed in what looked like men's clothing. She could see why her son thought it was a man. But after brushing a wave of blond hair from the person's face, she realized it was a woman. Susan placed two fingers on her neck to check her pulse. Again, nothing.

Susan was about to return to the trail when she noticed a checkbook protruding from the young woman's back pocket. Instinctively, she pulled it out to see whom it belonged to. According to the checkbook, the woman was Kimberly Wilson, from San Diego. How odd that someone from San Diego would wind up dead in Woodridge, she thought.

Kimberly Wilson. Susan had never heard the name before. But since it was Christmas, maybe she was a college student home for the holidays. Maybe she had been out with some friends to celebrate and had overdosed on drugs.

As Susan shuffled out onto the trail, she heard voices coming from a home nearby.

"Hello!" Susan called out. "Hello . . . there's a body out here. Could someone please call nine-one-one."

The neighbors yelled back that they would. Susan stood

alone on the trail, hoping the cops would get there soon. All
she could do was wait and wonder.

The call to Bellevue Police dispatchers came in at 11 A.M.
The precinct sat on a tree-lined street just east of downtown
Bellevue known as "Auto Row" because of the string of car
dealers that sprawled on either side. The call came in as a
"body found"—which could mean just about anything. Perhaps a drunken bum had collapsed or some addict had overdosed, or maybe it was a suicide. There were few police
calls to this neighborhood, fewer still to the specific location
where the body was found, in a popular neighborhood park.
Though the call raised a few eyebrows among the dispatchers on duty that day, it was nothing more than routine.

Detective Robert Thompson was driving through the
small town of Snohomish, just northeast of Seattle. He and
his wife were looking for a place to have lunch when his
pager went off just before noon. A forty-two-year-old tall,
slender man with short blond hair and a boyish face, he was
used to getting paged at any time of the day and stopping
whatever he was doing to head into work. He dialed the
number that popped up and spoke with a Bellevue Police
Department dispatcher who told him that a body had been
found at a park in the Woodridge neighborhood. The first detective on the scene, Jerry Johnson, was requesting assis-
tance.

Thompson didn't hesitate. He turned his car around and
dropped off his wife at their nearby home, then continued on
to Bellevue.

Thompson knew the neighborhood well from his early
days working in the Bellevue Police Department. When he'd
shown up at the department in 1982, Thompson started in
the patrol division, where he was assigned a section of
Bellevue to watch over. Woodridge was one of those areas,

so he didn't need a map now to point him in the right direction.

When Thompson arrived at the park just after noon, he noticed yellow crime-scene tape wrapped around a small portion of the park. He shook his head, frustrated at the apparent lack of precaution his colleagues had taken to secure the scene. The entire park should have been cordoned off by now. Like all good cops, Thompson had been trained to treat every death investigation as a crime scene. In this park, there was no telling where the potential crime scene began or ended, and crucial pieces of evidence might be lying scattered all over the place.

Thompson got out of his patrol car and made a beeline toward Johnson, who was standing in the parking lot talking to officers and bystanders.

Tall and trim, with salt-and-pepper hair and rectangular wire-rim glasses, Johnson had worked for the Bellevue Police Department for fourteen years, the last year of which he spent working directly with Thompson in the Crimes Against Persons Unit. Their professional lives paralleled. Both men had entered law enforcement in the late '70s. When they arrived in Bellevue, they worked together in the patrol unit. They moved to the narcotics division around the same time, and both wound up in the detectives unit, Thompson in '94 and Johnson a year later.

"There's a woman around the corner," Johnson said. "Some kids were here yesterday and saw a pile of clothes. They came back today and found out it was a body."

Thompson nodded his head, but said he would first have to get a roll of yellow tape and seal off the rest of the park.

In his almost fifteen years with the Bellevue Police Department, the last three of which had been investigating crimes against people, Thompson had learned that one mistake in a criminal investigation could jeopardize an entire case. He learned not to screw up, to use an overabundance of caution rather than too little.

Before going to see the body, Thompson taped off practically the entire park so no one could get in. A crucial step in criminal investigations is making sure the crime scene stays uncontaminated. No one but those involved in the investigation would be allowed inside the restricted areas.

Thompson then followed Johnson a few yards inside to check out the body. Although he had seen many dead bodies by then, Thompson had learned to never make assumptions about how a person had died. In police work, cops never exactly know the cause of death until the investigation is complete, and even then, in many cases, the how and the why remain mysteries. However, they do have hunches, and some clues at the scene can help investigators rule out certain scenarios.

Bob Thompson had investigated all manners of deaths, from suicides to accidents to homicides. One of his first assignments as a rookie in the Tri-Cities, Washington, area was to sit on a couch next to a dead man who had blown his own face off with a shotgun. He'd had to wait for the medical examiners to come and take the body away. That assignment had taught him well how to harden himself against gruesome scenes.

Thompson walked up the gravel trail and studied the body from the path. The woman appeared young. Thompson wondered where she came from. He scanned the area and took note of the position of her body, how she lay facedown in the dirt against the slope. He walked up the slope and stood on a patch of lawn above the body, looking for any disturbance in the dirt that could help explain how she got there. Maybe she fell down the hill and hit her head against a rock, knocking herself unconscious. But there were no marks. The grass above the woman's body had no indentations or skid marks.

Either she had died where she lay, or someone had dumped her there.

Thompson noted that the woman was fully clothed, and there were no apparent signs of trauma to her body. Her clothes were soiled, probably from being exposed, but they didn't look disheveled or torn. On the surface, it looked like a suicide.

Detective Johnson searched the woman's body for identification. Apparently, all she had on her was the checkbook that Susan Matney had pulled out of her back pocket. Johnson noticed a belt with a leather loop, the kind used to attach wallets, but there was nothing on it.

There was no way to tell how the woman had died until the King County Medical Examiners arrived and closely checked out the body.

It didn't take long for investigators from the ME's Office to reach the park. Medical Investigator Arleigh Marquis and Medical Examiner Kathy Raven were on duty that Sunday. Marquis snapped on a pair of latex gloves and, with help from Detective Johnson, rolled the body over.

When Marquis and Raven began inspecting the body, Thompson saw something that instantly changed his initial thoughts about the cause of death: a piece of braided rope, about a quarter of an inch thick, was twined tightly around the young woman's neck.

He immediately raised his eyes to the tree branches above him, searching for some sort of sign that this was a suicide.

"I remember looking in the tree thinking, 'I hope there's a rope broken off someplace to explain this,'" Thompson later recalled. "When there wasn't, I'm thinking, 'This is a homicide.'"

PART ONE

The Bodies

1 January 5, 1997 was forty-five degrees, cold and dewy, the kind of day better spent indoors with hot chocolate and a good book. Detective Jeff Gomes was busy in his shop behind his family's Woodinville home, dismantling a classic car. He had bought the broken-down vehicle just a few weeks earlier and was beginning his first attempt at rebuilding an old car. The holiday season had been unusually quiet as far as crime went in Bellevue. He hoped that trend would continue.

Gomes turned on some Hawaiian music and popped open a can of beer. It was his way of relaxing on his day off—listening to the tunes from back home, and pursuing a new hobby. But an afternoon phone call from one of his partners quickly brought an end to that peaceful day.

Gomes instantly recognized the friendly yet authoritative voice of Bob Thompson.

"Some kids found a body at a park in Woodridge. This one's yours," Thompson said.

Many police agencies across the country use rotation schedules among their top detectives to decide who gets to lead major investigations. Bellevue's police department was no different. Although the three members of the department's Crimes Against Persons Unit—Gomes, Thompson, and Jerry Johnson—inevitably worked together on every murder case, the men took turns serving as the point man for each case.

Gomes stripped off his coveralls, grabbed his car keys, and rushed out the door.

The drive to Bellevue from Woodinville, a piney suburb ringed by farmland, takes half an hour or more during rush hour. But on that Sunday afternoon, there was hardly any traffic. During the quick fifteen-minute drive that day, he scrolled through his mind a list of resources he would need to investigate the death. Like Thompson, Gomes knew Woodridge well from his own years of working patrol for the BPD. It was a clean, quiet place that had existed for years untouched by any major crimes. But tragedy doesn't discriminate. Gomes learned that long ago; his work took him from the city's worst neighborhoods to its best, chasing criminals both rich and poor, young and old.

As Gomes was making his way to Woodridge, King County Deputy Prosecutor Patricia Eakes was holed up in her office in downtown Seattle, scrambling to finish last-minute details on a major case that was about to go to trial. The fifth floor of the courthouse was empty. Built in 1914, the gray brick-and-granite structure hunkers on a slight hill on the southern flanks of downtown. It sits on a block whose corners and alleyways are populated by Seattle's street people—a sundry collection of drug addicts, homeless men and women and runaway teens.

The thirty-three-year-old prosecutor had come in on her day off to have some quiet in which to work. Thin and fit, Eakes had a subtle copper complexion that hinted at her Filipina blood. She was a tireless employee when it came to prosecuting any case. Days without interruptions were hard to come by during the workweek, and she wanted time alone to add some final touches to her case.

The Cronin and Roberts trial was set to begin in less than two weeks. The case involved two Canadian men who had escaped from prison and murdered a man in a community just north of Seattle. (Both men were eventually found guilty. One was sentenced to life imprisonment; the other received the death penalty.) The last thing Eakes needed was another huge case. But like the BPD, the King County Prosecutor's Office uses a rotation schedule among its prosecutors for handling major criminal cases. Eakes was up next.

At around 2:30 P.M., Eakes' pager beeped. She dialed the number and spoke to Lieutenant Jim Gasperetti of the Bellevue Police Department.

"Some kids found a body at a park in Bellevue, over in the Woodridge neighborhood," Gasperetti said evenly. "Could be a suicide. There's rope around her neck."

"Okay, I'll be right out." Eakes got off the phone and called home to talk with her husband, Mike Gray.

"I'm heading over to Bellevue." She would be a little late for dinner, she told him. "Looks like a suicide."

It was certainly possible. In the seven years she had been a prosecutor, Eakes had become used to answering calls in the middle of the night about bodies being found. She would hurry out to the scene, only to find someone had hanged himself or taken too many hits of cocaine. Unjaded, she was still eager to see for herself what had been discovered in Bellevue. Part of the excitement about her job was never knowing what she'd get into next.

As Gomes got off the freeway and headed into the Woodridge section, his mind began racing. A body in Woodridge? He couldn't remember when a body had ever been found in that part of town.

Gomes had worked for the Bellevue Police Department for two decades, starting as an intern fresh out of the police academy and then landing a full-time job in the traffic division. He had a well-rounded training background that included a stint on the SWAT team and a brief stint at a boot camp to learn about bomb investigations. He had only about a year in age and experience on Thompson. Tall and handsome with thick black hair, a full mustache, and mocha-colored skin, Gomes was considered his department's fashion guru, always wearing designer suits with matching tie and socks, and dress shoes. However svelte he appeared, he was an excellent cop and had built a reputation as a hard worker, thorough in his investigations, a master at precision. These qualities had earned him a promotion in later years to Accident Reconstruction and then Crimes Against Persons, the department he was working in on January 5, 1997.

Like most cops, Gomes had been in the business long enough, and had seen enough horrific crimes, to become hardened to the tragedies.

"You gotta have a hard shell to survive out there," he would later say. In order to survive, he had trained himself to separate his own life from the crimes he investigated, but sometimes they hit too close to home. Every now and again, there would be a crime so unspeakable and egregious, a victim so close in age, so similar to family and friends, that it would leave a new map of emotion on his face—rigid lines of grief etched in tight rows above his brows. Like many of his colleagues, Gomes used a dark humor to shield against the horrors he saw. Over the years, he had come to be known as his department's wise guy.

Gomes had become an expert in accident reconstruction. His meticulous attention to detail and his organizational skills made him perfect for the job. He had worked on one of Bellevue's most notorious homicide cases ever—a case involving an eighteen-year-old young man, Atif Rafay, and his best friend, Sebastian Burns, who were accused of bludgeoning to death Atif's parents and sister for an inheritance that would have equaled less than half a million dollars.

In 1994, police were called out to the Rafays' posh hilltop home in Bellevue's upper-class Somerset neighborhood. There they found Atif's parents in one room and his teenage sister in another room. Each had been brutally beaten. The killers made it look like a botched burglary: the furniture was turned over and the electronics were ripped out of the wall. At the time of publication this case was in the trial process.

Although it had happened years ago, the brutality of those slayings was something that had seared in Gomes' mind. Nothing could ever compare. Or so he thought.

Even though the sun had now reappeared, the plants were still wet and the ground saturated with dew. The sun filtered through the leaves as Gomes worked his way past several police cars, an ambulance, two county medical examiners, and a collection of curious onlookers. He stopped where the two MEs and his partners were standing and saw under a canopy of cedar branches the body of a young woman. Early twenties. White. Short blond hair. Dressed in blue jeans, and a sweat shirt over a plaid shirt matted to her body with the sticky seal of the previous night's rain. Clearly, she had been dead for some time. A piece of braided rope was twined tight around the folds of her neck, tied in a double knot, the way a kid would tie shoelaces. To Gomes, it looked like a piece of clothesline. The young woman's clothes were dirty, but not ripped. It appeared as if she had merely slipped down the hill. There were no signs of a struggle. Except on her face, which was dirty and bruised. Patches of black-and-blue marks covered her cheeks like continents on a map. It looked as if someone had beaten her with his fist. Again and again.

What a waste, Gomes thought. She looked so young, so bruised and broken, yet someone's daughter.

Detective Jerry Johnson had been working to track down whether the Kimberly Wilson who owned the checkbook had any local connections. He ran the woman's name through a series of computer databases and came up with a local address that matched.

"Gomes, you might want to check this out. Might be her family," Johnson said, handing the address to Gomes.

A Wilson family lived nearby, at 1521 121st Avenue Southeast, not even a half mile from where he was standing at Water Tower Park. Computer records showed that a Kimberly Wilson had lived at that address in the past. Gomes had no idea whether the Kimberly Wilson in the park was the same one who lived at the nearby address, but it was a starting point. He decided to go to the home to inform any potential survivors of the young woman of her death. He also wanted to get more information about her.

The body was lifted onto a gurney and carted away. Now came the hard part: delivering the bad news. Gomes got in his patrol car with Prosecutor Eakes and headed to the home to notify family members of the death. Marquis and Raven, from the Medical Examiner's Office, were already on their way with the body inside their van. As a matter of procedure, Gomes would have to ask Kimberly Wilson's survivors—if there were any—to identify her body.

No matter how many times Gomes delivered bad news, it was never easy telling people that someone in their family had just died. Sometimes they would stumble backward, shaking their heads and holding trembling hands to their mouths to catch the screams before they escaped. Other times they would simply stare wide-eyed, looking through the cop as if they were unable to understand. Occasionally, there was no one left to tell.

It was barely a three-minute cruise from Water Tower Park to 121st Avenue Southeast. The area was a typical suburban enclave: manicured lawns, minivans and Oldsmobiles hunched in winding driveways, and bright homes lined with flower beds. Police had responded to an occasional call of a car or home break-in, even vandalism. But never a murder victim, at least not in recent memory.

Gomes came to a stop at a well-maintained white, wood-frame, three-story structure. There were no lights on, except for the Christmas lights decorating the house, and the curtains on the ground floor were drawn, shutting out the possible shapes of family life. It was an average suburban home with trimmed trees and freshly swept walkways.

Immediately, something caught Gomes' attention. Two cars were parked in the driveway and another one was in front of the house, on the street. A golden retriever lay in the front yard.

The dog whimpered quietly but didn't bark as the four strangers—Gomes, Eakes, and the two MEs—approached the house. That was odd, Eakes thought to herself. Golden retrievers were known to fiercely protect their owners and their owners' property, but this dog didn't seem to care about the strangers wandering around the house that day. Only hours later did anyone notice blood on its body.

It was an eerie scene that gave Gomes a sinking feeling. Something wasn't right.

He knocked once on the white double doors. No answer. He knocked again, and paused before ringing the doorbell. Still no answer.

Thinking it odd, Gomes walked around the house and peered into the windows from the backyard. He didn't see anyone inside. Gomes and Eakes then circled the house and began looking in all the windows. The place was completely dark.

Curious as to where the family might have gone, the detective and the prosecutor went to the house next door. They spoke with Barbara Sauerbrey, a chatty and welcoming older woman, and the president of the Woodridge Homeowners' Association. Mrs. Sauerbrey kept pretty close tabs on the families who belonged to the association, which included the Wilsons. She told the detective and the prosecutor that all of the Wilson cars were home and that someone should be there, unless they were visiting other families in the neighborhood. However, Mrs. Sauerbrey thought it was strange that the Wilsons' dog, Moe, was roaming around the front yard unattended. The Wilsons never let Moe outdoors because he was old and had had hip surgery.

Gomes and Eakes asked a few more questions before cutting back across the lawn to the Wilson home. Mrs. Sauerbrey followed them to find Moe and bring him over to her house while the investigators continued their search for the dog's owners.

Gomes and Eakes went to the backyard, where Marquis and Raven were waiting.

"The door's unlocked," Marquis told Gomes, gesturing toward the sliding glass door.

"What do you think we should do?" Gomes asked Eakes.

From the looks of it, Eakes also had an uneasy feeling about the situation. The dead young woman could be related to the homeowners; three cars were parked at the house, a dog was moping around outside, and no one was answering the door.

"There was a definite part of me that thought something might be wrong, but you couldn't fathom what Gomes was going to find," Eakes would later recall. "It was just like, 'Something's funny here.' These people are gone. It was all dark in the house. It was the middle of the afternoon, on a Sunday. You would have the lights on."

Sensing trouble, Eakes suggested Gomes go inside and check things out.

"I think you might want to go in there. There might be something wrong," she said to Gomes.

Gomes and Eakes had worked on several other cases together and had maintained a good working relationship. They joked with each other constantly. Now Gomes was ribbing Eakes for jumping to conclusions that something terrible might have happened.

"No, really, something could be wrong," Eakes insisted. "You have enough probable cause to go in and check the welfare of whoever lives here."

Gomes' humor instantly disappeared. Eakes was giving him legal permission to enter the home. He knew he had a responsibility to make sure no one inside needed help.

"Okay. I'm going in."

Gomes drew his gun, slid the door open, and carefully stepped inside. The house was stuffy and a bad, rotting smell lingered in the air. From just one whiff, Gomes could distinguish that metallic odor from any other.

"Police," he announced, walking cautiously into the house. Again he was answered by silence.

Gomes went through the kitchen first, and then up a flight of stairs as Eakes, Marquis, and Raven watched him disappear. He wasn't sure yet just what he was looking for, but that would quickly become clear. He padded through the second-floor dining room in search of the residents before slowly making his way upstairs to the third floor. Gomes turned right, walked down a hallway, and glanced inside the bedroom at the end of the hall.

He stumbled onto a grotesque scene: a severely battered body lying in a pool of blood. Startled, Gomes felt his heart leap.

"One dead!" he shouted. Even though his SWAT-team days were over, Gomes still used the lingo out of force of habit.

Eakes, who had heard him call out, looked at the two MEs and rolled her eyes. Gomes was joking again, she thought. She didn't want to believe that another body had been found—this one inside the home.

"Oh, yeah, right, Gomes. Very funny," Eakes yelled through the sliding glass door.

Having worked as a prosecutor for the past seven years,

Eakes had honed her instincts so that she recognized when something was wrong. But there was no way of telling just how serious the situation was.

Eakes and the medical investigators waited on the back porch, where they continued to peer inside the house to try to see if anyone was around.

Inside, Gomes gripped his pistol tighter. He checked closets and looked behind doors. Now he knew what he was looking for: either the killer or more victims.

Gomes' heart pounded faster as he took a few more steps down the hallway and looked into the master bedroom. The sight was almost overwhelming: two more bodies beaten into bloody heaps. A figure that appeared to be a man sat slumped at the foot of the bed, and another body that looked like a woman still lay tucked under the comforter. Blood had already started to crust on the victims' pale skin.

"Two more dead!" Gomes shouted, his voice shaky.

A pang of fear coursed through Gomes' body. For all he knew, the killer could still be in the house and might attack him next. Gomes walked through the rest of the house, checking each room, gripping his pistol even tighter as he slowly, methodically searched each floor. He wanted to make sure no one else was in the house before going back outside.

After Gomes' second call, Eakes realized the detective wasn't joking at all. Moments later, Gomes came downstairs and back into view, his gun still drawn.

"There are three bodies in there," Gomes said, his eyes bulging. "Two in one bedroom and one in another."

"Are you fucking with me, Gomes?" Eakes asked impatiently.

"No, there are really three dead people in there."

"What happened to them?"

"I don't know. Looks like gunshot wounds. There's blood everywhere up there."

Gomes wasn't in an easygoing mood anymore. The casual grin he had been wearing earlier had been wiped from his face; it was replaced by a twisted look of shock.

The group decided to go in briefly to see for themselves the horror Gomes was describing so they could figure out what they needed to do next. Gomes led them, his gun still drawn, cautiously through the sliding glass door and up the stairs to the third floor, where he had discovered the bodies.

By around 4 P.M., the house was cloaked by a semidarkness that added an eerie tone to the discovery. It was hard to make out a couch or a chair, but Eakes could see the outlines of various things—a dresser, a bed, a body. She felt safe with three other people there with her, but she wondered whether the killer was still around.

"Frankly, I was afraid. I was unarmed, there were no cops there (except Gomes). At this juncture we had no idea if whoever killed them was still in the house," Eakes recalled.

No one went into the bedrooms. Gomes advised everyone to stay in the hallway so as not to contaminate the crime scenes. The prosecutor and the MEs didn't need to enter the bedrooms to see the carnage. In one room, Eakes could clearly see a young woman lying just inside the doorway.

"I just remember a lot of blood. Her face looked completely distorted, what I could see of it. She was pretty battered," Eakes said.

The group then went to the other end of the hallway, where the man and woman had been attacked.

"The woman was lying just like she was sleeping, except the whole side of her head was caved in," Eakes would later say.

From where they stood outside the doorway to the master bedroom, Eakes couldn't see too much of the man sitting slumped on the floor. But something caught her attention on the back of his white T-shirt—a bloody shoeprint. It was so clear, even in the dim light.

Then the group hurried back out of the house. There was no time to get sick over the gruesome scene. Immediately, everyone kicked into professional gear. Adrenaline coursing, Gomes and Eakes quickly made their way to the front of the house and got into Gomes' car, where he radioed for backup.

The scene had to be secured. Police officers needed to be available to keep bystanders out and talk to witnesses. Essentially, everybody who had been called out to the nearby park was asked to head over to the Wilson home, save for two patrol officers who were assigned to guard the park overnight so no one could get in.

A team of forensic scientists from the Washington State Patrol Crime Lab also were called to help process evidence at the Wilson home and assess the scene. Gomes' mind began spinning with thoughts on what could have happened.

"I started thinking about what needed to be done, and trying to process how this was connected to the girl in the park. You think you've identified everybody. You don't know if some other family member did it and is missing. Is this a murder-suicide? Is this a quadruple murder, which happens so rarely?" Gomes would later say.

The detective immediately got on his cell phone and called Lieutenant Ed Mott, the supervisor in command that day, who was still at the park.

"We've got three people dead in the house over here," Gomes said, without a hint of the usual sarcasm in his voice.

Like Eakes, Mott initially didn't believe Gomes. How could there be three more bodies? It had to be a joke.

Gomes handed the phone to Eakes.

"Gomes isn't kidding," Eakes said. "There are three people in that house. They're dead."

2 The tone of the afternoon had shifted dramatically from a casual pace to a frantic scramble for backup and more information about the family. There were two crime scenes now, and that meant double the resources. A team of about two dozen experts from the Bellevue Police Department, the ME's Office, the State Patrol Crime Lab, and the city's survey department had gathered at the home to begin the tedious work of tracking evidence and piecing together the crime scenes.

Lieutenant Mott ordered separate investigations of the crime scenes. He assigned Detective Johnson to oversee the investigation of the park, where the first body was found, and Detective Thompson to head the investigation at the Wilson home.

Eakes and Gomes, meanwhile, focused their efforts on getting legal permission to search the home and tracking down basic information about the family and who might have had access to the house. By this point, time became crucial, and Eakes didn't want to waste any by driving back to her office in Seattle to type out a search warrant, so she sat in the medical examiner's van and scribbled a handwritten warrant.

A few hours later, at around 8 P.M., the detectives got the warrant signed by a King County Superior Court judge who happened to live near Woodridge. Now, with the legal clearance needed to enter the home, Thompson slipped on boots and gloves and walked through the front door. He was followed by Detective Gary Forrest, a police photographer, Carl Nicoll, a forensic expert, and Gomes.

Thompson walked slowly and methodically through the bedrooms where the bodies lay. In the master bedroom, Thompson first noticed the amount of blood. A woman lay badly beaten in bed, where she'd been attacked. Blood drenched the pillow and comforter, and had sprayed on the wall and ceiling above her. Thompson then trained his flashlight on the man, and stopped the light on a huge hallmark the killer, or killers, had left behind. A full, bloody shoeprint with a diamond-patterned sole was stamped on the back of the man's T-shirt. It was so obvious that Thompson wondered whether the killer or killers were making a mockery of police, taunting investigators—*Come find me. Come track me down if you can . . .*

"It was almost staged there, like, 'Check this out,' " Thompson would later say. He found something else bizarre on the man's body—an AmeriCorps bumper sticker slapped onto his thigh, smeared with blood.

Thompson then proceeded down the hallway and saw what appeared to be a young woman's body just inside the doorway of her bedroom. As he took notes in the room where the young victim lay on the floor, Thompson couldn't help but feel like he was suffocating. The temperature outside was slowly dropping to the low thirties as the night wore on, but inside, the electric heat was still turned on. Thompson was starting to sweat.

He couldn't believe the carnage. He kept his notepad open during the walk-through, sketching positions of bodies and taking note of anything from the light switch in one of the rooms not working to the way the woman in the master bedroom lay in bed, in her natural sleeping state, probably without a chance to even wake up during the vicious attack.

Finally, Thompson explored the bedroom in the middle of the hallway. Nothing appeared to have been disturbed there, but he would later find blood on the light switch, as if the killer went from room to room, hunting down each of his victims until everyone in the house was dead.

The curtains had been taken down in all of the bedrooms. It appeared as if the family was in the middle of a major remodeling project that involved repainting the walls. Thompson glanced outside through one of the bedroom windows. He could see TV news crews and members of the press peering in from across the street. Worried that photographers would use their zoom lenses to get a closer shot of the ghastly specter inside the home, Thompson hastily hung bedsheets over the windows. The public did not need to see the destruction, he thought.

The next stop on his tour of the home was the second floor—the family room. Thompson was scanning the room, searching for anything that seemed out of place or awry, when his eyes locked onto the entertainment center. His heart stopped momentarily. The VCR was missing. Cords cut.

Thompson couldn't believe what he was seeing. The scenario at the Wilson home was so familiar to the one he had walked into when he and Gomes had investigated the Rafay killings—three bodies, that of a man, woman, and young woman, beaten and bludgeoned to death in their bedrooms, and the VCR ripped out of the wall. It was a bizarre and chilling coincidence. The number and gender of the victims were the same. The crime scene itself—an apparent staging of a botched robbery—also bore a striking resemblance to the Rafay case.

In the Rafay case, the suspected killers ended up being the Rafays' son and his friend. Now Thompson wondered whether the attackers who had entered the Wilson home were also part of the family, or maybe even someone close enough to be family.

3 About the same time that Eakes and Gomes were trying to get a search warrant signed, Julia Mahoney was in her house watching TV when the five o'clock news flashed on with breaking news.

"Children playing at a park in the Woodridge neighborhood in Bellevue this morning found the body of a young woman. That led police to three more bodies at a home nearby . . . The identities of the victims have not been released."

Mrs. Mahoney froze. The TV anchor was standing in front of what looked like the home of her daughter, Rose. No one at her daughter's house had answered the phone all day and night on Saturday, and no one had picked up that morning when she tried again to call her. They normally talked every day.

Mrs. Mahoney's attention was shattered by the sudden ring of her telephone.

"Julia, did you see what I just saw on TV?"

The voice was a familiar one to Mrs. Mahoney. Over the years, she had heard it so many times—it was Rose's best friend from college, Diana Funai, who lived nearby.

"Yes, I did."

"Well, I'm coming over to pick you up," Funai said. "We're going to make goddamn sure it's not their place."

Close to 8 P.M., Funai and Mrs. Mahoney pulled up to a police barricade about a block from Rose's home. Funai rolled down the window as Mrs. Mahoney leaned over to talk to the police officer.

"That's my daughter's house down there," Mrs. Mahoney told the officer.

The officer radioed Gomes, who ordered him to allow Mrs. Mahoney through. Funai parked her car along the street as police lights swirled in a dizzying pace nearby.

After introducing themselves to the two women, Gomes and Eakes piled into the backseat of Funai's car to talk to Mrs. Mahoney. From the frail woman they confirmed that the family members who lived at the home were her daughter, Rose, her son-in-law, Bill, and her granddaughters, Kim and Julia.

As they asked questions of Mrs. Mahoney, the detective and the prosecutor walked a fine line between the need for sensitivity and the need to press for more details about the dead family. Throughout the interrogation, Gomes would ask, "Do you feel okay? Do you want to continue?" to which Mrs. Mahoney would answer, "Yeah, I can answer questions. Go ahead."

"Did either of the girls bring anyone home lately? . . . Did Bill own a gun? . . . Did Kim do drugs?"

To all the questions, Mrs. Mahoney answered with a solemn "No" or "I don't know."

"Did they have any enemies?" Gomes asked.

"Rose? Oh, no. Bill? No, not an enemy in the world . . ."

The more questions Gomes and Eakes asked, the more worried Mrs. Mahoney became. Something terrible had happened to her family, and she didn't know what. As she realized her family had been murdered, tears began to pour from the seventy-eight-year-old woman's eyes. She had no idea what was going on and wanted reassurance that her family was okay. But it was reassurance that Gomes and Eakes could not give.

"I've been trying to call all day and no one has answered,"

Mrs. Mahoney told the investigators. She was starting to shake with fear. Her voice cracked as she asked the most terrifying question of all.

"How did they die?"

"We don't know," Eakes said. "We wish we could give you more information, Mrs. Mahoney, but we don't know very much at this point."

It was little consolation for a woman who had just seen her daughter's residence flashed on the evening news and a TV anchor announce that three bodies were found inside. *It had to be them,* Mrs. Mahoney thought. *Someone must have broken into the house and shot my family.*

There was nothing Mrs. Mahoney or Funai could do but go home and wait until the morning—until confirmation that the dead people inside the house were in fact the Wilsons.

Gomes and Eakes slipped back inside the command-post van. They hung their heads, angry and guilty that a family member had to learn about a death through the media. In murder cases, detectives can usually prevent that from happening by reaching the family first and informing them of the death. But in this case, there was no one in the immediate family left to tell.

"That was probably the most emotional part of the whole thing," Eakes would later say. "It was just awful to have this poor woman see it on TV. You feel terrible you couldn't notify anybody. Everybody told us the grandmother lived nearby, but no one knew where."

Just as Mrs. Mahoney learned of the murders on the TV news, so had the rest of the Bellevue community. But for many Woodridge residents, the news unfolded right before their eyes.

That Sunday night, many Woodridge residents were trundling home in their minivans and sports utility cars after weekend ski trips or other out-of-town vacations. As they neared the top of Woodridge Hill, they were met with a chaotic scene of ambulances and police cars jamming their street. Some parents had left their teenagers home alone and panicked that the medic and squad cars meant there was trouble at their homes. They pulled up to police barricades and demanded to get through. They lived down there, down where the red lights swirled with bad news. They pleaded with officers to let them through. When residents learned the address in question was not theirs, they drove home quietly, peering at the surreal scene as they slowly passed by.

Never before had there been this much commotion in the sheltered neighborhood. Families emerged from their homes and huddled in thirty-five-degree weather in front of the Wilson house, hoping to learn more about what terrible thing had happened inside, and to find out whether they were safe in their own homes.

Police officials wouldn't say whose bodies had been discovered, but neighbors who knew the family pieced it together on their own. Bill and Rose Wilson lived at that address with their two daughters, Kim and Julia.

Neighbors covered their mouths as tears began to well up in their eyes. They paced up and down the street, nervous, frightened, confused. Friends of Kim and Julia trembled and sobbed as they stared at the home, shaking their heads, wondering why.

The Wilsons were friendly, active people, neighbors told reporters. The Wilson girls swam on the Norwood Swim Team, and Bill and Rose Wilson were avid University of Washington Huskies fans, often seen coming and going from their house clad in purple and gold—Huskies colors—on game days. Like other families in Woodridge, they knew their immediate neighbors, but for the most part stayed to themselves. If there were any hints of trouble within the home, they remained tight-lipped about it.

A Woodridge resident, Dawn Stansfield, who had once

rented the Wilsons' former home in the neighborhood, said that the older daughter was rumored to have dabbled in drugs. In the past couple of years, she had started running with a tough crowd, Stansfield told reporters. She wondered whether the murders were the result of a drug deal gone bad.

The only unusual incident at the home was so minor it took up less than a few lines in a police report. On December 26, just a week earlier, a Bellevue police officer had been called out to the Wilson home for what eventually would be reported as a domestic-dispute call placed to 911 at around midnight.

While she was visiting her family over the holiday break, Kim had lost her driving privileges, so she depended on her parents or sister to take her places. That night, she went into her parents' bedroom and demanded that she be given a ride to a friend's house. Her parents refused.

The confrontation escalated into an argument. Kim's father threatened to call the cops if Kim didn't calm down. Bluffing, he picked up the phone, dialed 911, and immediately hung up. But the call went through to the police station. A Bellevue Police Department dispatcher traced it, and sent an officer to the home.

The officer who arrived to check on the family indicated in his report that the dispute was between Kim and her parents over Kim's career choice.

Other than that one visit to the house, police had no record of any disturbance at the Wilsons'.

Slowly, more and more neighbors appeared and spoke in hushed tones. They came out wanting answers, wanting, in any way they could, to help. But there was nothing they could do, so they went back inside their homes and locked the doors behind them.

At 7 P.M. Sunday night, Claire Hearn, a young woman who lived in Woodridge and was a friend of Kimberly Wilson, spotted the blinking lights of ambulances and police cars illuminating the sky from down the street. The commotion drew Claire to the Wilson home, where a group of neighbors and reporters had already arrived.

Police officers roamed the streets, talking to potential witnesses and trying to keep gawkers from cruising past the scene.

Worried that something bad had happened to Kim, Claire kept peering toward the home, where investigators walked in and out of the front door.

"What's going on?" Claire asked a uniformed police officer standing guard near the house.

The officer told her that three bodies had been found inside and that one had been found in a park nearby. He did not give any other information.

"Do you know who lives there?" the officer asked.

"Yeah," Claire said, panic rising. "My friend Kim and her sister, Julia, and their mom and dad."

Claire, one of Kim Wilson's closest childhood friends, was home for the holidays, staying with her parents. The Hearns lived in a modest wood-frame house just a few blocks from the Wilsons. Claire had not been living in Woodridge recently, but she kept in close contact with her friends in the neighborhood.

Claire had tried the college life after graduating from Bellevue High School in 1994, but school was not where she wanted to be. There was so much in the world for her to experience. She had grown up in Bellevue, and she wanted a change of pace, something different to challenge her.

That brought her to the Navy. In 1997, Claire was training to become an intelligence agent. She was a tall young woman, twenty years old, bright, and filled with ambition. She was also pretty, with long brunette hair that dipped just below her shoulders.

She had been a good friend of Kim's ever since the

Wilsons moved to Woodridge Hill in the mid-'80s. They had met in grade school. She had known the Wilsons long enough to enter their home without waiting for someone to let her in. The Wilsons always kept their doors unlocked. So did Claire's family, and others in the neighborhood.

On Friday morning, January 3, Claire and Kim met for breakfast. Kim had been in San Diego for the past few months, volunteering in President Clinton's AmeriCorps program, and this was Claire's chance to see her.

The young women caught up on each other's lives. They talked about the excitement and rigors involved in their respective jobs—Kim clearing trails at the San Diego Zoo, and Claire following a strict daily regime in the Navy.

After breakfast and a good talk, she and Kim hugged each other and said temporary good-byes. They agreed that if they were both free on Saturday, they would try to get together again. Kim was due to leave town that Sunday.

On Saturday, January 4, Claire spent most of the day running errands and visiting with friends she wanted to see before she had to leave town again. About 4 P.M. that day, she walked down the street to see Kim. She had noticed the cars parked in the driveway earlier in the day when she had driven by. As she approached the house, she could see that all the Wilsons' cars were still there: two in the driveway, and one—the Wilsons' minivan—parked out in front on the street. She figured someone had to be home. But it was odd that the house was so dark and quiet, and none of the cars had moved all day.

An uneasy feeling came over her, telling her not to barge in, as she was accustomed to doing. Claire approached the front door and decided to knock this time.

No one answered.

She rang the doorbell.

Still no answer.

As Claire stood on the porch, the family dog, Moe,

walked up beside her, whimpering and frantically wagging his tail. Claire thought that was strange; she couldn't ever remember seeing the dog outside, and she knew Rose would get upset if she knew Moe had escaped.

Claire stepped away from the house and looked through the curtains. All the lights were turned off.

Figuring the Wilsons were probably in the neighborhood somewhere, Claire sat down, leaning against the house and keeping Moe company as she waited for Kim to get home.

After about a half hour, Claire became worried that Moe hadn't been fed. She returned to her house and came back with some dry cat food, which she gave to the Wilsons' dog. It was starting to get dark, so Claire plugged in the Christmas lights to an outdoor socket and sat down again to wait for her friend. After about an hour, when the family still had not returned home, Claire gave up.

She would have to call Kim later to say her final good-bye before Kim left Bellevue the next day.

Then, on Sunday, January 5, curious about her friend's whereabouts, Claire drove by the house a couple of times to see if anyone was home. She wondered if Kim's parents were taking her to the airport. But the cars were in the exact same position as the day before, and still there were no lights on in the home. Thinking it odd, she telephoned Kim's good friend Sky Stewart to find out if she knew where Kim was.

Sky hadn't seen or spoken to Kim since Friday night, when she'd dropped Kim off at home after they had been hanging out at Denny's. She, too, had driven by the Wilson home and called to see if anyone was around, but no one had answered.

Throughout the day on Sunday, Claire had kept thinking about Kim. It would have been unlike her to leave town abruptly without calling to touch base with her friends.

The police officer questioning Claire wanted to know whether Kim had any enemies. While Claire couldn't think of anyone who would want to hurt Kim or her family, a vague memory came back to her. Approximately a year earlier, Kim had confided in Claire. Kim was worried that a guy she had dated briefly in middle school, David Anderson, and his friend, Alex, were planning to commit some sort of crime. Claire didn't know David or Alex well, but she had hung out with them a couple of times with Kim. She knew they were part of a tightly bonded raffish group of kids— many of whom were high school dropouts—who loitered at a nearby Denny's from midnight until dawn. Kim had started running with that crowd her senior year of high school—a group that flirted with drugs, alcohol, sex, and petty crimes like shoplifting and vandalism. Struggling through typical adolescent disagreements with her parents over homework and household chores, Kim had turned to the Denny's gang, defiantly embracing their delinquent lifestyle.

The kids who hung out at the twenty-four-hour diner were known to be part of the Gothic scene—a subculture marked by dark, dramatic clothing and white makeup. Goths enjoy a spectral, and at times vampiric, appearance, and often are preoccupied with death and the macabre. Bisexuality is also common in the Goth community. Some of the kids who hung out at Denny's claimed to be bisexual, dating friends of both genders.

Many of them were also involved in fantasy role-playing games like Dungeons and Dragons. The games are adult versions of "make-believe" in which players assume a character and act out a role in scenarios spiked with fantasy violence.

David and Alex were part of that subculture.

For the most part, Kim had spoken fondly of David whenever she mentioned his name, Claire told the officer. To Kim, he was good-looking and a fun guy to hang out with. He was adventurous. Charismatic. Kim liked the fact that David never followed a crowd. In fact, he led one—a crowd of girls who pined after him.

Alex, however, was a different story. A tall, shadowy kid with long, greasy hair tied in a ponytail, he was never friendly to Kim and he followed David wherever David went. His eerie and solemn nature frightened some people, especially whenever he sat back in a booth at Denny's and scowled at everyone. He was a relentless brooder, and even his friends wondered what might lie hidden beneath his silence.

"Kim was scared of Alex," Claire told the officer. "She thought he was creepy."

By the last newscast at 11 P.M. that Sunday, Woodridge residents were watching their own neighbors—their faces distorted with expressions of horror and disbelief—pace up and down the street as investigators worked through the night to process evidence.

Denial led many residents to believe it was an outside job, that the murderer or murderers did not live in Woodridge, or even in Bellevue, for that matter. It had to have been someone from out of town, they insisted, a coward who did his dirty deed while passing through. But why the Wilsons? And if it could happen to the Wilsons, could it happen to them? They wanted to know: Was a killer on the loose in Woodridge?

Fear, the primal, instinctual kind that makes a person all the more sensitive to sounds and strange sightings, engulfed the once tranquil neighborhood. It was an unusual phenomenon for Woodridge, so unusual that Bellevue police officials stepped up patrols in that part of town just to put its residents at ease.

Woodridge had always been a secure place, the residents insisted. And police reports backed them up. The most serious crimes were occasional burglaries and car prowls.

"This is one of the best places in town," Lieutenant Bill Ferguson, spokesman for the Bellevue Police Department, told reporters the night of the gruesome discoveries. "This is the first time I can recall a homicide occurring in this area."

But even in the best places like Woodridge, danger lurks.

4 Seattle, named after the Native American Chief Seattle whose tribe settled the shores of Puget Sound long before whites arrived, was a destination point in the '90s. Despite its paralyzing traffic, the metropolis twice in ten years garnered national recognition from *Forbes* magazine as the most desirable place to live in America—a designation the city owes, in large part, to its robust economy and family atmosphere.

Seattle's natural beauty gave the city much of its appeal. On clear days, spectacular views of several different mountains and lakes can be seen from various locations around the city. But people seemed too rushed in Seattle, and crime was as much a part of everyday life as lattes and computers.

To escape the swiftness and chaos of urbanity, families moved east, across Lake Washington, and out to the suburbs where a rustic smell lingered in the air. On the Eastside, as locals called it, the soil was dark and fertile, and the landscape was heavily forested. Bellevue rose rapidly out of the thick stands of cedar and Western hemlock about fifteen miles east of Seattle on the shores of Lake Washington. Interstate 90, a major thoroughfare, slices through the heart of the suburb, then charges east across the country.

Bellevue has always been a place for opportunity. The town's first white settlers were an odd assortment of European immigrants—bankers, loggers, land prospectors, attorneys, cabinetmakers, coal miners, bakers, farmers,

43

trappers—an eclectic yet practical blend of men in shiny shoes and work boots. The white settlers staked out lake-front property, which they subdivided and sold to prominent Seattle businessmen, who built summer-vacation cabins among the trees. Businesses sprouted almost immediately. Bellevue, like so many other cities that grew up in the era of railroads, prospered because of its natural resources. Logging and mining for coal were hard lives, but people made money. And with that money they built homes and schools and churches.

Nothing contributed more to Bellevue's growth than the construction of two bridges which linked the suburbs to Seattle by the 1940s. For years, Bellevue residents enjoyed a sense of being isolated and independent. Before the floating bridge was built, getting across Lake Washington to shop in Seattle for items like clothes and certain groceries would require rowing by canoe, or hailing a ferry on the shores with a blanket or apron. Roads were inadequate, and driving around the lake would take half a day.

The 520 floating bridge and Interstate 90 bridge marked Bellevue's rapid rise as a major Seattle suburb. In 1955, a year after the city officially incorporated, Bellevue was designated *Life* magazine's "All American City," and many locals believed it was true, up to and through the '90s. The city has always upheld its reputation as the place "Across the bridge to gracious living," as a 1940s real estate ad promoted.

People have flocked to the state's fifth largest city because of its reputation as the quintessential American suburb. They've come to enroll their kids in the top-notch school system, and to take in long afternoons at some of the best golf courses in the region. They've come because it is safe. They like the fact that the suburb is nothing like crime-infested Seattle. Bellevue claims one of the lowest per capita crime rates in the region. Murder happens less frequently than in Seattle.

By the 1980s, the city was edging toward becoming a metropolis. Its downtown fit together like a mathematical equation. At best, Bellevue radiates a drab sophistication, a soap-and-water cleanliness that evokes plainness and boredom. But beyond the glass buildings and high-rises, the city fans out in a vast spread of lush green and brown. Bellevue has remained faithful to its French-derived name: *belle vue*, a beautiful view. It is a natural playground for outdoor enthusiasts. To the east, the city is hemmed in by a jagged link of snowcapped peaks known as the Cascades—a popular mountain range to hike; and to the west, it is bordered by Lake Washington, where locals sail and swim during the sun-drenched summer months of July and August.

The people—more than 100,000 in all—are now a mix of longtime residents, who wear blue jeans and drive Honda Accords, and the nouveaux riches, who dress in high fashions and drive Mercedeses and BMWs. By the 1990s, out-of-state transplants made up most of the city's new growth. They were part of the smug bourgeoisie who collectively, because of their demand for luxurious homes, pushed up the average price of a home in town to nearly half a million dollars by 1997. Yet they were amicable and generous people just the same, given to donating large sums of cash to schools and charities. They spoke with the polished words and phrases that suggested book clubs and martini-mingled evenings. They were proud of their reputation for being conservative, and not particularly diverse.

For years, Bellevue had been known as a bastion of the white upper class. It was true, for the most part, but that was gradually changing. Signs of a more cultured enclave began springing up in visible numbers by the mid-'80s, when large waves of immigrants—Russians, Southeast Asians, and

South Africans, mostly—started moving into town. But these were not families of comfortable financial means. They were the day laborers who cut the lawns and washed the cars of the Microsoft millionaires.

To be sure, much of the wealth in Bellevue was a century old. Like so many cities in the Northwest, Bellevue was built on its resplendent supply of natural resources, namely coal and timber plucked from the mountains near the turn of the century. But by the 1980s, technology took hold and anchored itself on the Eastside, where Microsoft, Boeing, and Nintendo—a few of the biggest names in the nation's high-tech industry—had laid down roots. Acre after acre, high-tech campuses cropped up on what formerly had been farm fields. The buildings stood in neat, orderly rows, stacked like Lego blocks. The Eastside quickly became known as the "Silicon Valley of the Northwest."

The high-tech industry developed into somewhat of a tourist attraction in the '90s; people came to check out the Microsoft campus and Bill Gates' $40 million lakefront estate. Nintendo and Boeing commanded much attention as industry heavyweights, but it was Microsoft that made millionaires and front-page headlines in the local and national newspapers.

Despite the city's changing image as a high-tech hotbed, Bellevue still clings to its semirural charm. It is still a place where thousands turn out—even in the constant Northwest drizzle—for the Cow Parade at the annual Art Grazing festival, in which Star Valentine, a live and rather motley cow, serves nobly and nonchalantly as grand marshal. The parade snakes through the corridors of downtown and ends near Bellevue Square, a ritzy shopping center billed as the region's premier mall with high-class boutiques and retail stores. It is a place where the local cultural establishments consist of the botanical gardens and a doll museum. The city's moral tone and source of pride appear to be set by city codes. There had once been a topless dance bar, but a strict ordinance regulating that kind of unseemly adult entertainment ultimately forced the place to shut down.

It is easy, in a town saturated with prosperity, to miss the crevices of despair, the deep pockets of poverty lined with secrets so dark, few were willing to admit or even acknowledge they existed. But the poor in Bellevue *do* exist, although they remain mostly invisible and unaccounted for, hidden behind the glistening facade of so much money. Some of these families are made up of single parents who come home and collapse on the couch; who have neither the time nor the energy to keep tabs on their children all day and night. Others have children already reeling from their parents' authority, mere shadows who stalk the streets, stomping alone through the chaotic journey of adolescence.

Most parents, nonetheless, believed they were raising their children in a good, safe setting, far removed from the big-city crime and mayhem found in Seattle. By the 1990s, the Seattle area had gained a reputation as one of the most sinister edges of the world, home to infamous serial killer Ted Bundy, murderer and serial rapist George Russell, and the elusive Green River Killer, who to this day has not been tracked down. His killing spree resulted in the deaths of some fifty people.

For the most part, however, cities like Bellevue kept out of harm's way. Bellevue lacked the drama of larger cities where the screams of sirens invariably meant a gang shooting or robbery or brawl. Sirens in Bellevue, on the other hand, more likely meant a resident at the Garden Club retirement home had fallen off a chair and thrown out a hip, or a pedestrian had been hit while crossing the street.

But on that Sunday when the four bodies were discovered in Woodridge Hill, the residents of Bellevue realized their suburb was not immune from the sort of violent crime that infiltrated Seattle. They would not forget that day when a horrible thing happened, revealing a side to the city that no one wanted to acknowledge existed, and that would make some parents, at least for the moment, eye their own children with suspicion.

5 Many Bellevue children—the ones who dropped out of school, who ran away from home and responsibility, or who wanted nothing to do with mainstream society—ended up at Denny's. At the all-night diner in downtown Bellevue where David and Alex regularly hung out, news of the Wilson murders spread fast through the boys' circle of friends.

"Did you guys hear what happened to Kim and her family?" one person asked in a frantic whisper. "They were murdered. Someone broke into their home and stabbed them or something."

The group was stunned that someone they knew, someone they used to hang out with, had been murdered. Eager to find out more information, they questioned each other on when they had last seen Kim Wilson.

As some of the teenagers started to speculate what could have happened to Kim and her family, sixteen-year-old Korby Gerth piped in: "I wonder where David and Alex are. Someone said they skipped town because they might know something about the murders, or they might know who did it."

David and Alex were regulars at Denny's, but they had been conspicuously absent from Bellevue's late-night teenage Denny's scene in recent months. The kids wanted to find David now more than ever, because they knew David was close friends with Kim. If anyone had any more information about the homicides, they figured it would be David, who was friends with all of them. David had instantly bonded with the group of kids at the restaurant when he started hanging out there in his early teens. In the quiet of the night, the youths had created their own hybrid society, and many considered David their leader.

At midnight, when the streets are empty and darkness hovers over the city, a loose-knit cabal of about two dozen teenagers dressed in black slide into the squeaky brown vinyl seats at Denny's, where they drink coffee and smoke. Children of grocery clerks, computer consultants, teachers, truck drivers, even lawyers, they had parents who were too busy making a living to watch over them. So they started watching over each other.

In a way, for most of the kids, the Denny's gang was their surrogate family. When someone needed a place to crash, there were always other kids to take that person in. When a kid didn't have money for food and cigarettes, friends were there to buy lunch and loan him or her a pack of smokes.

Members of the Denny's gang lived for the dark. The joke among the group was that they ran on Denny's time, which usually meant they slept in until three or four in the afternoon and preferred the night because daylight was too cluttered with the chaos of ordinary living. Around the group swirled a universe of hip young families in BMWs, roll-top Peugeots, and sports utility jeeps. It was the sort of material world the Goths resented. All of them resisted a nine-to-five schedule and were uninterested in what they considered to be the mundane world of mainstream. Like the mythological immortals they attempted to portray with cheap makeup and secondhand clothes, these kids were creatures of the night.

Each wanted to feel as though he or she were a part of something bigger than his or her own life. So the kids turned to the Gothic subculture as a way of declaring their individuality. They worshiped heavy-metal rocks stars like Marilyn Manson and studied the poetry of Edgar Allan Poe. They believed the world was on the verge of an apocalypse, and so they lived as though they were already dead: sometimes wearing white powder on their faces, and often clad in all-black get-ups. Gothic teenagers knew they were on the fringes of their peer group, and they were proud of it, content to be regarded as oddities of society.

Dressed in their combat boots and ubiquitous black pants and miniskirts over ripped stockings, the girls titter around, mussing the boys' hair and snatching their cigarettes. The boys wear black leather pants or jeans, and some have pierced tongues and wear spiked dog collars around their necks and wrists. They talk about movies, music, and sex, their conversations livened with vulgarities. Gently stroking the inner thigh of his girlfriend, one of the boys makes sexual jokes and discusses breast sizes while the girls gossip about who among the boys can boast the biggest penis. Two of the boys toss tiny containers of half-and-half cream into each other's mouths, one of which pierces the boy's lips. He bleeds from the mouth and sucks it in, the taste of salty blood mixing with bitter coffee. The girls giggle and think it's gross; the boys think it's totally cool.

By 2 A.M., they are working on their second pack of cigarettes and, for some, their ninth cup of coffee. The phone rings, and it's for one of the girls in the Denny's gang. She walks behind the counter to take the call; it's a former friend who wants to kick her ass because of a dispute over a boy.

The girl returns to the table, and slumps down.

"That fucking bitch can't tell me what to do!" she complains.

Some of the boys have ordered food and ignore her. The greasy smell of scrambled eggs and hash browns mixes with the smells of sweat and cigarette smoke wafting through the air as some of the teens shovel eggs into their mouths. The

table is a sticky mess of grease, ashes, spilled coffee and
sugar.

They stay at Denny's, arriving alone or sometimes in
groups, and they often don't leave until just before the morning rush beginning at 7 A.M. with business men and women
catching a quick bite to eat before they head into the office.
The only people to eat so late besides these kids are truck
drivers.

For these kids, hanging out at Denny's was the popular
thing to do, especially because everything closes so early in
Bellevue. Denny's had become their living room. The disen-
franchised teenagers had broken away from parental authority and created their own primitive society based on
adolescent virtues like sex, drugs, and fantasy games. Most
members of the group were unaware of the irony of their situation: Here, in a family restaurant, the only thing missing
for these kids was their families.

A couple of days after the grisly discoveries in Woodridge,
some members of the Denny's crowd finally caught up with
David.

Korby, a sixteen-year-old runaway who favored oufits of
black miniskirts with chains around her waist and torn fish-
net pantyhose, said that she noticed David leaning against a
black pickup truck in the Denny's parking lot a few days after the murders. She approached him to ask if he knew what
was going on.

"Don't look at me," David said. "You know as much as I
do."

Korby also noted a change in David. He had cut his hair
and it had been dyed black. She thought this was odd. In the
year that she had known David, she got the impression that
he loved his shoulder-length blond hair and would rather die
before getting it butchered. David denied any involvement in

the murders, but it was strange that he would cut and dye his hair if he had nothing to hide.

His golden hair was a great part of his attraction for the girls in the Denny's crowd. They also loved seeing his body.

David prided himself on his good looks. At 5 feet 7 inches, he was well built, with bulging biceps and broad shoulders. He had the physique of a baseball player. Next to body-building, that was one of his favorite sports. He kept several baseball bats in the closet and under his bed. Behind closed doors, he would practice swinging at a make-believe ball.

Through the fogged windows of the Denny's restaurant, the girls in the Denny's crowd would turn their heads when they saw his silhouette swagger down the sidewalk and push through the swinging glass doors at the twenty-four-hour hangout. He was confident and always in control.

"Here comes loverboy," some surly teenage boy would blurt out as David strutted over to where his comrades took up an entire corner.

Tammy, one of the waitresses, would swirl around to where the teens sat and whip out a notepad and pen. "What do you girls want?"

They wanted him, David Anderson. They considered him a total babe and a Goth jock. He was outgoing and charis-matic, buoyed by attention from his peers. The girls hung on to every word he spoke.

For many years, David had worked to perfect his image as a man with a slightly rebellious side that made him mysteri-ous and all the more desirable. He spent more time building up his body than his life, hanging out at the gym bench pressing with the boys.

"Where's my bitch?" David would bark at the crowd, snapping his eyes from corner to corner around the restau-rant.

His "bitch" was Marsha Joy Rash, a tall, blond young

woman and the latest lover in David's ever-growing stock-pile of girlfriends.

Like his other girls, Marsha remained at David's beck and call. Always there to light his cigarettes. To fetch him more coffee. To cook him "poor boy's beef-a-roni"—a mixture of pasta noodles, ground beef, chunks of cream cheese, and tomato sauce. David's girls were more like mothers than girlfriends. They cooked for him, washed his clothes, paid his rent, even gave him money and cigarettes. And he reveled in their idolization of him. Marsha knew David could have any girl he wanted, but he chose her.

It seemed, though, that there was more to Marsha than her looks that was keeping David's attention. He had been going out with her for three solid months with no downtime in between. Just a few weeks after hooking up, they were already sharing an apartment with one other roommate in Seattle's southern working-class suburb of Renton, known for its cheap apartment rents and high crime.

Some of the girls in the Denny's crowd knew he wanted only one thing: sex. And they didn't mind giving it to him. He, in turn, showered them with compliments on how beautiful they were. But David was smart. He seemed to select the girls he knew he could easily manipulate. For the most part, David's girlfriends were an eclectic mix of punk girls who dyed their hair purple and wore spikes, and girls who wore glasses and hit the books hard, but dated him to elevate their status—they wanted to be cool. When he met girls, he seemed to control them with relative ease. And if he—David Anderson—had one thing going for him, it was complete and utter control.

Members of the Denny's gang began wondering whether David and Alex were deep into another game of Dungeons and Dragons—a fantasy role-playing game popular among the Denny's kids—and that was why they weren't around. It was a game the boys had become addicted to in their early teens, and they were good at it. Other times they would sit in front of the computer for hours, mesmerized by the images jerking and sliding across a computer screen and machine-gun noises emanating from speakers. And sometimes they acted out their fantasies in a live setting. Their friends knew whenever they got involved in a game, they were lost to a world of fantasy and darkness. One game was like any other.

They would come out at night when the streets emptied out and there was room to prowl. They would ride wide plains of darkness, zigzagging across town, through neighborhoods, and into abandoned parks. There they would don their capes and white makeup, pull out their fake swords, and stalk through the trees and bushes, searching for the enemy. Trained to kill.

Through streetlamp-punctured twilight, they would hunt Woodridge's Water Tower Park in search of each other. They became shadows, dressed in black, gliding in and out of moonbeams as they would plunge their swords through the air.

Alex would come out of the trees and step onto a path. He would hear a rustling in the bushes nearby, and before he would have a chance to turn around, he would feel a sharp object sticking him in the back.

"You're dead!" David would shout, tapping Alex with his fake sword to indicate a fatal blow that would end this session of Dungeons and Dragons role-playing.

"I am Slicer Thunderclap, god of evil. I am immortal, you fool," Alex would carp, running off into the trees. "I will never die. I will never die . . ."

On that Sunday, January 5, David and Alex spent all day in their Dungeons and Dragons roles, oblivious to the chaos surrounding the gruesome discovery on Woodridge Hill.

Later that night, after returning to their separate homes,

David went to his room and fell asleep. A few miles away, Alex was at the home of Ron and Valerie Boyd, where he rented a room. He was watching the 11 P.M. news with his friend and peer, Bob Boyd. Boyd was surprised to hear that a member of the group he and Alex hung out with at Denny's was brutally murdered. He knew David had been good friends with Kim, and so he figured Alex would have heard from David what had happened to her. Bob looked at him with an imploring gaze.

"Don't look at me, dude," Alex said, chuckling. "I didn't do it."

By midnight, an oily darkness had spread across the sky. At the Wilson home, the Christmas lights blinking along the gutters were a bizarre counterpart to the grisly scene inside. It was too dark to accomplish much more in the investigation. Gomes and members of the State Patrol Crime Lab agreed that it would be better to call it a night and come back fresh in the morning, when there would be much more light to work with. Detectives agreed to leave the bodies in the home until then.

As the street began to slowly empty out around midnight, the only things that remained were a few patrol cars and two on-duty police officers in charge of keeping vigil at the house. The officers had been instructed to patrol the area throughout the night to ensure no one could get in and tamper with the evidence.

That night, Gomes did something he ordinarily did not do. When he arrived home, he rechecked to make sure the garage doors and front door were locked before going to bed. He could not get the image of those people out of his mind. Although he couldn't tell for sure just how old each victim was, the family structure looked a lot like his own: mom and dad, and two young daughters in or approaching adulthood.

Never before had Gomes felt so vulnerable.

"If it could happen to the Wilsons, it could happen to my family," Gomes would later say.

Gomes went to bed that night without a clue as to who the killer or killers might be. All he knew was that the bodies were fresh—meaning the victims had died recently—and so the perpetrators could not be too far away. The next morning, he would hear about Claire Hearn and meet with her. Gomes would spend the next several days hunting down the attackers in much the same way it seemed the killers had hunted down the Wilsons.

6 At 6 A.M., Monday morning, Jeff Gomes hurried down the stairwell at the Bellevue Police Department and headed to his desk in the basement of the building. It was cluttered with tips from the previous night scrawled on scraps of paper and Post-it notes.

He rummaged through the notes and rewrote each on an 8½-by-11 sheet of white paper. He had investigated enough cases to know how important it was to stay organized, to keep information in one place so it's accessible later.

Bob Thompson and Jerry Johnson also showed up early that morning, knowing they each had a long day ahead of them.

At 9 A.M., the traffic division conference room filled with uniformed officers, detectives, prosecutors, members of the State Patrol Crime Lab, and top brass at the Bellevue Police Department. Gomes had called for a briefing so everyone could share information and find out what new leads and duties would have to be pursued or performed that day.

Thompson was to go back to the Wilson home with a crew from the State Patrol Crime Lab; Johnson was to go to Water Tower Park and begin processing that crime scene. Several officers were sent to Woodridge to canvass the neighborhood, to talk to neighbors and anyone who knew the Wilson family in order to get more information.

The officer who had spoken with Claire Hearn the previous night told Gomes about her and gave him her phone number. Claire seemed to know Kim and her family pretty well, he said. Gomes agreed to check her out that afternoon.

The briefing lasted less than an hour, and immediately afterward, Gomes and Patty Eakes, who had also attended the briefing, drove to Woodridge to find Claire Hearn.

They arrived at a house just up the street from the Wilson residence and knocked on the door. Claire answered and invited Gomes and Eakes inside. She responded to the detective's questions eagerly, hoping to provide whatever information she could to help the investigation. Claire told the detective and the prosecutor of the conversation she had had with Kim about David Anderson and his friend Alex, whose last name she didn't know.

After questioning Claire for about an hour, Gomes asked if she would mind showing them around Woodridge. They wanted to know where this David Anderson lived. She agreed and hopped in the backseat of Gomes' patrol car.

As Gomes' car wound its way around the hill, Claire pointed out the home on Southeast 25th Street where David grew up, and where his parents still lived. Next, Gomes drove past Norwood Park—another neighborhood park where Kim used to hang out with her friends. Claire herself had been in that park numerous times with Kim, swinging or just sitting on the grass and talking. Then Claire agreed to accompany Gomes and Eakes to Seattle to point out the apartment of Sarah Lamp.

Claire told the detective and the prosecutor that Sarah was good friends with Kim and had once dated her. She went on to explain how Kim, in the past two or three years, had started experimenting with her sexuality. She had not come out to her parents, and only a few of her friends knew about her bisexuality. Sarah, apparently, was one of Kim's first girlfriends.

"Do you know why they broke up?" Eakes asked.

"No. I think they just wanted to move on."

Gomes' ears perked up. Whoever this Sarah woman was, Gomes knew he needed to reach her. Surviving family members, lovers, or friends can often lead detectives in the right direction on their hunt for the killers. Detectives frequently don't have to go further than that to find their suspects.

But before speaking to Sarah Lamp, he wanted to first talk to the person who saw Kim last on Friday night. Claire believed that would have been Sky Stewart, another of Kim's friends, and former girlfriends.

That afternoon, Gomes paged Sky—a young, soft-spoken woman with red hair and several piercings on her ears, nose, and eyebrow. Sky had been a friend of Kim's since 1995, when the women met at Denny's. She'd been working Sunday and hadn't heard the news that Kim and her family had been murdered.

Sky didn't recognize the number that popped up on her pager, but she called it anyway. She talked to Gomes, who broke the news. Trying to hold back tears, Sky agreed to meet with Gomes to tell him more about Kim.

At police headquarters, Sky told the detective that Kim was a close friend. That Friday night, they'd had plans to spend time together before Kim was to leave town Sunday morning to return to her job with AmeriCorps.

Sky recounted the night's events for Gomes, which sounded like nothing more than an evening of running errands. She'd picked Kim up at her house just after 9 P.M. after Kim had returned from a walk with her high school pal, Erin Gauntlett. They headed to the Best electronic store so Sky could buy an alarm clock. The women then went to the Bon Marche at Bellevue Square shopping mall so Sky could pay her bills. Finally, they drove to McDonald's to get snacks, then headed to Denny's in Issaquah. Kim had hoped to find a friend of hers whom she thought would be there. Kim and Sky shared a booth and a pack of cigarettes. They talked for about forty-five minutes and decided to leave when they couldn't find Kim's friend.

It was around 10:30 P.M. by then, still a little too early for these night owls to turn in, but Kim had to pack the next day and Sky wanted to meet up with her boyfriend. The girls called it a night, and Sky zipped back across town to drop Kim off at home. Lights around the city blinked off one by one as the girls wound their way through Woodridge and finally came to a stop in front of Kim's house. It was just after 11 P.M.

They made a date to see a movie the next day, on Saturday. Kim promised to call. Sky lit a cigarette and drove away. The next day, she waited to hear from her friend.

But Kim never called.

As Monday wore on, who the Wilsons were—or had been— grew more clear.

Unlike many of the families who moved to Bellevue, the Wilson family was not part of the nouveaux riches who had big show homes, flashy cars, and sailboats. They did not come to Bellevue for the high-tech jobs that attracted so many others. Both Bill and Rose Wilson, who had met at the University of Washington's business school, worked as accountants: Rose, for the University of Washington's library; Bill, for a construction company called Graham Steel in the neighboring city of Kirkland. Rose drove a minivan and took her kids to family-style restaurants rather than to the upscale restaurants scattered throughout downtown. They had a strong twenty-five-year marriage, and with their daughters, Kim and Julia, and the family dog, Moe, appeared to be a typical suburban family.

Bill and Rose decided to move to Bellevue in 1984, and specifically to the Woodridge neighborhood in search of a good place to raise a family. Woodridge was already an established middle- and upper-middle-class area by the time they arrived. While many retirees lived there in the '90s, it has remained mostly a family enclave.

Not everyone on Woodridge Hill belongs to the same socioeconomic strata. A family's placement on the hill indicates its income level. Toward the bottom of the hill, the homes are small, wood-frame, two- or three-bedroom structures with a limited patch of lawn and no sidewalks. Farther up the hill, where the views of downtown Bellevue and the Seattle skyline are more pronounced, the homes are more lavish, some with winding driveways that cut through fresh layers of bark dust and expensive landscaping.

At Christmas, families string up lights along their gutters and windows—a ritual that makes the entire neighborhood glow like candles under the marble-gray December moon. Holidays in Woodridge seem to endure longer than elsewhere in town. Even in January, many homes are still washed in that red-and-green lollipop glow.

Bill and Rose Wilson were more conservative when it came to decorating their house for the holidays; it lacked the plastic lawn ornaments and fancy lighting systems seen on other homes on their street. Every year, Bill hung a single strand of lights on the rain gutters and a wreath on the door. They were festive without being excessive.

The Wilsons had been moving up the hill. They built their life around their children and their home, remodeling this, redecorating that. They spent entire weekends hammering nails into wood planks on their deck or reorganizing closets. They bought their first home in Woodridge in 1984, a starter home toward the bottom of the hill that they purchased for $167,000. But in 1990, after saving enough money to move closer to the top of the hill, the couple spent just over $200,000 on 1521 121st Avenue Southeast. The remodeling alone in the new home cost the Wilsons thousands of dollars more, so if they had the money to spend, they figured they might as well invest it in their home and get a higher return when and if they ever decided to sell it. By 1997, the home was valued at $240,000. But they weren't at all nouveaux riches.

At 5 feet 8 inches, Bill was of average height, and he balanced his 200 pounds on sturdy legs that carried him over high mountain trails and across vast stretches of beaches. He remained active—even into his fifties—hiking, walking, biking; and at the end of January 1997, he and his wife had planned to be parasailing off the picture-postcard-perfect coasts of Hawaii to celebrate their twenty-fifth anniversary. Bill's physical activity had a lot to do with his wife; he followed Rose along hiking trails and beaches to keep her company, and also to make sure nothing bad happened to her.

Rose was an expert scuba diver and was excited about diving in the deep-sea waters of Hawaii during the upcoming anniversary trip. She had, on many instances, plunged into the chilly Puget Sound with her scuba club. Much smaller than her husband, at 5 feet 2 inches and 150 pounds, Rose easily and excitedly propelled herself through the water.

Bill was a man with an admirable work ethic and compassion. Once, when a new employee at his company needed a place to stay while looking for housing, Bill put him up in a hotel. He cared about people, whether they were friends or strangers. And he took pride in being a family man, helping his wife raise their two daughters. Rose also placed a high priority on family. She would shuttle her daughters to piano practice and swim meets, and in her spare time would volunteer as a "Brownie Mom" in their Girl Scouts troops. Both she and Bill worked hard to be able to provide these avenues of improvement for their girls.

The Wilson sisters competed on the Norwood Swim Team, one of two private swimming clubs in their neighborhood. They both were active members of the youth group at

First Presbyterian Church. One year, they spent the summer in Halfway, Oregon, helping build homes for the poor. Another summer, they participated in a Love of God retreat in which church members are encouraged to find peace with God. The sisters also were regularly called on to baby-sit neighborhood kids. They were dependable and responsible when it came to caring for kids; both were favorite picks on the neighborhood's co-op list of baby-sitters.

However, while Kim and Julia were sisters, they were very different in character. Kim was the rebel of the two, the one who cupped her baseball cap and wore it backward—the final touch to her usual outfit of blue jeans, black combat boots, and plaid shirts. Julia preferred a softer, more feminine style of flower-patterned dresses and skirts with blouses. She loved spending the day at the mall; Kim, on the other hand, preferred to spend her free moments getting grease under her chewed-up fingernails as she helped her dad rebuild a Mustang in the garage.

Kim and Julia got along well, for the most part, but as they both maneuvered their way through high school and adolescence, they were given to sisterly squabbling and complaining about the other talking on the phone too much or not doing a fair share of household chores. Kim's mercurial temper often stoked the flames of what exploded into epic battles between them. Julia was more reserved, yet stubborn and unwilling to surrender to her bigger sister.

One weekend morning, Rose was awakened to ear-piercing shouting. She jumped out of bed and hurried downstairs, only to be greeted by a box of macaroni and cheese flying through the air. It crashed into the far wall of the kitchen, just above Kim's head, and spilled noodles everywhere on the floor. Kim had been taunting Julia, telling her that eating mac and cheese would make her fat. Rose put an end to the arguing, and the sisters each went their separate ways, at least for the moment.

Some of the more worrisome family conflicts occurred between mother and daughter. Rose and Kim had been at odds with each other since Kim started high school. Kim had taken to hanging out with what Rose considered to be some underachieving friends at school. She started cutting classes, and she blamed it on the pain from her bad back. But Rose refused to let Kim use her pain as a crutch. If Kim was feigning pain, she was to go to school immediately. No buts about it.

Much of the time, though, the pain was real.

As a kid, Kim began feeling a tight knot in her lower back, as if someone had just stepped on that part of her body. She bent down one day to tie her shoe and it was as if her spine had snapped in the middle. A sharp pain coursed through her body, a pain that never completely left her.

Doctors diagnosed a congenital back problem. They had tried several times to alleviate the excruciating twinges for Kim, offering drugs and finally, as a last resource, surgery. Kim had gone through several rounds of back surgery. Then it all stopped in 1991, when she was fifteen years old. Doctors attempted a bone graft to correct her problem. The surgery seemed to take forever, and after it was all over, there was only disappointment. Kim was not relieved of the pain, the operation wasn't successful, and the doctors threw up their hands. At that point, there was nothing more they could do.

When the hope of a cure for her persistent pain was ruled out, and she was left with a bad scar and years of wasted effort, this was probably the biggest disappointment of Kim's life.

The pain had followed Kim from her early childhood into adolescence. By her senior year of high school, it had become so bad she began to miss classes more regularly. A day here, a day there. So many absent days stacked up by the end of the year that she nearly failed her courses. She had spent the better part of her senior year negotiating with teachers for a good grade. It was the back pain, she would tell them. The pain was a shadow on her life; she couldn't concentrate on anything.

But Rose, graceful, diplomatic Rose, turned the situation into a challenge rather than an obstacle in Kim's life. She helped her elder daughter learn how to cope with the pain, how to manage it so that it didn't consume her life.

Kim grew up in a household with a lot of freedom. Bill and Rose chose not to impose curfews on their girls. They raised their daughters with few boundaries, the extent of which appalled Rose's brothers, who, along with her, had been brought up under the rigid constraints of Catholicism. But Rose didn't want her children to feel confined. She encouraged them to venture out, to explore new places and things. Rose wanted her children to grow up and be able to think for themselves and make their own decisions, which Kim ultimately did.

While she appeared to be a model daughter who baby-sat neighborhood kids, attended church regularly, and competed on the swim team, there was another side to Kim. She enjoyed spending her free time at Denny's with her buddies, and, like them, she started wearing black clothes and combat boots. In her last two years of high school, Kim distanced herself from her family and moved further into the world of dropout friends and few responsibilities. She started smoking, hoping to soothe some of her back pain, friends said, but it was also a habit her parents would complain about. She started running with a different crowd, a tougher, more rebellious group of kids who were less interested in graduating and going to college than in chain-smoking and killing time at local Denny's restaurants.

It was Kim's friends whom Rose felt most uneasy about.

"Oh, God, one of Kim's friends is sleeping on the couch again," Rose blurted out to co-worker Tasha Taylor as she arrived at work one morning. It was not unusual for the Wilsons to have teenagers crashing at their home. These were friends of Kim's who had been kicked out or who had run away from home; and sometimes homeless kids who just needed a place to stay for a couple of nights as they rotated among their friends where they would sleep. At the Wilson home, there was no telling who would show up for breakfast.

No matter whom their children were friends with, Bill and Rose always had an open-door policy. But no one could have known that the Wilsons' trust in people—friends or strangers—would be an open invitation for evil to enter their home and impinge on the sanctity of family life.

That Monday morning, as Detective Gomes and Patty Eakes were being driven around Woodridge with Claire Hearn in the backseat, King County Senior Deputy Prosecutor Jeff Baird was getting to know the Wilsons in a much more personal way, not by interviewing friends or relatives of the deceased, but by learning just how they had died.

Eakes, who knew she would be overwhelmed with the quadruple slayings, called on the veteran prosecutor to assist her. Baird was a thirty-five-year-old dynamo with an unblemished record at the King County Prosecutor's Office. He started the Violent Offenders Program just a few years earlier, which allowed prosecutors to be more extensively involved with police investigations of major crimes.

Baird's first task in helping out with the Wilson murder case was to spend the morning at the King County Medical Examiner's Office and observe and take notes during the postmortem examinations. Two workers at the ME's Office were in charge of the autopsies on all four bodies—a long and tedious process that involved cutting, probing, and reexamining every inch of the body to determine exactly how and possibly even when each person had died.

Dr. Richard C. Harruff is a small, soft-spoken man, trained as a general forensic pathologist. As an associate medical examiner for King County, he is involved with almost all of the county's 1,000 or so autopsies each year, and since 1983, he has performed or supervised some 10,000 postmortem examinations with that office. He thought he had seen all manners of grotesque murders until that Monday, January 6, when he supervised the examination of the body of Kim Wilson. Performed by Dr. Raven, a pathology fellow in training, it would be the first autopsy of an entire family brutally murdered at once.

Kim Wilson, Dr. Harruff noted, was a normally developed white female, age twenty, 156 pounds, and 5 feet 7 inches tall, dressed in several articles of clothing and a few items of jewelry. Her clothes—a University of Washington Huskies sweatshirt over a blue-plaid shirt, blue jeans, and hiking boots—had been soiled from her lying outside in the dirt. A brown leather belt was fastened around her waist, and on it was a small leather loop with a metal ring. There should have been a wallet or key chain there, Dr. Harruff surmised. But there was nothing on the ring.

Dr. Harruff noted that Kim had a quarter-inch-thick cord of rope wrapped twice around her neck within which two necklaces were tangled. The rope was wrapped so tightly that it had caused blood vessels in her eyes to pop, dotting the whites of her eyeballs with red specks.

Just above the rope, Kim's neck bore the signs of ligature furrows, caused by movement of the rope. From these chafing patterns, it appeared that the rope had been tied once, undone, and retied.

Dr. Harruff determined that Kim had died of asphyxia, or strangulation. From experience, he knew Kim had not lived long while she was being strangled. Without oxygen to her brain, she probably would have become unconscious after ten seconds and died within four minutes.

Undressed, Kim's body bore the clear signs of abuse—her back was covered with blue bruises. Her face was spotted with abrasions and was bruised or scraped over her cheeks, eyes, nose, and the left side of her chin—injuries Dr. Harruff believes were caused by a blunt object. Several areas of skin on her face had rubbed off, but, given the circumstance in which she was found—outdoors, facedown, in a park—Dr. Harruff had difficulty determining how much of that was caused by the attack and how much was caused by insects eating away at her skin.

The injuries did not stop there. Inside Kim's body, Dr. Harruff discovered unusual damage to her internal organs. Kim's left flank, the part of the torso between the hip and the ribs, was covered with striated reddish-purple marks. One bone in her left rib and two in her right were fractured. Beneath the bruises, Kim's kidney and spleen had been torn—an injury that Dr. Harruff would later testify could be caused only by extreme force. A simple kick could not cause that kind of internal damage, he would later declare. More likely, Kim's upper body had been crushed. For instance, Kim might have been lying on the ground and her attackers had repeatedly stomped on her, Harruff said. The kind of force it would take to bring about the sorts of internal injuries Kim had suffered would equal her having been in a car and hitting something while traveling about thirty miles per hour.

A small amount of bleeding that occurred internally around those organs means Kim was probably still alive when she received the wounds to her left flank. The dead do not bleed. But it's likely she did not live very long after that.

7 Like the other Woodridge kids, Kim Wilson loved Water Tower Park, a place she seemed to spend more time in than her own bedroom. As a kid, she loved to swing through the trees and play hide and seek along the trails and among the cavernous bushes. The park was so close to her home, it was like having a second backyard. Well into her teens, Kim continued to go there to get away from the world, to find peace when everything seemed as if it were spinning out of control.

The news of Kim's death sent a ripple of shock through her group of friends. Just days after the murders, they left bouquets of flowers for her at the park, under the cedar tree where her body had been found. Along with the flowers, they left notes flooded with a mixture of emotions, grief and sorrow, anger and confusion; the pain bled off the pages as the rain pelted the stark white sheets. Day after day, the part of the trail where her body had been found was turned into a makeshift memorial. The friends who came hoped to feel her spirit among the trees she used to hide under as a child. They stood, shaking their heads and sobbing, holding each other as they trembled beneath the wet January sky.

She was born Kimberly Ann Wilson on September 21, 1976—a cute little baby with bright blond hair and big blue luminous eyes. She had an innocent smile and rosy cheeks that masked the mischief in her. When she was barely two, she was already getting into trouble, yanking pots and pans from cupboards and pulling on just about everything within reach: the tablecloth, phone cord, chairs. Once, she tried to climb a ladder to the top of her family's house, where workers were installing a new roof. This behavior was typical of any two-year-old, but Kim was particularly precocious. Rose always had to keep an eye on her because she had an infinite supply of energy, more so than most kids. Kim had an inborn curiosity; she wanted to know everything. Like her parents, she grew up to be compassionate and kind, offering help to anyone who needed it.

Kim was a healthy, happy kid, until she started having back problems. The pain somehow hardened her. She developed an edge, assuming the role of a tough street kid who could fight her own fights and start them, too. By the time she entered high school, Kim had become a strong-willed, independent young woman, unafraid of anyone or anything.

The Wilsons had only one other child, a daughter who was born three years after Kim.

On the Fourth of July in 1979, Julia Wilson emerged into the world, becoming the little sister whom Kim could pick on and to whom she would pass hand-me-downs and sisterly advice on anything from guys to friends to teachers.

Julia was much more shy than her sister; she focused on school rather than a social life. In her adolescence, while most teenagers wouldn't be caught dead with their parents, she worked out at the gym with her mother. At first glance, Julia appeared to be a pretty girl with a sweet smile and timid eyes. But a closer look revealed a droopy left eye—a birth defect that required surgery, which left her with a tiny metal plate behind the globe. Unlike her sister, Julia had only a few close friends with whom she ate lunch, went to the movies, and shopped.

Outgoing and buoyant, Kim was always on the hunt for adventure and new friends. In grade school, she met a cute little blond boy named David Anderson, who she later discovered lived just down the street from her family's first Woodridge home. David was younger than Kim; in fact, he was Julia's age. But the two grew close anyway. By the time David started middle school, he and Kim began dating off and on. They were an item for three consecutive summers. During that time, they would meet on the weekends and go for long walks at Norwood Park or Water Tower Park in their neighborhood. But the puppy-love relationship ended as Kim found herself immersed in high school activities. By then, she was also interested in someone else. Kim's childhood friendship with David would be one of the earliest and most important relationships in her life. Only later—several years later—would anyone realize just how significant it was.

In high school, Kim kept up a frenetic pace of life. She became a student body officer, and she would walk around the hallways asking her friends what they would like to see changed in school. She was outspoken about her concerns, and wanted to hear what others had to say, too. Kim made a name for herself as a "natural helper"—a student who is nominated by his or her peers as the person you would most likely go to if you had a problem. Natural helpers attend a weekend training course to teach them how to respond to friends in trouble. One of the most helpful things to do, she learned, was to just listen.

Kim was skilled at just that. One of her favorite pastimes was to go on walks in Water Tower Park, where she would listen to her friends talk about their problems at home or at school, or about trouble in their love lives. She and her friends also would hang out in the evenings at Norwood Park, where they would sit on the swings and talk. They liked the peace out there, the solitude that daylight made impossible. At night, they felt as if the world were theirs alone.

Kim encouraged people to stay in school. She would talk

to her friends in the Denny's crowd who had dropped out, urging them to reenroll and to at least get their high school diploma, because that way they could still get a good job somewhere. She convinced her best friend, Sky Stewart, to finish high school, and tried to persuade her ex-boyfriend Bill Krock to go to college.

Kim met Bill when she was a junior and he was a senior at Bellevue High School. The son of a BHS math teacher, Bill carved his own path in life; his plans after high school did not include going to college. Instead, he worked odd jobs until finally getting a job at Fitz Autoparts, one of the Seattle area's largest auto-body shops.

But Kim's imposition of her morals and values onto others caused her relationship with Bill to fracture and finally end.

Unlike Julia, Kim was not so motivated to go to college, but instead had her own ideas for what she would do after leaving the security of high school. She got a job in the administrative office at Costco—a popular wholesale store—and she took night classes at Bellevue Community College. It was Kim's strategy to buy time, to give herself a chance to decide what she wanted to do with the rest of her life, or at least with the next few years of it. While taking college classes, Kim continued to live at home. At night, she grabbed her books and took them to a corner table at Denny's, where she would study until her friends showed up to talk with her.

Kim's life had been an unplanned chain of events that had no sense of order and no sense of urgency. She took each day as it came, and the future was someplace she wasn't sure she wanted to go, even to visit. It seemed so distant.

Her approach to life was simple. She decided that she was young, and she'd be young only once, so she was determined to have as much fun as possible. Going to the movies, hanging out with friends, staying out late, and meeting new people every day. That was one thing that there was no shortage of in Kim's life—friends.

Kim became friends with just about anyone and everyone. She was known for having a diverse combination of friends from church, school, the neighborhood, and Denny's. Surprisingly, it was hard, at first, to get to know her. She put up her guard, and until she felt comfortable with someone new, she would keep it up. But once a person made it past that threshold, Kim was a loyal, dependable friend. She loaned her friends money, bought them cigarettes, drove them just about anywhere they wanted to go. They all knew they could turn to her when they were having trouble at home. And they did.

Kim kept an assortment of friends from the Denny's crowd in the basement, where they slept on the couch. One of the Wilsons' more frequent guests was David Anderson. David had been one of Kim's few childhood friends whom she kept in contact with, and he was so close to the Wilsons that he was considered part of the family. If he wasn't spending the night, Bill and Rose often saw him when he stopped by to meet Kim so they could walk around the neighborhood together. They also enjoyed cruising around Woodridge Hill and Bellevue.

There was always someone coming or going in the Wilson home, so Bill and Rose never locked their doors. And there really wasn't any need to. The Woodridge neighborhood was one of the safest in the city. People regularly left their garages open and their car doors unlocked.

That home life, and that sense of comfort, were foreign to a lot of kids in the Denny's gang. When Kim's friends slept on the couch, they awoke to a warm room and breakfast, to a mom and dad at home and the family dog sniffing around their shoes. Despite some conflicts the Wilsons faced, they tried to be a family—something that so many in the Denny's crowd didn't have.

Rose never questioned her daughters' choice of friends. She raised Kim and Julia to make their own friends. Still, there were times when Kim brought kids home from the Denny's crowd whom Rose watched suspiciously.

"But she's a good kid," Rose would say. Rose taught her children to judge people not by outward appearances but by their inner souls, the things that made them good people.

That's why Kim had so many friends. They now wanted to know who could commit such a hideous crime. In their minds, they scrolled through the list of possible suspects— old boyfriends, estranged relatives, even possible admirers—but they were unable to come up with any names that they could, with certainty, offer to investigators. Each friend seemed sure of the same thing: Kim had no enemies.

If anything, the twenty-year-old young woman was the perfect friend. Her buddies knew they could count on her night and day. Like many teenagers in this suburban town, she kept a pager clipped to her blue jeans everywhere she went, and passed out the number to all her friends. While most teens carried pagers to be cool, Kim kept the leash on out of a sense of duty. It was a way for her to be a twenty-four-hour friend.

"Call me any time," she said, and meant it. She would answer pages in the middle of the night or while she was eating breakfast; to her, every call was an emergency. She was always prepared to handle any number of crises among her cadre of friends. She never let any of her calls go unanswered.

In fact, if this young woman had any faults, it was that she had too many friends. She cared passionately about all those who crossed her path, loaning them money, giving them food, a place to stay, even offering advice.

But in the end, she had trusted two too many people.

8 By Tuesday morning, January 7, police had received no viable leads. The more time that elapsed, the more detectives in the Bellevue Police Department worried that the suspects might never be found. In police work, there's a golden forty-eight hours after a crime has been committed in which investigators have to find a suspect, or else the chances of solving the case dramatically decrease. Gomes had already passed forty-eight hours. But he did not let the pressure get to him. He worked at his own steady, methodical pace, and it never failed him.

That day, he focused on finding two people: Sarah Lamp and Bill Krock, both of whom reportedly had had romantic relationships with Kim Wilson. Gomes had no reason to believe they were in any way involved in the murders, but it was a starting point to learn more about Kim and possibly others in her life who might have wanted her dead. However, before Gomes could follow up on either of those leads, a new, more solid one surfaced.

Kevin Wulff, the principal at Bellevue High School, where both Wilson girls were educated, called to say he had two students who had important information to share with police. It was to be the first big break in the case.

Gomes sent the husband-and-wife team of Detective John McBride and Officer Molly McBride—both veterans of the BPD—to check out the tip. John McBride was a short, heavyset man with silvery hair and a friendly face. He was working in the department's Personal Crimes/Special Assault Unit when he was called on to help with the Wilson investigation. Molly McBride was a petite woman with long blond hair. She was soft-spoken, and her years in the department's Special Assault Unit, where, among other duties, she interviewed abuse and sexual-assault victims, had helped hone her skills as a good listener. She had previously held the title of detective, but in order to qualify for advancement under the BPD's promotion system, she had to go back to patrol and work up from there. Together, the McBrides complemented each other in their investigative techniques.

When they arrived at the school, perched on a bluff in downtown Bellevue, they met two nervous young women in the counselor's office, their eyes wide with fear.

Amryn Decker and Danielle Berry were seniors at BHS. They were good friends and had a lot in common—one of which was a guy named David Anderson. Both were his ex-girlfriends. When they heard about the Wilson murders, the news triggered a disturbing memory—something David had told them separately when they were going out with him.

The young women told the McBrides that they believed David Anderson had something to do with the murders. The secret fantasy David shared with each of them had finally come true.

David had boasted that he was planning to commit a murder. He spoke of his plans in great detail, saying he would use knives and a baseball bat, and that he would do it before he turned seventeen so he wouldn't have to spend his life in jail. (David, as it turns out, was misinformed about Washington State law and believed that if he commited a felony before age eighteen, he would be eligible for release on his twenty-first birthday.) Although they didn't know whom David planned to kill, they felt like he had to have been involved in the Wilson murders. They didn't know Kim Wilson personally, but they knew David had had some sort of falling-out with her. Over the course of a year, he had developed a hatred toward Kim, although they weren't exactly sure why. She, on the other hand, still trusted him with her life.

Danielle and Amryn wept and trembled as they told the police about the separate conversations they had had with David.

"It was him," they agreed. "David had something to do with it."

While the McBrides were questioning the two students at BHS, police officers were scouring through Water Tower Park in search of possible evidence.

Because Detective Jerry Johnson was the first detective to arrive at the park in response to the call of a dead body, he had been placed in charge of processing the evidence there. On Tuesday morning, Johnson and several officers continued to comb the area, on hands and knees, searching for any small clue that might tell them more about what had happened that fatal night.

On the path, near where Kim's body was found, Johnson picked up an empty pack of Dave's cigarettes, a Marlboro cigarette butt, and a Rainier Ale bottle cap, among other items.

Johnson also carefully went through the contents of a garbage can in the parking lot. However, he would find nothing connecting to the crime.

Over the next few days, he and his crew would keep on with their tedious search, scavenging for any sliver of evidence that might help lead them to the killers.

That same morning, in Seattle, Prosecutor Baird again spent the day with two medical examiners as they autopsied the three bodies of Rose, Bill, and Julia Wilson. Unlike Kim

Wilson's, these bodies were covered in blood, which had soaked into their clothes and caked onto their skin. Dr. Harruff knew from the start that these autopsies would take much longer than Kim's, because there were a lot more injuries to examine.

Rose Wilson had died from a blunt-force injury to her head. She was dressed in a nightgown. Her head had been so badly beaten, it was misshapen; the right side had been driven in for two inches. Her left hand had received a slight blunt-force injury, and the stone in her wedding ring had been knocked out.

Whatever it was that hit her, the force of the impact had shattered her skull, which crushed into her brain. She suffered severe brain damage, which was the principal cause of her death, Dr. Harruff determined.

Rose's head and neck also were covered with stab wounds. More than once, the weapon had been forced all the way through her neck, coming out the other side and piercing her left shoulder. Dr. Harruff would conclude that it would take a sharp weapon at least eight inches long to cause such an injury.

The wound pattern showed that Rose's injuries were lined up in neat clusters. From that, Dr. Harruff could deduce that she was not moving—was probably asleep—when she was attacked.

She did not live long. The damage caused to her brain would have resulted in almost immediate death, Dr. Harruff estimated.

For Baird, witnessing the autopsies was a helpful yet exhausting task. He knew the importance of learning just how each victim was killed.

"It's the most important scene of the crime," Baird would later say.

One of the most significant things Baird learned from the pattern of injuries and wounds was what type of person would do this. The murders were clearly overkill and deliberately gratuitous.

"I knew this was someone for whom killing had been its own motive," Baird would later say. "It was almost as if the people had died before the killers were gratified. They had to continue to mutilate them after their deaths because the mere act of killing was not adequate."

In the postmortem examination of Bill Wilson, Dr. Harruff determined he had died from a combination of blunt-force and sharp-force injuries. Similar to his wife's, Bill's injuries were limited to his head and neck.

Bill's skull had cracked in triangular pieces. He suffered a total of a dozen stab wounds and cuts, and a dozen blunt-force injuries. One of the stab wounds—a through-and-through wound—measured five and a half inches long. The wound started under Bill's left ear, went deep through the neck, sliced through the spinal cord, and finally cut through an artery that supplies blood to the brain. That blow would have immediately paralyzed Bill. He was probably still alive at that point, but unable to crawl or move away.

Human skulls are generally about a quarter inch thick. It would take considerable force to drive a knife right through the skull, but that's what happened to Bill. As Dr. Harruff cut a piece of the skull away to x-ray it, he noticed a tiny piece of metal stuck in the bone. The tip of a knife blade had apparently broken off during the attack.

"It could mean that when the blade was in, it was twisted, causing a can-opener effect, to pop open a piece of skull," Dr. Harruff would later testify.

Unlike Rose's injuries, Bill's wounds were chaotically distributed on his head and neck. He was probably moving at the time of the attack, perhaps struggling to escape as the attacker continued to rain blows down on him.

Both Bill and Rose were clearly caught off guard when they were attacked, as their injuries suggested. But the injuries suffered by their younger daughter, Julia, suggested she was the only one who had struggled for her life.

Julia's body was the only one that bore signs of defensive wounds—generally, wounds to the hands, arms, legs, and feet that indicate a person is trying to protect himself against the attacker. Julia had died from multiple stab wounds delivered to her body, Dr. Harruff determined.

During the attack, two of Julia's teeth had been knocked out; someone had hit her in the face, either with a fist or some other heavy object. Dr. Harruff reported again that it would take considerable force to cause these kinds of injuries.

He offered two different scenarios on what could have happened: Julia's head was either lifted and pounded repeatedly onto the floor, or her head was on the floor and the attacker kicked or stomped it.

Julia's right forearm was broken, which suggests she put up her arms to ward off her attacker, Dr. Harruff later testified.

A large reddish bruise stained Julia's right foot, which possibly could have been caused by someone stomping on it with a heavy shoe, Dr. Harruff said.

Julia also had sustained two stab wounds to the left side of her chest, one which measured one and a half inches long and the other a quarter inch deep, plus several stab wounds to her face and several more on her neck.

On Julia's neck, Dr. Harruff noted five cuts, one of which was a lethal wound, cutting her jugular vein and carotid artery. Julia had aspirated a lot of blood, which would have caused her to go into shock.

Among the stab wounds to Julia's neck, one went all the way through the trachea, severing the windpipe. At that point, she would have been unable to scream for help.

Like he did with her father, the killer left a piece of his weapon behind. Dr. Harruff found a sliver of metal lodged in

Julia's skull. X-rays showed it was probably iron, because of the rust discoloration.

Dr. Harruff put both pieces of metal—the one found in Bill Wilson's skull and that found in Julia Wilson's—under the microscope. What he found was startling.

"It appears that the two pieces of metal came from the same source, but the actual tip of the blade is in Mr. Wilson's skull and then the second piece broken from the same blade is in Julia's skull." That meant that Bill must have been attacked before the killer went after his younger daughter with the same sharp weapon.

In all, Julia suffered twenty-four sharp wound injuries.

But there was something particularly disturbing about Julia's injuries. She suffered three stab wounds to her left eye. The knife went straight into the eye socket. One of the wounds was so deep it cut the globe, causing it to collapse, totally destroying her left eye.

The killer obviously spared no mercy during his attack on Julia. In fact, it appeared the killer was enjoying his assault, and continued to plunge the knife into her even after she was probably already critically wounded or dead.

In death investigations, so often the last witness, and sometimes the most crucial witnesses, are the victims themselves. Their bodies, however broken and battered, can often tell when they died, and the order in which the wounds were inflicted.

Sometimes they can even pinpoint the weapons used.

One of the injuries of particular interest to Dr. Harruff was on Julia's head. There, toward the top of her head, a huge, gaping cut had been inflicted, what Dr. Harruff would later describe as a "chopping" type of injury. From the size of the injury, Dr. Harruff determined the weapon would have had to be an exceptionally long knife.

Maybe even a sword.

9 At noon on Wednesday, January 8, Gomes sent the McBrides to track down David Anderson. It was clear that the two Bellevue High School students who had come forward with revealing information about David and his boasts of committing a violent crime were scared of him; the McBrides wanted to check him out for themselves. They pulled up to a two-story nondescript home in Bellevue where they had been told David rented a room with his brothers. The boys no longer living with their parents on Southeast 25th Street. Four cars were parked in the driveway, and when John McBride knocked on the door, a tall young man with short blond hair appeared.

The McBrides introduced themselves as detectives with the Bellevue Police Department, and asked the young man if he had heard about the murders of the Wilson family. The man identified himself as Mike Anderson, and yes, he had heard about it on the news.

"We're looking for friends of Kim Wilson," John McBride said. "Did you know her?"

"Yeah, we were friends," Mike said. "You might want to talk to my brother Dave. He knows Kim."

"Would you mind getting him for us?"

"Sure."

Mike invited the McBrides inside and then disappeared into a bedroom at the end of the hallway. A few seconds later, Mike came back, followed by David Anderson, who stumbled down the hallway and into the living room. He had obviously just woken up.

As the McBrides followed the men into the living room, they noticed another young man on the floor playing a video game and a young woman sitting on the couch watching.

Mike introduced the young man as Joe Kern, a friend of theirs, and the woman on the couch as Marsha Rash, David's live-in girlfriend.

David slumped down next to Marsha with his legs spread apart and his head tilted back.

Molly McBride bent to her knees in front of David and Marsha. She wanted to get on eye level with them. Meanwhile, John McBride remained standing so he could gauge each person's reaction to his wife's interrogation.

Molly McBride asked David whether he had heard about the murders.

"Yeah, my dad called me on Monday and said there was a murder in Woodridge. He said Kim was a victim," David said, his head lolling with sleep.

David said he knew Kim and went out with her in the sixth, seventh, and eighth grades. The last time he saw her was right after Christmas, on December 28, from the back-seat of his parents' car as they drove by the house while running errands, and he had seen her in the fall before she left for AmeriCorps.

As David answered the McBrides' questions, he was calm, relaxed, and appeared ready to fall back asleep at any moment. He seemed unshaken by the bad news that a woman he considered his friend, and at one time dated, had been murdered.

"It's too bad," David said. "Woodridge used to be a place where you could leave your doors unlocked."

Nothing the young man did or said alerted the McBrides to anything unusual. The detectives thanked the group and left. However, they forgot one crucial step in the investigation: asking the young people for their alibis.

On their way back to police headquarters, Molly McBride phoned Detective Gomes to tell him they had just talked to some people who knew Kim Wilson, but they didn't have much information to add to the investigation.

Molly McBride insisted that David Anderson couldn't possibly be a suspect.

"This isn't the guy we want, Jeff," she said.

But Gomes, making sure he covered his bases, asked several questions of the McBrides. Specifically, he wanted to know if they had asked David where he was on the night of the murders.

No, they hadn't, they told Gomes, as they believed this David guy had nothing to do with the crime.

Gomes asked the McBrides to go back and ask where everyone had been the Friday night the Wilson family was killed. John McBride made a U-turn. At around 1:30 P.M., the McBrides were back to where the Anderson boys lived. This time, the group had gathered outside to smoke near the front door, obeying the household rules of no smoking inside.

John McBride started with Mike, and asked him where he was the night of the murders. Mike said that he had been working; then, later that night, he went out dancing with some buddies.

Marsha said she had been working all evening at Radio-Shack in nearby Factoria. David, who was driving her step-father's pickup truck, came by to pick her up around 9:30 P.M. and take her home. Once home, she went straight to sleep.

David was questioned next. He remained cool as he answered the detectives' questions. David said that after he dropped Marsha off at home, he had been with his friend Alex at the house where Alex rented a room. They had been playing video games the rest of the night until 5 A.M., he said.

Joe said he spent all day Saturday playing Dungeons and Dragons, but David butted in and corrected him.

"No, Joe. You and me and Alex played D and D all day Sunday."

John McBride also asked if each of them would mind showing him the bottom of their shoes. He and the other investigators were specifically on a hunt for the boots that had made the bloody prints inside the Wilson home. They all volunteered and lifted their shoes to humor the detective. They looked at each other and couldn't stop giggling. They couldn't believe that the cops actually thought they might be suspects.

The McBrides wanted to see other shoes that belonged to the kids, especially to Mike and David. So the brothers went to their respective rooms and tossed several pairs of shoes out into the hallway. John McBride looked at the soles of each shoe; they were all smooth. Definitely not like the shoe which had made the distinct bloody print on the back of Bill Wilson's T-shirt.

"Have you guys ever been in the Wilson home?" McBride wanted to know.

"Yeah," David said. "But it was more than a year ago."

John McBride explained how he was trying to eliminate suspects, including friends of Kim Wilson. As a procedure during this particular type of investigation, McBride asked if the boys would be willing to go with him to the police station for fingerprinting and to get their mug shots taken. In Washington State, there is no law that requires detectives to obtain parental permission before fingerprinting a teenager if he or she voluneers to do so.

"Sure, that's fine," David said, cooperating fully. Whatever the investigators' suspicions, they seemed not to bother David.

On the way to the station, David was polite, bantering with the cops. Molly McBride asked David if he knew Alex's address. David eagerly volunteered to show the cops where his best friend lived, pointing out the Boyd family's house on the way to the station.

David radiated supreme confidence. He wanted to give the impression he had nothing to hide. In David's mind, the McBrides were wasting their time and his.

10 About 5 P.M. that Wednesday, the McBrides went back to the house that David had pointed out on their earlier drive to the police station. Now they wanted to contact this Alex Baranyi.

Alex answered a knock at the basement door to find two plainclothes police officers. John McBride introduced himself and his wife, Molly. Alex, without hesitation, invited them in. He gestured for the McBrides to follow him back to his bedroom, which he had been renting for the past few months from Ronald and Valerie Boyd. Their son Bob was one of Alex's school buddies.

Fifteen-year-old Bob Boyd was in Alex's room playing video games, so Alex asked him to leave, which he reluctantly did.

John McBride asked whether Alex had heard about the murders, and Alex said he had: on the TV news.

"Do you know Kim Wilson?" Molly McBride asked.

"She was more of David's friend," Alex said, maintaining eye contact with her. He paused, then added: "I didn't really like her."

"Why not?" Molly McBride asked.

"She was selfish. She would never share her cigarettes with me." Alex appeared calm and nonchalant as he spoke. Someone he knew had just been murdered and he didn't seem to care. Whether he liked Kim or not, news of her violent death should have at least surprised or stunned him.

As Molly McBride continued her queries, John McBride glanced around the room. His gaze fell on a pair of yellow work boots on the floor.

Alex told John McBride that that was the only pair of shoes he owned. He laughed and said he should probably buy a pair of black boots to match his dark wardrobe.

Then the McBrides asked the crucial question. They wanted to know where he was on the night of January 3.

"Me and David were here playing video games," he said, without a hint of nervousness in his voice. "David came in the evening, and he went home around five A.M." That sounded about right to the McBrides; David had just told them the same thing.

John McBride continued to look around the room as Alex responded to his wife's questions. He noticed a sword in a corner of the bedroom, and vertical gashes along the wood panel that lined the walls. More cuts had been inflicted on a lounge chair in the corner. McBride recalled that during the police briefings, it was mentioned that a sword might have been used in the attacks. Curious, he asked more questions about the destruction he saw in Alex's room. McBride wanted to know how the cuts got on the chair.

"I used my sword," Alex said casually.

Later that night, Detectives John McBride and Bob Thompson returned to the Boyd residence. McBride wanted to get the sword in Alex's room, since he suspected it might have been used in the attack on the Wilsons, and he also hoped Alex would come to the police station for the fingerprinting process.

The moss-covered Boyd home was a split-level, wood-frame structure with a mother-in-law apartment in the basement. It had gone an entire generation without repair. The gray paint had dulled, making the house look ghostly. Ronald and Valerie Boyd originally rented the five-bedroom home to raise their three sons, two of whom were grown men and had since moved out.

Their youngest son, Bob, was a sophomore at Bellevue High School and good friends with both David and Alex.

Since the two older boys had gone, no one was using the downstairs bedrooms, so Ron and Val decided to rent them out. Christine Sheridan, Ron's sister, rented one room, where she lived with her eight-year-old son, Stephen, and an adult son, Ed; Alex Baranyi paid $50 a month to rent the other bedroom.

McBride and Thompson knocked on the basement door just off the driveway. Again Alex happily invited his guests in.

McBride asked if Alex was willing to come down to the police station to get fingerprinted and have his mug shot taken as a matter of procedure. The detective assured him he was not under arrest. They simply needed to exclude him as a suspect.

Alex agreed to go along. At McBride's request, he brought his sword with him.

At police headquarters, Thompson pulled the double-edged sword out of its metal sheath. He noted that dust flew into the air. Thompson had heard from other detectives in the case that David and Alex enjoyed collecting swords and knives, and that, according to Dr. Harruff's findings, a sword might have been used in the attack on Julia Wilson. But the sword now in Thompson's hands obviously hadn't been un-sheathed in a long time.

Meanwhile, McBride had taken Alex to the processing room, where he was fingerprinted and photographed.

"This should be pretty easy," McBride said, reaching for Alex's hand.

He pressed the boy's thumb into ink and then onto paper. But Alex's hands were sweaty. The first print completely smeared on the paper.

"I'm pretty nervous just being here," Alex said. His hands were somewhat fidgety.

McBride got a paper towel for Alex to wipe his clammy hands with, and he tried to roll another print. But as soon as Alex's fingers touched the paper, it smeared again. After several attempts with different fingers, McBride gave up. He got only a partial print and told Alex they would have to try some other time.

Detective McBride was still convinced he and his colleagues were on a cold trail. This David and Alex duo were definitely weird, he thought. They played too many computer games and collected swords. But to McBride, they appeared to be just boys, not mass murderers.

PART TWO

David and Alex

11 In 1995, Kim Wilson dragged through her last year of high school and started spending more and more time at Denny's. There, that summer, she reconnected with a friend she hadn't seen in a long time—David Anderson.

Kim was hunched over in a corner of Denny's, smoking a cigarette and drinking coffee, when Mike Anderson, David's brother, sauntered into the diner, followed by David and another boy. He noticed Kim sitting in a back booth and made a beeline toward her.

"Hey, Kim, how's it going," Mike said, squeezing himself into the booth to join her. He motioned for David and his friend Alex to slide in next to Kim.

The Andersons were longtime Woodridge residents. Kim went to school with both Mike and David; Mike was a grade ahead and David three grades behind her.

Kim was happy to see David. She had lost touch with him since she'd gone on to high school, leaving him to finish off his last year at Chinook Middle School.

When they first met in grade school, they were simply friends. But by middle school, they shared a mutual attraction. Throughout their early teens, they dated off and on during summer vacations.

Kim started high school in 1991, and consequently, she saw less and less of David. They no longer went to the same school or ran with the same crowd. Kim had wondered when she would bump into David again.

"Hi, Dave," Kim said as David settled into the vinyl seat.

"What's up?' " David said. Alex slipped in next to David. "You remember Alex from Chinook, right?"

Kim did remember Alex from school, but only vaguely. He wasn't someone she would have chosen to hang out with.

She smiled lightly, but Alex didn't smile back. Instead, he looked off toward the waitress, hoping she would come soon to take his order.

Kim thought Alex was weird and unfriendly. She was put off by his cold demeanor, and ignored him the rest of the night.

Kim talked a lot to David that night, and from then on, when they bumped into each other at Denny's, they shared a booth and hung out together.

In the summer of 1995, Kim and David were dating again, much to Alex's dismay. He was growing to hate Kim. He thought she was selfish with her cigarettes, unwilling to loan him a pack or buy one for him. Alex also hated the fact that David was spending more time with her than with him. He wondered why David was attracted to her when, more than once, he called her "dumpy" and an "ugly bitch" behind her back. But as he did with so many others, Alex tolerated Kim because she was David's girlfriend, and he didn't want to do or say anything to upset David.

For her part, Kim didn't let Alex get in the way of her pursuing David. She had a renewed interest in him, and was easily charmed by the good-looking Goth jock. Soon enough, she became one of Dave's girls. Kim and David spent hours taking walks together through Woodridge, and through Water Tower Park. She hung pictures of David in her bedroom, and in her day planner, his was the first name and phone number on her list of contacts.

But the relationship was only a brief fling; they both knew

it would not last. Soon she became part of David's growing number of ex-girlfriends. It was all for the best anyway, she thought. At least now they could be friends.

Over time, Kim turned into somewhat of an older-sister figure and mentor to David, loaning him cash when he needed food, and letting him crash on her family's couch when he ran away from home. He, on the other hand, was still upset that the relationship had ended before he scored. But Kim wasn't that type of girl.

After the breakup, the two remained close. In fact, Kim considered David one of her closest friends. She didn't realize that he never forgot or forgave the rejection. The fact that Kim refused to have sex with him was a personal affront. The rejection cut too deep, and was too unexpected. David carried it with him like a great black stone in the pit of his stomach. Every so often, he erupted into a tirade.

"That dumpy bitch must be a dyke or something," he would say, the words spewing out of his mouth. "I just want to kill her."

But back then, no one believed him.

12 At the northern entrance to Woodridge, visitors are greeted with a "Welcome to Woodridge" wooden sign, at the base of which a cherry tree grows. The sign and the tree sit at the mouth of 121st Avenue Southeast, just before drivers crawl up a windy hill into the cluster of homes. Several residents volunteered to set down a memorial plaque and to plant flowers around the tree, which they patted into the cool spring earth in the lemon light of a Saturday morning. In memory of the Wilson family.

Neither the tree nor the plaque below it was there when the Anderson family moved to Southeast 25th Street, on the south slope of Woodridge Hill, in the early '80s. The family—Bruce, Leslie, and their three sons, Michael, Troy, and David—arrived via Texas in search of a fresh start, a good place to live life.

Bruce, a big man with rectangular wire-rim glasses and a swift, deliberate pace, was a security systems operator who liked nothing better than to fire up the grill for a barbecue with his boys. Leslie, a rather shy, endearing woman who radiated calm and favored long dresses in pastels, worked as a nursing assistant in the maternity ward at a Bellevue hospital. It was clear to those who visited the Andersons that this was a family with traditional virtues—Bruce assumed the role of disciplinarian, while Leslie focused her efforts on cooking and cleaning. David learned by his father's example that men call the shots—a message so ingrained into David's head that he would be the dominant one in his future relationships with women.

In March of 1979, before the family moved to Woodridge, Leslie Anderson gave birth to her third son, David Carpenter Anderson. She had hoped for a girl this time, as it would have been nice to have at least one daughter. But it wasn't meant to be, and even her last child, whom she would give birth to a few years later, turned out to be a boy, named Stephen.

Bruce and Leslie Anderson had found the perfect home for their family. They paid $76,000 for the simple five-bedroom rambler with a square patch of lawn. The Andersons lived on a part of Woodridge Hill that wasn't particularly known for its extravagance.

On 25th Street, there were no sidewalks and no gutters. People liked the semirural feel, even though they were in the middle of a burgeoning metropolis. There was nothing particularly special about the wedge of neighborhood where the Anderson boys were raised. It was a reasonable place to live, considering it was Bellevue, and that was good enough for Bruce and Leslie.

Bruce was not a man to be fooled with. He worked long hours and his patience was low, especially when it came to bringing up his sons. If the boys didn't want to live by his rules, they were not welcome to live in his home. When Mike and Troy dropped out of high school, Bruce kicked them out of the house. They lived with friends and eventually found a house of their own to rent together.

Without his two brothers at home, David lost his sense of direction and grew angry at his parents. Leslie tried to be the peacemaker in the family, quelling conflicts between father and son before they erupted into serious battles. She raised her boys the best she knew how, making their dinner and folding their laundry. She loved them, no matter what they did.

When the kids were younger, Leslie ferried her boys to and from baseball practice, summer camps, and their friends' houses. She came home Saturday afternoons with her arms full of groceries. And while the boys lounged on the couch watching the game—it didn't matter which one, so long as it was a game—Leslie scurried back and forth between the family minivan and the house to retrieve more bags of groceries. When the boys refused to come out of their basement rooms for dinner, Leslie brought food down to them.

The Andersons hoped to bring up their boys with the same set of moral codes that their own parents had passed down to them. The family went to a Baptist church regularly. Following the strict Baptist ways, Bruce was a swift and merciless disciplinarian. He wanted his sons to grow up and be respectable men. To be obedient. To have manners. To respect authority. Punishment was at times harsh in the Anderson home. In fact, according to Alex, if the boys got poor grades, Bruce had no qualms about hitting them. And if they ever disobeyed their father, they did not leave home the next day without bruises and red marks on their bodies.

When David and Alex were in middle school, Alex remembers David showing up for school with bruises on his arms every now and then.

"They looked like knuckle marks," Alex would later say.

David didn't try to explain the marks, except to say he hated his dad, and Alex didn't probe. But Alex had been in the Anderson home enough times to observe Bruce Anderson's violent temper. Alex was sure those bruises were made by Bruce.

The Anderson boys cringed every time they did something bad, but the more they were punished, the more they rebelled.

Over the course of time, it was no surprise that both Michael and Troy dropped out of high school, and David followed step by step behind them.

Troy Anderson appeared to be the biggest rebel in the family. In 1991, a neighbor called the police after he and a friend had been throwing large knives into the air and watching them land. The woman was worried that one of those knives might hit her. She also told the police Troy was tossing firecrackers into a barbecue, pouring lighter fluid on them, and torching them, just to watch the flames kick and fly wildly into the air.

After Michael and Troy had moved out, the boys fought back anytime their father tried to hit them. In 1995, Alex recalled a time when Bruce attempted to strike Troy. Troy hit him back, throwing punches and lunging toward his father. After that incident, Alex noticed the abuse by Bruce had stopped. The boys were now men and stronger than he was.

The brothers ran with a rough crowd, and by the time they had reached adulthood, each had his rap sheet of minor run-ins with the law.

David, who looked up to his big brothers, learned from their example.

His blond-haired charm was only surface-level. Beneath it lay a cold, angry, short-tempered boy—a match that could burst into flames with the slightest friction. As he grew older, David grew more hostile. He took great pride and pleasure in beating up other kids. His glamour-boy physique was the result of endless hours of bench-pressing in the eighth grade. He looked hard. Mean. A natural-born rebel.

It was at night, when everyone else was asleep, that David came alive as he entered the world of fantasy and mystery. He read the book *Magic's Price* by Mercedes Lackey, a novel about the fantasy life of a teenager in a make-believe kingdom, and he enjoyed entering the domain of death-row prison inmates in Stephen King's *The Green Mile*, part of a book series. David devoted his free time to reading about criminals. He was intrigued by how the prisoners found themselves behind bars, what evil acts they'd committed to be stripped of their freedom and identity. These men who defied authority became David's role models. They were demagogues in a world they believed was too rigid with rules. David decided he would never allow anyone to have any power over him. He alone would determine the rules by which he would live.

In his adolescence, he became nervous and more agitated. He increasingly resented the demands of his parents, and the weight of their authority seemed heavier than that which he had endured at school. He hated being told what to do and how to do it. He hated living at home and being chauffered around town by his two older brothers because his parents would not buy him a car.

By the time he reached middle school, David was already shaping up to be like his older brother Michael: toned and healthy, with the rippling good looks of video-game heroes. He was even becoming the same kind of rebel as his brothers: failing to do his chores and homework, talking back to his parents, staying out late at night against his parents' wishes, and skipping school. David had also picked up the habit of using women for sex. He defied authority with malice and arrogance. He liked the fact that no one could tell him what to do, and he reminded people of that on a daily basis.

When his parents asked him to do his homework or help clean the house, David shrugged it off. His parents' words were wasted on a boy unwilling to be bothered by anyone, especially his own parents.

"Fuck that shit," he would hiss. "I'm leaving this fucking dump."

He would run away, sleeping in abandoned cars and

crashing at friends' homes. David felt as though he had no one to turn to, no one to confide in and with whom he could share his interests and dreams, until a new family moved to the Woodridge neighborhood, delivering him a new friend.

13 In 1989, just a few years after the Andersons moved to Woodridge, Alex Baranyi Sr., his new bride, Mary Beth, and his son and namesake moved into a tree-lined cul-de-sac two blocks away. By settling there, Alex Sr. hoped to put some distance between himself and his ex-wife, Alex Jr.'s mother, Patricia. Their divorce had been so bitter, he and Patricia had long since taken to calling their son by his middle name, Kevin, because Alex Sr. didn't want to share his name or identity with the offspring of a woman he had grown to despise. (Their son, however, continued to call himself Alex, the name by which his classmates, teachers, and friends knew him.) Alex Sr. also had asked for a restraining order and he had ultimately won custody of their child.

Patricia remained in Snohomish County, about a ninety-minute drive north of Bellevue. It was a distance that Alex Jr. would grow to dread. He visited his mother once every month, sometimes less frequently, and only when he could bum a ride from one of his friends. His father had left it up to him to keep in touch with his mother if he chose to. Alex Sr. wanted nothing to do with Patricia and would have preferred that his son forget her, too. *She* was the one who'd walked out on them, he reminded Alex Jr.

But Alex Jr. needed no reminding. He would never forget that point when his parents' relationship began to sour. He was young, confused, and utterly lost in the tempest that raged around him. Soon enough, he would grow to resent his father, who kept him from his mother, not out of love, but out of spite for Patricia. Later in his life, Alex Jr. would come to realize it was his father who was the bad parent.

Alex Baranyi Sr. was born and raised in Pittsburgh, but his family had come from Hungary, where the Baranyi clan lived collectively as farmers and goat herders. Baranyi means "lamb" in Hungarian.

Alex Sr.'s father was a swift disciplinarian. When Alex Sr. and his younger brother, Larry, misbehaved, their father whipped them with a belt and ordered them to kneel on a steel grate until their knees chafed against the metal, according to Alex Jr.

Alex Jr. couldn't recall his grandfather's name, only that he was a brooding man, prone to outbursts. He had served in the Navy, fighting on the shores of Normandy, and he still suffered from post-traumatic stress disorder. When he returned to the states, he struggled with his demons—nightmares from the bloody battles which he would often relate to his wife, Betty. The sounds of bombing and gunfire shattered his sleep. He would wake up crying. He hated killing people, he would tell Betty. He had killed so many strangers and had watched many of his own friends die.

Nonetheless, he was able to provide for Alex Jr.'s father and uncle. Alex Sr. grew up in a modest Pittsburgh neighborhood and took classes at Dale Carnegie, where he studied to be a salesman. He dated infrequently, focusing instead on his studies.

After finishing school, Alex Sr. returned to his family's home, where he met a neighborhood girl who would later become his wife.

Patricia Stephan was barely into her twenties and eager to leave home when Alex Baranyi Sr., a good-looking young man with tufts of naturally curly, coarse dark hair, appeared

in her life in 1970. She had lived with her two brothers, Tom
and Gary, and their mother, Ellen Stephan, since age nine.
That's when, according to Alex Jr., her father walked out on
the family. It's unclear exactly why he left, but his actions
would leave a lasting impression on Patricia, who, years
later would follow in her father's footsteps by leaving her
own family. When Alex Sr. appeared in her life, Patricia
thought he was a godsend. It wasn't that she fell madly in
love with him. She did love him, but her decision to rush
headlong into his arms had more to do with her need to escape a tempestuous home life than it did with wanting to
marry the right man. Ellen Stephan kept close tabs on her
only daughter. She didn't allow Patricia to date, fearing Patricia might make the same mistake she had—marrying
someone whom she considered a creep. Patricia hated staying at home and listening to her mother's tirades about men,
her relentless nagging. Get the house clean, stop smoking,
and get a job, Ellen would rant.

Instead, Patricia got married to Alex Baranyi. After a
small, unremarkable wedding ceremony, the Baranyis
moved into a quaint apartment in Pittsburgh. They had
tossed around the idea of moving in with Alex's parents to
save money, but both wanted to escape their families.

Alex's job as a computer software salesman meant he had
to make frequent business trips, leaving his young wife
home alone to watch TV, cook, and clean.

Even though the Baranyis were living in their own apartment, Pittsburgh was still too close to home. In 1979, the
couple moved to Cleveland, Ohio, where they would be just
far enough away from their families yet close enough to visit
when they wanted to.

The Baranyis enjoyed their life. It was simple and peaceful, uncluttered by children and obligations. But after a few
years of marriage, conflict began driving the couple apart.
They would argue over little things, like the sugar bowl not

being filled. As the marriage started to disintegrate, the Baranyis decided maybe what they needed was children. Patricia didn't think she was prepared to be a mother, but she went along, hoping to save her marriage. She worried that she wouldn't know how to take care of a baby or provide for the child. Alex Sr, wasn't interested in starting a family, either. But the couple was at an impasse; something needed to change.

In 1979, Patricia gave birth to her first and only child.

Alex Kevin Baranyi was born in a Cleveland hospital on May 14, a healthy, eight-pound baby. But it was not an easy birth. Patricia Baranyi struggled through thirty hours of labor before doctors decided to perform a C-section. Baby Alex had an unusually large head and large hips.

"You just didn't want to come," Patricia Baranyi would tell her son.

That early resistance into entering this world seemed to set the tone for the rest of Alex Jr.'s life. He hated this world from the beginning, and by the time he would enter adolescence, he would choose to live within the boundaries of a make-believe one.

Little Alex was never an outgoing child. His isolation from the social world began when he was a toddler, living in his family's Cleveland neighborhood, which was populated by retirees. Even then, Alex Jr. didn't have any friends, at least not any human friends.

At age three, Alex Jr. found a best friend in a neighbor's dog, Smokey. While his father was away on business trips and his mother stayed inside watching TV, little Alex played alone, riding tight circles on his tricycle in the driveway and running around with Smokey in the yard.

Sometimes he would play in the backyard on the swing set, gliding down the slide and propelling himself through the air on the swings. Even as a toddler, Alex felt the sting of solitude.

"I remember sitting on top of the slide. I had a profound feeling of loneliness," he recalled. "I never had any kid friends."

Because he lacked companions, Alex Jr. turned to books. The boy had an aptitude for language and learned to read by age three. He enjoyed nature books, and in his later years would delve deep into science-fiction novels.

Alex Jr. doesn't remember much about his father during those formative years of his childhood, other than the fact that he was often gone on sales trips. When he returned, he always walked through the door with a suitcase in one hand and a stuffed animal tucked under his arm.

Alex Sr. brought his son a stuffed toy every time he went away. By the time the Baranyis moved across the country, young Alex's bedroom was lined from wall to wall with the cottony creatures.

"They were my 'babies,' " Alex Jr. would later say. "My room was coated in them."

The Baranyis decided not to have any more children. They had hoped having children would slow the disintegration of their relationship. But Alex Jr.'s birth might have only added momentum to it.

When it came to child-rearing, Alex Sr. operated under traditional codes: his wife's duty was to take care of the child, and his was to go out and make money.

Patricia began seeing the injustices and inequities pervasive in their relationship. Not only had her husband relegated the majority of child-rearing responsibilities to her, but he began waging verbal attacks on her.

The couple began fighting over who was pulling more of the weight in the family. But before the fighting got much worse, Alex Sr. decided to move his family to Washington State. By then, he was more interested in computers than working as a salesman. Washington was the perfect place for a computer job with its booming high-tech corridor. Perhaps a job in that industry would solve the family's financial problems and ease the tension in their marriage.

In 1982, when Alex was three years old, the family packed what little they owned and moved to Everett, a growing suburb north of Seattle where the airplane manufacturer Boeing had long operated, and where other high-tech companies had sprung up around it. An educated man with a penchant for computers, Alex Sr. immediately started up his own computer-consulting business, while Patricia found work at the Lake Stevens School District as a teacher's assistant. But the change of scenery and new job opportunities didn't help Alex and Patricia's marriage. By 1987, the fault line had grown too wide, and the end was in sight.

Their arguments grew more fierce and regular. First, it was little things. *You forgot to fill the sugar bowl. You left the front door open again. You haven't paid the bills.* Then, gradually, the bickering turned more personal. *You can't do anything right. You're a controlling, abusive jerk.*

When his parents fought, Alex Jr. would rush into his bedroom, shut the door, jam a thumb into his mouth, and cuddle with his stuffed animals. He would continue to soothe his insecurities by sucking his thumb, a habit he finally gave up at age fifteen. He would then rock himself to sleep, covering his ear with one hand, trying not to cry. He didn't understand why his parents just couldn't get along, why they didn't like each other anymore.

On July 1, 1987, before the Baranyis had a chance to plan their Fourth of July weekend, without warning, Patricia packed her bags and walked out on her family. She had had enough of her verbally abusive husband. She later told her son that she left him behind because she believed his father could better provide for him—he was the one with the career. Alex Sr. was infuriated that his wife would dare leave him; even more upset that she would leave the kid behind.

Suddenly, alone with a child, Alex Sr. was faced with the

challenging new role of being a single parent. He continued
to work at his consulting business, and came home with
burgers and fries from McDonald's. Alex Jr., who at the time
was enrolled at Hillcrest Elementary School in Everett, also
remembers eating a lot of rice—one of few dishes his father
could cook.

It was not long after Patricia left that Alex Sr. found himself standing in front of a judge, asking to divorce his wife.
Alex Jr. felt like a pawn his father was using against his
mother. During their lengthy divorce battle that year, Patricia and Alex Sr. were each unwilling to completely give up
their son, but for different reasons. Alex Jr. was at the center
of it all, mentioned in divorce-court records as if he were a
rag doll, wrenched from one parent's hands to the other's.
Throughout the process, he was yanked in and out of
schools, relocated back and forth between Washington and
Pennsylvania. He had moved five times in as many years.

Amid the turmoil in the Baranyi home, Alex Jr. became a
quiet, brooding, sulky child whose personality fluctuated between explosive outbursts and intense, unbreakable silences.
He was extremely shy, often sitting by himself during school
recess and watching the currents of activity swirl around
him, but he was never a part of that activity. Awkward in social settings, Alex Jr. longingly toed the margins of his peer
group. All he wanted was a friend. Just one. Someone to
walk beside him so that he wouldn't be so utterly alone.

Young Alex felt the loneliest at home. His father was
moving on with his life, and now that his mother was out of
the picture, Alex Sr. was eager to find someone to fill the
void. In the summer of 1988, when Alex Jr. was nine years
old, Alex Sr. moved back to the East Coast to woo an old
high school sweetheart, Mary Beth Uhlig. Worried that his
son might get in the way of the courtship, he left Alex Jr. behind to stay with his mother. That fall, Alex Jr. enrolled in
the fourth grade at Pilchuck Elementary School in Lake

Stevens, where Patricia had rented an apartment in the cheap
Shadow Creek apartment complex.

In grade school, he was constantly the underdog and a
magnet for bullies. It was rough being the new kid on the
block. Again. But it was a routine with which Alex Jr. had
become painfully familiar. As usual, he was easy prey for
bullies.

Once, he was accosted while standing at the bus stop on
the first day of school in the fourth grade. From the corner
of his eye he saw several bigger boys approaching him. A
kid named Shane was the first to shout names at Alex Jr.,
and his two cohorts quickly chimed in with insults of their
own. Shane ordered one of his pals, a bigger kid—about
100 pounds—to lay into Alex Jr. The boys pushed and
punched each other as a crowd of children waiting for their
ride to school cheered them on. After kicking one of the
kids in the ribs, Alex Jr. took off running in no particular direction. His long legs just carried him, propelling him forward with the kind of fear-induced speed that surprised
even him.

He never made it to school that day. Instead, he spent the
day hiding in bushes and behind fences, around corners and
behind cars. He would stop every now and then to look behind him. To see if those bullies were about to catch up
with him.

That was in 1988. And it seems that since then, Alex Jr.
kept running and never really stopped. Running from home.
Running from bullies. Running until one crisp fall day in
Bellevue in 1991, when a surprising thing happened—he became someone's friend.

14 Within months after leaving Alex Jr. with his mother in Washington, Alex Sr. called Patricia to ask her to send his son to Pennsylvania, where he was living with Mary Beth. He wanted to test whether Alex Jr. would be able to get along with the woman he might someday call his stepmother. Patricia Baranyi purchased a one-way airplane ticket for her son and, reluctantly, sent him back to the East Coast, where she and Alex Sr. first met. As much as she wanted to keep Alex Jr., Patricia felt obligated to satisfy her ex-husband's demand, worried that he might find a way to keep Alex Jr. from her forever.

Alex Jr. enrolled in Trafford Elementary School in Pennsylvania halfway through the school year. But by that summer, his father sent him back to Lake Stevens to live with his mother. Alex Sr. and Mary Beth were getting married and would eventually return to Washington. To help make a smooth transition, Alex Sr. dumped his son back on his ex-wife so she could take care of him during the transition period.

There was no stability in Alex Jr.'s life, but that was something he was learning to live with. In his early childhood, Alex Jr.'s father expected him to set his own alarm clock and prepare his own breakfast. He was so focused on making his new relationship with Mary Beth work that he didn't care whether his son needed new school clothes or supplies. Alex Jr. soon learned to count on no one but himself.

To make up for all the bad times, Alex Sr. bought his son a Nintendo computer game set, and over the years, Alex Jr. would collect a number of fantasy video games like Dungeons and Dragons and Rifts. Without knowing it, Alex Sr. had set his son on the early path of darkness. Nintendo became a great source of escape for the boy, who spent countless hours playing video games seeded with violence and destruction.

But Alex Sr. realized buying games and toys was not enough to bring his son out of his shell, so he started taking Alex Jr. to see a therapist through the Lutheran Counseling Network. Alex Sr. believed his son was suffering from depression. He told the therapist that Alex Jr. didn't talk anymore and seemed uninterested and unable to make friends. It wasn't that he didn't want any friends; Alex Jr. never stayed anywhere long enough to make any.

Patricia Baranyi noticed her son's dark moods, too. In 1989, shortly after Alex Jr. started the fifth grade at Pilchuck Elementary, Patricia Baranyi asked a school psychologist to talk with her brooding son. But before the psychologist had a chance, Alex Sr. pulled his son out of that school and enrolled him in yet another new school in Bellevue. Alex Sr. and Mary Beth had relocated to the Woodridge neighborhood in Bellevue, and they were ready for Alex Jr. to come live with them. With every move he was forced to make, Alex Jr. grew increasingly resentful of his father. He had enjoyed living with his mother, and grew to hate his father for continuously forcing him to uproot.

It was in Bellevue that Alex began a rocky entrance into adolescence. He was fighting with his father more frequently. He had become even more withdrawn than in previous years. He was growing increasingly despondent and cynical about the world.

In 1991, Alex was starting the seventh grade at Chinook Middle School, yet another new school. For Alex, it was just one more chance at being the new kid on the block, the outcast who couldn't fit into any social groups. He was already preparing himself to be picked on.

As it happened, David Anderson was enrolling in the same grade at Chinook, and he was scoping the campus for someone to bully around.

Before the fall of 1991, David and Alex had never met, despite living less than two blocks from each other. They would have had no reason to cross paths, until their first day at Chinook.

It had been a difficult first day of school for Alex. He didn't know a soul and already wondered how he could avoid being picked on.

Alex was playing wallball by himself in gym class when he first bumped into the blue-eyed bully with a wicked grin. David came up from behind him, appearing out of nowhere.

"Hey, can I play?" David asked.

Alex caught the ball with both of his hands and looked at David suspiciously. He had never had friends before, and wondered why this boy wanted to play with him. He hesitated, then agreed.

"Sure," he said.

Alex handed David the ball, and David threw it hard against the wall, angling the ball so that it would bounce back and hit Alex. He broke out in uproarious laughter when the ball slammed into Alex's chest.

Alex scowled, regretting that he had ever let this kid into his game.

Sensing Alex's anger, David chased after the ball and ran back to return it to him. He apologized and said he didn't mean to hit Alex.

Alex thought about it, then nodded his head, accepting the apology.

In the following days, whenever David saw Alex in the hallways, he made it a point to harass him.

"Where are you going, geek?" David would yell across the hall.

Alex would pretend he hadn't heard and just keep moving along. Trying to escape trouble, he would turn and walk in the other direction. When David shoved him from behind, Alex would pick up his pace, while David taunted him, pushing and prodding him as if he were cattle.

After school, David continued his attack. After they had gotten off at the same bus stop, he would follow Alex, throwing pine cones at him, and whenever he got close enough, he would punch Alex in the arm.

For David, it was a game. To see if the wimp would fight back or just keep taking it. David wanted to know if the nerd had enough guts to stand up for himself. Alex did not. That's exactly what David had hoped for: someone less confident than he, a personal punching bag he could abuse when he needed to take out some aggressions, and who always would be around to be abused. Alex continued to take the harassment, but in a way, he kind of liked the fact that one of the most popular boys at school was paying him attention at all. In a weird way, he felt privileged that David chose to pick on *him*.

The friendship began with violence, and that was the one constant that remained in the relationship as the boys quickly gravitated toward each other.

"The more he beat up on me, the more we had a chance to talk," Alex would later say.

After a year, the two were joined at the hip. They took long walks together around the neighborhood. Played video games, ate frozen pizza, chased cats, and fashioned pretend swords. The boys often walked home together, and hung out at each other's homes. They were as inseparable as any best friends could be, forging a friendship that bordered on obsessiveness.

The more they talked, the more they realized they had a

lot in common—a love of fast food, science-fiction and thriller novels, and a penchant for dark clothes and fantasy role-playing games.

The boys started playing fantasy games in earnest in the eighth grade, while attending Chinook Middle School. The games would generally involve a group of about a half-dozen kids who don medieval outfits and paint their faces white. They would gather at a player's backyard or a city park to act out a scenario. Many players use props including swords, wands, and bottles of magic potion to navigate their way past evil as they hunt for treasures. Along the route, players are awarded points for killing monsters and other characters in the game.

David often chose characters of gnomes, thieves, or mercenaries. But Alex had one character he favored and used most frequently in the games.

In his own world of make-believe, Alex was the god of evil. At times, he was Set Typhon Tanis, the Greek god of night, darkness, storms, and catastrophe. In mythology, Set ravaged the land and killed his father and brother.

But most of the time, he liked to play the role of Slicer Thunderclap—a half-cyborg mercenary, cold and unfeeling, but possessing many skills, including the ability to pick pockets and move silently through a crowd without being detected. This character was in love with a mythical woman named Rose—a beautiful mistress who was compassionate, strong, and loyal. In letters to his friends, Alex would sign his character initials ST in a sharp, cryptic medieval style, the beginning and ends of each letter pointed like the fine tip of a blade.

The boys also hunted for bugs to mutilate and cats to taunt. They caught flies and plucked off the wings, then watched them hobble around helplessly on the cement driveway. They teased girls and squandered long afternoons playing video games. They stole cigarettes from David's brothers or from local convenience stores and took puffs when no one was looking. And most of all, they loved to sword-fight. David and Alex made fake swords out of PVC pipe and duct tape. Often, they jousted back and forth down the street in front of the Anderson home. Neighbors simply shook their heads and drew their curtains.

Sometimes the boys used real swords. Neighbors wondered how two boys so young could acquire such weapons. They wondered if the Andersons knew their son was horsing around with deadly weapons. In the summer, neighbors out watering their shrubs and washing their cars remembered seeing David and Alex perform a pretend sword fight in the street, the sharp metal edges of their swords glinting spectacularly in the afternoon sunlight.

The two friends weren't really doing anything too unusual. They were typical teenage rebels out to have a good time. The duo even became known in Woodridge as the "Blues Brothers," because they were constantly seen together dressed in black from head to toe. They would walk side by side to and from each other's homes, their heads bent against the lashing Northwest rains and their black trench coats snapping like sails in the wind.

While they shared many interests, their differences were obvious. Of the two, David was the more outgoing. He seemed to exude testosterone with every step he took, and would strut down Woodridge's streets in a steely silence— the measured stride of a young man confident in his good looks and charm.

Alex, on the other hand, was quiet and temperamental; the slightest insult could make him explode into a violent rage. Whereas David was well proportioned for his height and weight, Alex was tall and wiry. He was a few inches taller than David, but they weighed the same. Alex, thin-lipped and a shadow of a young man, would slouch when he walked, always shrinking into his own shell. He hated standing out. For the most part, he didn't care much about his physical appearance, and often wore the same clothes to school several days in a row. He showered only occasionally, and there was something menacing about him. His face was a constellation of craters and pimples, dominated by thick black brows above brooding green eyes. Those eyes made people uneasy when they first met him. They were devoid of any warmth; they swallowed light. His rope of black hair was long and greasy and hung a few inches below the collar line. He loved to tie it in a tight ponytail, resembling that of his sword-wielding hero, Connor MacLeod, in the TV series *Highlander*. The sword-and-sorcery epic is about an immortal who travels through the centuries, gaining power and strength by decapitating other immortals in sword battles.

Both boys were rootless in their daily lives. They had no academic ambition, nor did they want to become professional baseball players or rock stars. The future for them was a place that seemed impossible to reach. They existed each day with no structure or schedule, no responsibility, and no sense of commitment to anything or anyone except themselves.

David and Alex were a curious couple and people wondered what could possibly bind them so closely. Their appearances and personalities were complete opposites. It was strange that two boys so different could be so close, but nobody in the Denny's group was bothered by it.

Between the two of them, David was the one the girls wanted. When the boys went to the Sun Villa Lanes—a popular teenage hangout a few miles from the Woodridge neighborhood—David would immediately scan every inch of the bowling alley to scope out girls. When he spotted one, he would move in like a tiger, approaching a gaggle of girls with a broad smile. He would sidle into a seat next to them in the snack bar, where they munched on nachos and slurped

Coke, or lean up against a wall and make catcalls as each went up for her turn to bowl.

David hung out a lot at Sun Villa because, for a short while, his brother Troy worked behind the counter at the cash register. Neither David nor Alex was a good bowler. They went to Sun Villa mostly for the scene. In Bellevue, that's where many adolescent romances played out like prime-time soaps. Relationships were formed and broken between strikes and gutter balls.

Alex slogged along behind as David hunted for the babes. Once David spotted a girl, he would order Alex to stay put while he went to hit on her, treating Alex as if he were a dog.

Alex stood in the darkest spots of the bowling alley alone, often dumping quarters into video games in the arcade. When he mustered enough courage to go talk to a girl, he stumbled over himself in awkward nervousness. David knew all the right things to say, while Alex struggled with his words around girls. And while David could be, and often was, a jerk to young women, they chose him over Alex because there was something especially eerie about Alex.

The girls knew David and Alex played fantasy games, but Alex often stayed in character as the demigod Slicer Thunderclap. When he spoke, he used big words that intimidated girls in the Denny's crowd, making them feel as if they had to use a dictionary when talking with him. But a few girls liked Alex because he was quiet, nice, and polite. And there was something appealing about his green eyes. Some of the young women also thought his long hair was sexy.

But Alex knew the routine well. As soon as he met a girl and she showed signs of interest in him, David would come along and start flirting with her.

"Aren't you going to introduce me to this pretty girl?" David would ask, winking at and nudging Alex.

When Alex introduced them, David would smile and

shoot off a series of compliments directed at the girl's shoes, her nice hair, her cute ass.

"I haven't seen you here before . . ." David would say. The next thing Alex knew, the girl's attention turned to David and the new couple would walk off to another corner of the bowling alley to make out.

Alex hated this, but it became routine and he had to accept it, clenching his teeth each time. If David hadn't been such a good friend, Alex swore he'd beat the asshole to a bloody pulp.

By the end of the night, David's pocket would bulge with scraps of napkins and torn edges of scorecards covered with the phone numbers of girls he'd met. It was so easy and natural for him to socialize with women. He'd grown up in a family of men, after all, and he had two older brothers whose macho images he emulated.

Whenever they were at Denny's, David always took over conversations. He would order for Alex and talk for Alex. It was almost as if Alex were nothing more than a faithful servant who deferred to the overbearing pretty boy.

"Get me a smoke," David would bark at Alex, leaning into some girl he had just met. Then he would drape his arm over her shoulder and saunter off, expecting Alex to follow orders and bum a cigarette off someone, then track him down in the chaotic establishment. The girls David dated thought it was cool that he had someone to serve him, always at his beck and call.

But while he played Mr. Smooth, the girls knew David had a mean streak. He could be an asshole when he wanted to be; he was sweet only during that brief time he was courting a girl. Once he got her, he called her a whore and a bitch behind her back, and believed she was good only for sex.

"Dave is such a womanizer," Alex would later say. "He stole girls from everyone. He stole girls from me."

But the one girl who mattered most to Alex, the first and

only girl he bought flowers for, was not stolen by his best friend, but lured away by someone else. Someone he barely knew, but whom he had grown to resent among the Denny's gang.

Her name was Kim Wilson.

15 By midwinter of 1995, Kim was beginning to have more frequent run-ins with her parents. She was graduating from high school that year, and had no immediate plans to go to college. Bill and Rose Wilson were frustrated at their daughter's apparent lack of direction and motivation. They finally gave Kim an ultimatum: go to college, get a job, or move out.

By this point, Kim no longer cared about her schoolwork. She wasn't doing her homework, especially when her parents ordered it. Instead, she started hanging out at Denny's, dabbling in drugs and alcohol, even experimenting with her sexuality. She was beginning to realize that she was attracted to women. Kim made a point to meet new women who loitered at Denny's. But she had not come out to her parents or her friends. She continued to eye women longingly, and discreetly.

In January, she ran into her old friend Mike Anderson at the Quality Food Center grocery store in Factoria, the strip-mall city next to Woodridge.

Mike was planning to see his on-again, off-again girlfriend, Sarah Lamp, that evening and asked Kim to join them. Kim agreed to go along and jumped into Mike's car so they could pick up Sarah.

That night, Mike, Sarah, and Kim went to Denny's to talk and smoke cigarettes. Kim and Sarah found they had a lot in common. The entire night, Kim smiled nervously at Sarah.

Sarah was a slight woman with long blond hair, a soft face, and a gentle smile. She was funny, smart, and easygoing. Kim went home that night in a daze of emotions, floating into her room and finally collapsing onto her bed with a tremendous smile. She was falling in love.

Soon after that initial meeting, Kim called Sarah and asked her if she wanted to hang out. Sarah seemed to respond to Kim. Kim was caring, compassionate, generous. She was a good listener and was clearly interested in Sarah. When Sarah and Mike broke up again a short while later, Kim and Sarah met for coffee. In her diary, Kim began recording her meetings with Sarah, how they got along, and how they kissed.

The friends soon became an item, although they kept their relationship secret from the Denny's circle. They went to movies and took long walks around Kim's neighborhood. However, to this day, Sarah denies a romantic involvement with Kim.

After those walks, they often ended up at Denny's, where they would bump into mutual friends, including David and Alex. Kim seemed to thrive in her new life; she had a girlfriend, a good job, and she made new friends every day.

What Kim didn't know was that she had also made at least one enemy.

Alex Baranyi had met Sarah Lamp a couple of months before she started dating Kim and, like Kim, he had fallen deeply in love with her. She was the only woman he had ever been attracted to. He would do anything for her, and he told her as much.

Alex and Sarah went on two dates in November 1994 before Sarah quickly called off the relationship. She apologized, explaining to him that she was getting back together with Mike Anderson.

In early 1995, Kim, Sarah, David, and Alex met frequently at Denny's. Alex hated being in the same room as Kim, because he had heard that Kim and Sarah were dating. He wanted Sarah desperately. And now the girl he loved was dating another woman. It was a huge insult to Alex's ego, and he seethed with anger every time he was anywhere near Kim.

Kim sensed Alex's anger, but shrugged it off. *Alex was just a coldhearted person who needed to get over himself.*

Alex didn't have much time to be jealous of Kim. Sarah and Kim continued to date each other for a couple of months, until Sarah decided to end that relationship, too. She went back to Mike Anderson. Kim was sad to see the relationship end, but she made an effort to remain friends with Sarah long afterward.

Alex was growing increasingly obsessive over Sarah. Now that she was dating Mike again, Alex recognized he had a lot more competition. That summer of 1995, he called and paged her several times a week, but Sarah didn't take the calls or return his pages.

Finally, Alex decided to try and contact her by mail.

In August, Alex sent off his second letter to Sarah after the first went unanswered. He wrote:

Dear Sarah,

Have you noticed that just about every damn song on the radio has to do with a guy being really happy with a woman, a guy being real sad because he doesn't have a woman, or it's a guy wishing he had a woman in his life. I sat and listened to the radio for a couple of hours and I've never been so depressed in my entire life!

Sorry, I don't like not being able to talk to you. Your [sic] the only woman I've ever really felt comfortable talking to. This being grounded really sucks. No

*phone, TV, or friends. I think I'm going to have to kill
my parents very soon. At least they let me listen to the
radio. Big whoop there! I'm so depressed and emotionally empty that suicide seems like a nice thing to
do. Death sounds pretty relaxing. But then I wouldn't
be able to see you. Hmmmm . . . I'm starting to think
that there really is something fundamentally wrong
with everything in general. Nothing really fits in place.
Life itself is like reading every other page in a novel;
you get the general idea but it never totally makes
sense. And all-in-all, it's not very interesting.*

Slicer Thunderclap

Sarah thought it was bizarre that he would use his role-
playing name in the letter. She worried that he was at a
breaking point and that he might hurt himself, so she
showed the letter to her mother. But Sarah and her mother
decided not to take any action; they figured Alex was merely
making veiled threats to win Sarah back. It didn't work.

Alex couldn't get Sarah out of his mind. She was everything he wanted in a girlfriend—sensitive, kind, beautiful,
funny. Once again, she belonged to his best friend's brother.

That summer, Alex was spending the night at the Anderson home when he started acting strange. As usual, he
crashed in David's room. In the middle of the night, David
woke up and saw Alex's sleeping bag was empty. He got up
to make sure Alex was okay.

As David tiptoed down the hallway, he peered into Mike's
bedroom. To his surprise, there stood Alex holding a knife
over Mike, who was sleeping peacefully.

"What are you doing?" David asked in an urgent whisper.

Alex turned his head and grinned at David. He slowly
lowered the knife.

He was just trying to give Mike a good scare, he ex-

plained to David, laughing as he stalked back to David's
room clutching the knife in his hand.

But David wasn't laughing.

For the rest of the night, David slept uneasily, waking at
the slightest sound. Worried that he might wake up and find
Alex standing over *him* with a knife.

The idea of his closest friend possibly trying to kill his
brother seared in David's mind. He was stunned and it made
him feel vulnerable. It also may have excited him. He began
to wonder whether Alex might someday kill for real.

16 By 1995, David had become bored with his life. He began having more clashes with his parents and continued to skip school. He was getting to a breaking point. That year, he became obsessed with making money, and doing something—anything—to quench his thirst for a cheap thrill. He wanted to take a trip to Mexico with some buddies. Or travel somewhere overseas. But David was lazy. The last thing on his mind was working for cash.

At Denny's, David started to plot. He, Alex, and Sarah were drinking coffee and smoking one night when David came up with a plan to commit the perfect crime.

"We could break into people's homes and steal their valuables," David said as Alex and Sarah nodded in agreement.

"But what if the people woke up?" Sarah asked.

"We'd have to kill them if they could identify us," David said, reasonably calm. "We wouldn't keep any witnesses alive."

The friends laughed and egged each other on to come up with as many creative ideas as possible. They talked about robbing an armored car, or being lowered by helicopter into a bank and stealing bags of cash. As it happened, David didn't steal money from strangers; he took it from his own parents.

By late summer of 1995, David had grown very restless. He was killing time at the mall and in front of the computer.

He also spent a lot of time in the open Bellevue fields chasing his friends in a game of pretend sword-fighting called Kinabota.

In September, David and Alex started their sophomore year at Bellevue High School. On the first day of class, David played hooky, he hated school so much. In his mind, it was a total waste of time.

David was beginning to drink and smoke pot heavily. He convinced a group of his friends to skip class and go with him to Canada, where they had heard they could get some good weed. David masterminded the trip, stealing his parents' ATM card. He and four of his friends piled into one of the boys' Cutlass Supremes and raced north to the Canadian border. Alex had been grounded and couldn't go. Along the way, they stopped at more than a dozen ATM machines, drawing out cash and leaving a spending trail behind them. They bought soda, chips, and cigarettes at service stations, and several bags of marijuana in Canada. They also ate out at restaurants and paid for overnight lodging.

By the time the boys returned to Bellevue, David and his buddies had emptied $1,800 from Bruce and Leslie Anderson's savings account. When Bruce found out, he demanded that David somehow repay the money. Hoping to shirk that responsibility, David ran away from home a couple of weeks later.

When he was picked up by a Seattle Police officer, he was taken to the Child Protective Services. David admitted he was using drugs, and he was being investigated for various petty crimes, including property damage in a hit-and-run incident; arson, for trying to light a political yard sign on fire; and grand theft, for stealing $1,800 from his parents. His parents refused to let him come back home.

David again turned to the streets. Wanting to stay loyal to his friend and stand by him, Alex sneaked out of the house to hang out with David at night. The boys would often head to the 7-Eleven in downtown Bellevue where Alex would buy $20 worth of candy, chips, and Big Gulps for David. They would walk to an underground parking lot nearby to feast and smoke, blowing smoke rings all night until Alex had to sneak back home.

David slept in an abandoned car in the Eastgate area behind the Sun Villa Bowling Lanes, and sometimes he crashed with his friend Bob Boyd. The only other person he knew he could always stay with was Kim Wilson.

When Kim found out David had run away from home, she offered to let him crash on the couch. That month, he spent so much time at the Wilson home that one neighbor asked Kim if David was her boyfriend. "No," Kim said, chuckling. "We're just friends."

By December, David was back at his parents' home, but this time more restless than ever. He started to obsess about the idea of killing someone. He wanted to be famous, like the criminals in the thriller novels he read. He dreamed of the day when everyone would know his name.

17 Mike Dickinson was a slight young man with short dark hair and a baby face that made him look much younger than his true age. He enjoyed playing Dungeons and Dragons and other role-playing games—a hobby he shared with David Anderson.

They met in the eighth grade at Chinook Middle School and soon became close buddies. David routinely invited Mike to sit with him and Alex during lunch. The three boys occupied a corner of a table where they would swap stories about teachers they hated and make catcalls to girls.

From the beginning, it was clear that Alex hated Mike. He considered Mike a tagalong who, rather than stealing other people's friends, should find his own. But Alex tolerated him because he was David's friend. Alex would tolerate anyone whom David chose to hang out with, even though he hated sharing David.

It wasn't long before Mike began spending the night at the Anderson home and vice versa.

In the fall of 1995, the boys had started their sophomore year at Bellevue High School. During Christmas break, after David had returned home to his parents from a month-long foray of living on the streets, Mike spent the night at David's house. It would be a night Mike would never forget.

The boys talked about the latest girls they were interested in, and David told Mike about his life on the run. Then, out of the blue, David locked onto an eerie topic: murder.

"I've done it before," he said, sitting in a chair next to his bed, on which Mike was lounging. "I've already killed fifteen people and I'm going to do it again."

Mike rolled onto his side and looked up at David, who was touching his fingers together and raising them to his chest—a gesture that suggested he was making a business deal.

"A group of us are going to break into a house at night and rob the family," David said. "We're going to take their cars and sell 'em to chop shops to make money. And we're going to take CDs, VCRs, stereo equipment, whatever they've got."

David grew excited as he talked about the plan, speaking faster and louder. He paused, drawing out his next words slowly. "We're going to kill anyone inside the house so they can't identify us."

Mike sat straight up. He wasn't sure whether he should believe David or dismiss his remarks as teenage boasting. David seemed serious, but his voice was spiked with sarcasm.

"We're going to stab them in their arteries, you know, in the heart and neck so they'll die faster."

Mike started to laugh.

"I'm serious. I've got the weapons to prove it. Look under the bed."

Mike reached under David's bed and pulled out two baseball bats—one metal and one wooden—and laid them on the floor. He reached farther under the bed and pulled out a black nylon pouch.

"What's this?" Mike asked.

"Open it up."

Mike unrolled the pouch on the bed; tucked in individual pockets were a butcher knife with a wooden handle and two paring knives, polished and shining in the bedroom light. David had got into the habit of stealing his parents' kitchen knives and stashing them under his bed. He would keep them there until his father confiscated them and returned them to the kitchen.

"We're going to do this. Do you want to join in?"

Mike was dumbfounded. "Hell, no," he said, shaking his head.

"Well, then don't go blabbing this to anyone," David said, leaning in close to Mike. "And don't tell Alex."

Mike swore that he wouldn't tell, but he thought David was nuts.

A few weeks later, Mike and David were shooting pool at the Ground Zero teen center in downtown Bellevue when David brought up the plan again.

"Kim and her family are on the list," David whispered, smiling as he walked past Mike to get around the pool table.

"What?" Mike said.

"I said, Kim and her family are on the list, you know, to be taken out."

Here he goes again, Mike thought. David was still talking about his big plan for murder, but Mike decided it was teenage posturing and kept the conversations to himself. He didn't even want to tell his parents. David was known for making comments purely for their shock value, to see how his friends would react. It was all talk. That was David.

18 In early 1996, Kim began focusing on work and school. Consequently, she was slowly losing touch with her friends in the Denny's crowd. She was still living at home, and taking part-time classes at the community college in town. She had thought about moving out and getting an apartment on her own, but she didn't earn enough money at her part-time job in the administrative office at Costco Wholesale, a discount outlet chain in the Northwest.

At home, she continued to argue with her parents over her future: she remained uncertain about what she wanted to do; they urged her to focus on school full-time. Kim knew she needed a change, but she wasn't ready yet to go to college. That drew her to AmeriCorps. Not only would she get to travel, which she loved to do, but she would be able to earn tuition money under the national volunteer program.

Later that spring, she applied for the program and was accepted. Figuring she would need some spending cash while she was in San Diego, she decided to call up her old friend David. More than once during the year, she had complained to a friend in her radio-broadcasting class at Bellevue Community College that David owed her some money, and now she planned to collect on the loans and all the money she had spent over the years taking him out to dinner.

But the request came as a surprise to David. He assumed that the money Kim had given him was not a loan, but a gift.

After all, she had said herself so many times that she would do anything she could to help him. He grew angry that she was now demanding the money back.

In June, Kim finally pressured David to sign a contract that stated he would repay her $350 by September. David was furious, and humiliated that Kim would ask Julia to sign on as a witness. He later told his friends, and his brother Mike, that Kim had forced him to sign the contract while he was drunk. He was still trying to repay his parents for putting a huge dent in their savings account during his escapade in Canada. There was no way he could get the cash Kim demanded by the September deadline she had set. And he was having a hard enough time trying to keep his own life from completely falling apart.

In the fall of 1995 and early 1996, as Kim was hitting the books, David had dropped out of Bellevue High School. Soon after, Alex followed suit. Alex did whatever David did, and followed behind wherever David went. David was the only thing that mattered in Alex's life. He lived to please David, to be there for David, because David was there for him. The boys were enamored with each other. Their bond was undeniably strong.

In early 1996, David was growing increasingly obsessed with two things—murder and girls. He was getting desperate for a change.

David continued to talk to his Denny's friends about doing "something big" to get attention. He continued to plan the perfect crime with Alex and Sarah. But now his plans became more detailed.

"You know who has a lot of property?" David asked. "Kim Wilson and her family. We could break into their home and take the electronics and steal the cars."

"Yeah, we'd make a shitload of money," Alex piped in.

"But those losers never leave the house," David said.

"We'd have to do it while they were still at home. If they caught us, we'd have to kill them."

There was a pause in the conversation as everyone in the group pondered that scenario.

"What could we use as the murder weapons?" Sarah asked.

"We could use a lamp or a phone, hit the people over the head with that," Alex responded.

The three friends laughed and bantered about their ideal crime—conversations that would continue over the course of several months. David discussed the plan while sitting at Denny's, walking around Woodridge, or shooting pool with his buddies.

The more he talked about it, the more he convinced himself that that was what he needed to do. His life was going nowhere; he had nothing to lose. David was thirsty for fame, for everyone to know who he was. In his mind, killing someone was one way to gain notoriety. He wore a laconic smile every time he brought up the subject of murder, which made none of his friends take him seriously.

Even his girlfriends didn't believe him. He started going through girlfriends like through packs of cigarettes, swearing his love and allegiance if they slept with him. For David, that's what relationships were all about: sex.

"He doesn't know what the word 'love' means," Alex would later say. The girls he chose were wholly naive, easily manipulated, according to Alex. "It takes him a week to break them down. They just blindly follow him. They turn into sheep, so docile. He told me, 'I just use women as a wipe rag when I don't want to jack off on myself.' "

David was dating someone new toward the end of 1995 and early 1996: a blond-haired, blue-eyed girl who also attended BHS.

When Danielle Berry first met David Anderson, he seemed like one incredible guy. Good looks. Lots of friends.

And loaded with charisma. It wasn't long—barely two weeks—before the two started dating.

Like most teenage romances, theirs was marked by movie dates and by hanging out in parks and at the mall. David knew the best movies to see, and while strolling through Factoria Mall, Danielle was impressed by how many friends he bumped into.

One of David's favorite places to take girls was Water Tower Park. He knew all the ins and outs. The little caverns of trees and bushes were perfect for hiding in when he played elaborate role-playing games there with friends. He and Danielle would saunter along the trails, sharing cigarettes and holding hands.

For the first couple of months of their relationship, Danielle believed she had made a surprisingly great catch. David was cute, adventurous, and seductive. But there was another, darker side to him that she gradually came to recognize. She got her first glimpse of it just a few months after they started dating.

"I'm going to kill someone before I turn eighteen," David announced evenly. "I've done some research. I know the laws and how to get around them. If I do it before I turn eighteen, I'll still be a minor, and so I'll get a lesser sentence."

Danielle was shocked. She wasn't sure if David was just joking or if he was being serious. But the more details David went into, the more Danielle assumed he was not kidding.

"I want to experience the power of killing someone with my own hands," he said, his face void of expression.

For the first time in their relationship, Danielle was becoming scared of David. She didn't want to hear any more. But he kept talking.

"It's going to be very violent. It's going to be a very special murder. I want my victims to feel pain. I want them to experience the pain I felt all my life."

David said he played baseball in middle school and so was skilled at using a baseball bat. He intended to use a metal baseball bat to smash his victims in the head, and he mentioned that he enjoyed collecting knives, which he would use as weapons also.

Not wanting to believe him, Danielle changed the subject and they went on to talk about movies and school.

In early March, David gave her the same news he had delivered to so many other women: he wanted to break up.

"We're better friends than a couple," David said in a nonchalant voice.

Danielle agreed. She, too, had been planning to end the relationship. Danielle decided not to tell anyone about David's comments, not even her parents. He couldn't possibly be serious about wanting to kill someone, she thought. He was just a teenager—an angry, venting teenager who could talk a good game but never play one.

As the weeks wore on, the friendship started to fray. David later admitted to Danielle that he was dating her friend Amryn Decker. But by March, David was in yet another new relationship.

Laurie Buehler was a petite young woman with long chestnut hair. A year older than David, she was a senior at Bellevue High School when she met him while hanging out at Denny's. By then, David was enrolled in Bellevue's alternative high school, Off Campus School, and was still skipping class regularly.

In March of 1996, David began dating Laurie, taking her on long walks through the Woodridge neighborhood and park. Although they barely knew each other, their relationship quickly grew intense and intimate. David would eventually suggest they get married. She started calling him "my sweetie." It was a term that she never stopped using; years after they had broken up, she would continue to use that term of endearment.

In April, when the first signs of spring began appearing on the trees and bushes, Laurie was with David and Alex at the Anderson home, playing basketball. As David dribbled up his parents' driveway, Laurie noticed a car pull up on the other side of the street. It was Kim Wilson.

David glared at Kim as she walked over to where the boys were playing.

"Hey, guys, what's going on?" Kim asked.

She moved over to where David was standing and whispered in his ear. She told him they needed to talk.

The two turned and strolled up the front lawn, safely out of earshot from Alex and Laurie. Alex kept shooting the ball into the air as Laurie egged him on.

Kim told David she needed her $350 back because she planned to go to a concert in Florida at the end of the summer. But David disagreed with how much he owed her. Growing impatient with him, Kim threatened to talk to his parents if he didn't pay up.

She headed back to her car as David rejoined Laurie and Alex.

Laurie asked David why Kim had come by.

"She thinks I owe her three hundred and fifty dollars," David said.

Laurie wanted to know whether David did, in fact, owe Kim any money. He admitted that he did, but that he owed her only about $100 for buying him dinner at Denny's and letting him sleep on her family's couch.

By that time, David was seething. "I'm so mad I could kill her."

"Yeah, we could kill her and we could take her car and take it to a chop shop," Alex butted in. "We could make some money."

"Yeah," David agreed. "It sounds like a good idea."

David's lips twisted into a sinister grin. He slapped the ball out of Alex's hands and started dribbling away. Alex chased him down the driveway, and within minutes they were playing again and had forgotten about Kim for the time being.

From then on, anytime anyone mentioned Kim's name, David's demeanor changed dramatically. His face turned red and his muscles tightened.

One afternoon Laurie was in David's room talking when he pulled out a baseball bat and started swinging it in the air, hitting an imaginary ball. He extended the bat out in front of his body, drew it back over his head, and let loose, recharging and swinging again and again.

"You could do a lot of damage with a baseball bat," he said, cupping it in his hands, then tossing a glance at Laurie. He told her that a person could break bones, even a human skull, with a bat.

Again David brought up the idea of killing someone and said he had the weapons under his bed: bats and knives. Laurie knew about his interest in blades. He often thumbed through the magazine *Excaliber*, a catalog of all sorts of collectible knives and combat equipment. David wore a knife in a nylon sheath that he strapped underneath his shirt with brass knuckle-duster grips. He also had a combat knife that his father bought him for his birthday; this he kept on a belt near his waist. They looked frightening, but Laurie had no reason to be afraid of David. In bed, he was kind, polite, and gentle.

David confided in Laurie, telling her about his supposed terrible childhood, how he and his brothers had endured physical and sexual abuse from their father. The sexual abuse has not been confirmed, and it's possible that David created the story to make people feel sorry for him, which Laurie did. *No wonder he ran away from home*, she thought.

But their relationship was not meant to be. By June, David and Laurie had broken up, and David was on to the next girlfriend. This time, she was a shy woman nearly three years his senior and recently divorced. Her name was Marsha Rash.

David realized he was getting involved in empty relationships with women, but he needed their comfort and their money. Almost all of the women he dated bought him cigarettes. Marsha even paid his rent. Over the course of several months, something had shifted inside him, something grew darker. He noted that in his journal.

The flame that I once possessed, emitting from my soul—the flame of friendship, love, compassion, carring [sic] and happiness—is now gone.

I once possed [sic] a great flame that spread warmth and a knowing light to all those who were close enough to me to receive the light, but now it's gone. I don't even know how long it's been gone, my attention strayed to petty pleasures and meaningless relationships . . .

I see myself walking my own path of darkness and light. I see people fall to my touch of extacy [sic], and I see people fall to my charming smile of friendship. And I wonder which of those smiles I have feigned and which ones are true.

In the faded light at Denny's, David, Alex, and Sarah continued to meet to talk about the murder plan. It never occurred to Sarah that David was serious, and so she mostly kept it to herself. But one day she slipped up and told someone—Kim Wilson.

Sometime in the spring of 1996, Sarah told Kim that David was planning to kill her and her family. Kim became angry that David would even suggest such a thing. Shortly after her conversation with Sarah, she bumped into David at the Bellevue Square shopping mall, where she confronted him about his plan.

It's likely that David simply laughed it off, hoping Kim would just get over it, but inside, he was seething. He contacted Sarah and berated her for telling Kim. He was furious that she would open her mouth to someone named as a potential victim. David had told several people about the plan, but Kim was the only one who confronted him. His outrage intensified. The secret was out, and now he had to do something about it.

19 In the summer of 1996, David and Alex now had every day to spend together, plotting and planning. The two seventeen-year-olds padded their regular routes around the Woodridge neighborhood, walking aimlessly up and down the hills, side by side along the edges of the streets. Sometimes the boys would stop at Norwood Park and play on the swing set, or they would walk to Woodridge Elementary School and scavenge for rocks to throw at the school windows.

As they ambled along, the boys talked about school and family life. They hated both. They also discussed their dream jobs.

"I want to be a soldier of fortune in a Third World country," David said, smiling as he closed his eyes to imagine himself in that nomadic lifestyle. He liked the idea of getting paid to travel to other countries and earn cash for killing people. It was an unusual aspiration, but to David, it seemed perfectly normal.

"Yeah, that would be cool," Alex said, nodding in agreement.

A wicked smile appeared on David's face as he continued to talk about a life of constant battle, constant killing. The thrill of hunting down the bad guy and exterminating him made David more excited.

During role-playing games, David had killed countless characters, slicing their heads off with his fake swords or

142

simply chanting, "You're dead," over and over again until the player was eliminated from the game. Now he was beginning to wonder what it might be like to take his games to the ultimate level, to experience the real thing—to kill someone.

"What do you think it would be like to kill somebody for profit?" David asked Alex. He paused to watch for Alex's reaction.

"I don't know." Alex shrugged.

"Well, why not kill someone you don't like?" David asked.

Alex smiled. In his mind, it wasn't a half bad idea. He could think of plenty of people he wouldn't mind killing, his father for starters. But David had someone else in mind.

"How about Kim Wilson?" David asked. He was no longer smiling. He was serious.

David hated Kim. She was dumpy, he told his friends, and she was constantly nagging him to go back to school and do something with his life. She was threatening to talk to his parents if he didn't pay back the money he owed her, and he had no idea where he was going to get it. But more than that, she knew about the murder plan he'd discussed with his friends while at Denny's.

Kim would be a perfect candidate for murder as far as David was concerned.

But like Mike and Danielle, Alex didn't take David seriously. Especially when he started couching the idea of murdering Kim in role-playing jargon. David created a fantasy scenario with characters and a story line, just as they did with their role-playing games. It was fun to imagine, so Alex played along.

"Let's say there's this game Dungeons and Dragonesque," David said. "What would happen if this dragon had stolen something from you, you'd want to slay the dragon."

Alex nodded to show he was listening and following along.

"So if Kim is the Dragonesque, we would have to kill her."

"Yeah, that sounds like a good idea," Alex said, offering his support and encouragement. "I would help you do it."

David smiled, slinging one arm around Alex's neck and pulling him close. "You and I have an understanding. We'll always be friends."

Alex grinned and the boys kept walking, separated by a gulf of silence as each contemplated the game and how exactly it would be played.

As the summer of 1996 progressed, David became increasingly excited every time he talked about the plan to kill Kim Wilson and her family. His face reddened with rage and his eyes bulged when anyone mentioned her name. He blamed Kim for all of the stress in his life. When Kim devised a contract that detailed when David would have to pay back her money, David's growing hatred for Kim was fueled even more. Now he wanted to kill her more than ever.

"You know, Alex, this is something that could be done in real life," David said one afternoon as the boys were once again strolling through the Woodridge area. "We could do this for real. We could lure Kim out of her house, you know, to a park or some place where there's no phone. We gotta get her where there are no houses, no lights, no cars coming by. We could kill her and dump her out in Issaquah or somewhere in the mountains over there. Then we could go to her house and kill her family and take their cars and VCR and stuff like that."

Alex couldn't believe that David was actually serious about the whole thing, that he had been thinking about it that long and hard as to come up with details on how to go about committing the murders and how to dispose of the bodies. But as he always did, Alex went along.

Alex felt like he owed David his life because David was his only friend. David gave him support and attention. David also provided Alex with access to a much wider circle of friends, and because of that, Alex had a chance at the dating scene. Mostly, David was the one constant thing in Alex's unstable life, the one thing he could count on when everything else in his world was slipping out of his control.

"He made me feel like he and I were soul mates," Alex would later say. "I believed it. I was an immature kid. What the hell did I know? He was my only friend."

Because of all this, he wanted to remain loyal to David. He would lie and steal for David. He would die for David. He vowed he would even kill for David.

More than anyone, David wanted Kim Wilson dead. And in her own plans, she would unwittingly fall into the destructive path David had laid.

But then Kim was on a plane bound for San Diego to begin the first part of her stint as a volunteer with AmeriCorps, and David soon stopped talking about her. He was happier, as if some great weight had been miraculously and suddenly lifted from his shoulders. And the plan to murder the Wilsons also faded, and apparently was dropped.

20 Over time, Alex Baranyi had grown to hate his father. He blamed him for his parents' failed marriage and resented him for fighting so fiercely to get custody of him. Alex Jr. felt ignored and neglected once his father remarried. It seemed that Alex Sr. didn't want his son.

Behind closed doors, Alex became increasingly despondent and withdrawn, barely addressing either his father or his stepmother. At the end of each day, Alex would come home, toss his keys into a bowl in the kitchen, grab several cans of Coke, and bound downstairs to his bedroom in the basement, where he would seal himself up for the rest of the night.

"I was the troll," Alex would later say. "I spent all my time down there."

He logged long hours in front of the TV either playing SuperNintendo or watching *Star Trek*. When he wasn't blowing things up on the computer or drowsing in front of the TV, Alex read. Science fiction, mystery novels, and medieval literature lined his bookshelf, the titles of which included *The Book of Runes; Moral Reasoning, the Value of Life; Elemental Power, Celtic Faerie Craft & Druidic Magic;* and "Liber Astarte," an article by renowned black-magic and occult author Aleister Crowley. He thumbed through issues of *Excaliber* magazine in search of new swords and knives he would buy once he had saved enough

146

money. He even ate meals downstairs, shoveling in piles of rice as the washer droned in the laundry room nearby.

Alex channeled his rage into poetry, prose, letters, and art. Darkness and death were common themes that showed up again and again in his writing. Between the lines lay hints of his propensity for violence and a sinister foreshadowing of the brutal crimes he would later commit.

In a notebook filled with musings, Alex wrote:

"What appears to you as 'nice Alex' is actually merely wisps of what was once a normal human being. These wisps of humanity float about the surface when I am with friends. A simili [sic]: The wisps of fog here cover the gloomy mountain (me). They add to the atmosphere (my personality) but they are truely [sic] part of the mountain and can not significantly change it. And so like wisps of fog, my wisps of humanity will soon fade into nothingness. You are warned . . . I will continue to be 'Mr. Hyde.' It is who I am. Jeckle [sic] was plagued by Hyde. I am Hyde who is plaged [sic] by Jeckle [sic]. It is who I am. I am not sorry. And it will get worse. Far worse. For one day, my humanity, my cherity [sic], my goodness of heart will be forever dissolved and I will truely [sic] be pure . . . and free."

Whereas he lacked in the social graces, Alex soared in intelligence. By middle school, he had become a prolific writer and artist. When he was tested at age eighteen, Alex's IQ placed him just three points shy of being a genius. Although he hated math and was bad at it, he excelled in his English classes. But even in the classes he liked, he failed to apply himself, and barely skimmed by most classes with D's. Those grades did not go unnoticed by Alex Sr.

One afternoon Alex Jr. came home from school to find his father, red-faced, clenching Alex Jr.'s report card in his fist and shaking it at him.

"You're a crappy kid! You can't do better than this?" Alex

Sr. shouted. "What's wrong with you? Can't you do anything right?"

Alex Jr., by then used to his father's tirades, scowled at him but said nothing.

"My dad brutally whipped down my ego at home," Alex would later say.

" 'All I want is for you to do your best,' " Alex Sr. would tell his son.

But Alex Jr. didn't want to hear it.

"Fuck you!" he would bark back, and then storm down the stairs into his dungeon.

As far as Alex was concerned, he was good at something. During his freshman year of high school, he began shoplifting, following David's lead. At first, Alex stole small things—candy bars, beer—whatever would fit into his pockets. As he began pefecting his habit, he started stealing much larger things like laptop computers and trench coats.

Alex was proud of his skill, and considered himself an expert when it came to shoplifting. He even took notes about how to succeed at shoplifting. In outline form in a green notebook, Alex wrote:

- a shoplifter must be seen taking something
- don't take stuff out of your pockets once outside
- shoppers ignore people and look at merchandise
- bags or big coats are watched more
- be confident
- large stores prosecute more
- discounts such as K-mart prosecutes heavy
- most guarded are cds, jewelry, leather goods
- rarely stolen are children's clothing, men's clothing, women's clothing by men, household items
- steal one at a time
- make a scene, refuse to go to the office
- when in the office, be calm and demand a lawyer

He would later brag that he never got caught. The few times he had been close, he made such a fuss about the situation that security guards let him go. Alex would threaten the security guards by saying if they searched his body and didn't find any stolen property, he would sue.

Alex had also perfected with David a system of sneaking out. Several nights a week, after midnight, Alex would see a silhouette bent over outside his bedroom window, then a flicker of light, followed by a tapping at the window. That was David's signal. David would leave and wait at the stop sign at the end of the street.

Alex Sr. knew his son was sneaking out with David. He despised David and scowled at him every time he came around the house. In Alex Sr.'s mind, David was manipulative, cocky, and lazy. He was trouble. Alex Sr. simply didn't trust him. But there was little Alex Sr. could do to prevent his son from hanging out with David, and in a way, he was glad to know that for the first time in his life, Alex Jr. had a friend.

Nonetheless, he was angry that Alex Jr. kept sneaking out at night, so he installed a security alarm that was left on even when everyone was home. Anytime Alex tried to sneak out, the alarm sounded and Alex Sr. raced downstairs to drag Alex back in the house. Finally, to make sure Alex didn't get out, Alex Sr. "superglued" his son's bedroom windows shut. Alex Sr. also ended the sleepovers; Alex Jr. was no longer allowed to spend the night with David at the Anderson home.

But Alex and David always found a way to get together. Nothing, not even their parents, could keep them apart.

In the summer of 1996, Alex was beginning to feel more confident around girls. He was seventeen years old, and by then, he had grown into his features. No longer the tall, awkward nerd he was considered to be in middle school, girls in the Denny's gang found him strikingly good-looking.

Now that David and Laurie Buehler were no longer dating, Alex started spending time with her.

Laurie lay sprawled out on Alex's bed one afternoon and Alex sat nearby on the floor. Finally, Alex thought, there was a chance to have a girlfriend.

But that bliss was interrupted when Alex's stepmother went downstairs to do a load of laundry. Curious about what was happening inside her stepson's room, she glanced through the door and saw a young woman lying on his bed.

Shocked at the apparent impropriety, Mary Beth hurried back upstairs to tell Alex's father.

"Fuck," Alex said, sighing as he listened to Mary Beth's petite footsteps bounce up the stairs. "I guess I'm in trouble now."

"For what?" Laurie said, raising herself up from the bed.

"Beats me. I guess I'll find out."

Laurie left through the sliding basement door and headed back to her friend Jamie Rivas' house.

When Alex went upstairs to get a Coke, he was confronted by his father in the living room.

Alex Sr. reminded his son that he was not allowed to have girls in the house.

Alex Jr. insisted that he wasn't doing anything, but his father became angry and lunged at him. Alex Jr. responded by kicking his father in the stomach and side.

"Die, motherfucker!" Alex Jr. shouted as Alex Sr. stood up and held a hand over his heart, gasping.

Worried that her husband might get hurt, Mary Beth threatened to call the cops if the two men didn't stop.

Alex left his father in the living room and went downstairs, where he grabbed some socks, T-shirts, and a pair of black jeans. He picked up the phone and dialed David's number.

"Dave, I just had a fight with my dad. Come get me," Alex said.

David said he would be right over.

When the boys got back to the Anderson residence, Alex approached Bruce Anderson and explained what had just happened.

"I got into a fight with my dad. Can I stay overnight?"

"Just one night," Bruce said sternly. "You have to go home tomorrow. You have to talk to your dad, Alex."

That night, Alex rolled out a sleeping bag and slept on the floor in David's room.

"So what happened?" David asked as he lay in bed and stared at the ceiling.

"Laurie was over and she was on my bed. Mary Beth walked by and saw her and thought we were doing something. So my dad said I couldn't have any girls in the house. He rushed me."

"Let's go over and kick his ass some more," David said, growing excited.

"No," Alex said, laughing. "We don't need to do that."

That night, Bruce called Alex Sr.

"Alex is here. He said you guys got into a fight. What's going on?"

Alex Sr. explained how his son broke the house rules by bringing girls over.

"I've raised four boys. I've been through this. They grow up and think they can do whatever they want. But they learn. You guys need to get back together."

The next morning, Alex gathered his belongings and David dropped him off at home. When he walked through the door, Alex Sr. was waiting for him.

"Kevin, I'm sorry," Alex Sr. said. Tears began to well up in his eyes. "I love you. You're my only son."

Alex rolled his eyes.

"Bullshit," he mumbled as he returned to his world downstairs.

* * *

By the end of the summer, both David's and Alex's lives were in flux. Each had left his home: David, to live with his older brothers, who were renting a home near Woodridge; and Alex, with Bob Boyd's family.

With a debt to Kim and to his parents hanging over his head, David took a job at Rite-Way Waterproofing in Seattle as a day laborer. A few months later, in October, he helped Alex also get a job there.

Alex was usually the first one to show up for work and the last to leave. Because he didn't have his driver's license, he had to wait for Marsha, David's girlfriend at the time, to drop him off each morning at 7 A.M. and pick him up at 7 P.M.

David worked only when he felt like it. When he did, Marsha would drive both of them to and from work. But by October, David had missed so many days of work that he was fired.

Alex was the more industrious of the two. He worked forty to sixty hours a week. On his day off, he went grocery shopping with Val Boyd, loading up on Top Ramen instant noodles. It was the only thing he knew how to make, and it was cheap.

Ron and Valerie Boyd enjoyed having Alex around. "He's a good kid," Ron Boyd would later say. He was polite. Respectful. A hard worker. He was part of the family.

In Alex's mind, living with the Boyds felt more like family than living with his own father. Now he had a job, a good place to live, and new friends.

On the surface, Alex seemed to have shaken off his delinquent habits and was turning his life around. For the first time in his life, things looked promising.

But what people didn't see was a simmering psychosis inside Alex. In his room, behind closed doors, he retreated deeper and deeper into his fantasy world. He began practicing how to use swords. He chopped off the head of a life-size cardboard cutout of his favorite actor, Mel Gibson, as

William Wallace in *Braveheart*. He hacked at a stuffed chair and other pieces of furniture in his room. Gouge marks lined his bedroom wall where he swung the sword and missed his target.

Alex entertained fantasies of killing certain people—anyone who had ever slighted him. He wanted to kill Mike Anderson because Mike had something he desperately wanted—Sarah Lamp. He wanted to kill David and the rest of the Anderson family. He wanted to kill Kim Wilson because he hated her. And more than once, he had thought about killing his own father for the constant verbal abuse that made him feel small, insignificant, unwanted. He would sculpt the air with his sword, making wide arches and criss-crossing swings above his head. When the time was right, he promised himself, he would put his fighting skills to the test.

21 In the meantime, Alex continued to satisfy his hunger for killing by playing live-action fantasy role-playing games. He was not alone in his active interests in the fantasy realm. Alex and David were both part of more than 3,000 people across the Seattle area who peeled away their weekday personas to become vampires and fallen angels in various games. The gamers included an eclectic mix of people such as Microsoft engineers, janitors, high school students, and fast-food restaurant employees.

These participants would gather on a Friday or Saturday night, turning parks and living rooms into temporary stages for a game. In fantasy role-playing, group members choose a character which they act out in adventure scenarios set by a "storyteller." The participants dress the part, paint their faces white with thick lines of black eye shadow, and sometimes use props such as swords or daggers to help make the simulation more real.

Fantasy role-playing games are a multimillion-dollar industry in the United States. There are dozens of magazines, hundreds of websites and computer games, and new role-playing clubs sprouting up each year. Role-playing games evolved from war games in southern European regions that date as far back as the third millennium B.C. to a board-and-dice adaptation in the 1950s. The games were taken to a live version in the 1970s, and were set into computer games by the 1980s, the first of which was Dungeons and Dragons.

In Bellevue, D&D gained an impressive following among the children who hung out at Denny's. David and Alex and their friends often played the games at local Bellevue parks and gathered at Denny's afterward to smoke and munch on French fries and talk about the games.

David often played a mischievous dwarf in the games, while Alex enjoyed the role of a mercenary character he created called Slicer Thunderclap.

What made Alex stand out was that long after the games had ended, he was known for his unwillingness to come out of character. He liked to think he was Slicer Thunderclap and encouraged his friends to call him that.

In Bellevue's role-playing community, David and Alex had gained a reputation as poor sports. Twice in the same year, they were kicked out of role-playing sessions held by the group Camarilla for taking the games too far and violating the no-contact rules.

That did not stop the best friends from playing. They merely created their own hybrid world of fake swords and mock battle games, chasing each other through parks and fields. Over time, they made up their own story lines and played by their own rules.

The more Alex used the character Slicer Thunderclap in fantasy role-playing games, the more he believed he truly was that character.

In his journal, penned in small, even letters, Alex pontificated about death and killing, and signed "ST" at the end:

All things deserve life. And as such, many things deserve death. Those that sing praise of killing have never done it. Killing is very hard. It pushes our minds to the limit. It crashes our egoes against the jagged shores of our conscience. Ask yourself: "Do those in my family deserve to be wiped from existence?" It's a hard choice if you think about it for awhile.

I have done the unspeakable. Death and killing neither worries or scares me. I have seen and done far worse. Death is supreme. There is nothing beyond death. Within our hands we hold the flame of life. I have done the unspeakable. I have become a god for I keep my lips close to others' flames. Ready to blow the wind of judgement. Through my power I am god. There are those higher than me but their power is no greater. Fear not death; respect it.

ST

He preferred living in this fantasy world where he could be king, a hero who saved pretty girls from villains.

In reality, Alex was painfully aware of his own place in life. In journal entries, he writes, ". . . My entire life has been one insult after another. Eventually, my ego and self-consciousness were torn down until only emptiness filled me. You see, in emotional terms, the feelings of pain and anger come quickest and last longest. So when I became empty, I filled that space with pain, anger, hatred, and evil . . ."

Every day Alex descended further and further into his maniacal make-believe world; even David was growing scared of his best friend.

A few years after the boys met, David wrote about those fears on a plain sheet of white paper, in neat penmanship.

I do not trust him, I have every cause to fear him as much as he should fear me, but we are the best of friends—or so he pretends. Possibly he is trying to do the same thing to me as I will do to Kim.

At times I think that our friendship will last forever, and then there are those times when he talks about his ambitions and about Rose, I try to keep myself from laughing, and when I think back on it I think that he is totally insane and I wonder who I've been talking to for the past 3 years.

I feel like his friendship to me is like a flame from a candle—starting out with just a spark of life—then growing and staying constantly strong, bright, warm, and melting all the waxy problems of life. Then the flame flickers, and sometimes goes out altogether, but always the flame was lit again—and again constantly strong, bright, and warm, but this time the wick is not as long, the flame not quite as strong. And I sometimes find myself wondering when the wick will run out, or when the flame won't be re-lit.

I also wonder who is the monster, is it him? Is it me? Or are we just children playing a child's game while waiting to grow up? It never hurts to wonder, but I'm very careful on which actions I choose to take from my decisions baised [sic] on my wonderings.

22 It rained on Friday, January 3, as Kim Wilson stepped out of the front door of her family's white wood-frame home on Woodridge Hill. She had returned home December 20, 1996 from AmeriCorps for Christmas break and was scheduled to fly back to San Diego on Sunday, January 5.

That day, Kim planned a quick trip to Bellevue High School for a special visit. She wanted to thank certain teachers and her guidance counselor for their help. After all, had it not been for them, she would still be there, scrambling to pass enough classes to graduate. Friday was her last chance to see any of those staff members at the school.

Now that she had been indoctrinated into the real world, Kim walked with a confident stride down the long corridors of her alma mater. Although it was winter, she wore only a light jacket and her usual casual attire of blue jeans and boots.

Kim had no other plans for the day, so there was plenty of time to catch up with former teachers. With each of them, she painted the same picture of her life after high school: it was hard at first, not knowing which direction to turn in, where to begin. But she had joined AmeriCorps to buy some time, and it was giving her a sense of direction. She was feeling more sure about going to college.

Things at home were still difficult, but improving, she told her former counselor. Kim realized that she would always be at odds with her parents over certain points and she just had to learn to compromise.

About ten miles away, at the University of Washington campus in Seattle, Rose Wilson was beginning her day with a cup of coffee and an early morning chat with her friend and co-worker Tasha Taylor.

Rose bounced into the office, smiling at everyone. She was always in high spirits and never looked tired, despite the constant home-improvement projects and the work of raising her daughters. That Friday, Rose was particularly excited. For the first time in many months, there was exceptionally good news. Rose had made a breakthrough with Kim.

"She finally gets it," Rose said, her voice elated. "Kim finally understands what being an adult means."

Rose and Bill hoped against hope that joining the Ameri-Corps program would provide Kim with a focus to her life. All these years, Rose had struggled with her elder daughter. There would be no more battles, Rose said, her mood ecstatic.

It was hard not to be excited when Rose was happy. Her joy was contagious; it worked its way from one person to the next until the whole office was in stitches over her stories of family struggles and triumphs. Friday was one of those rare days of triumph. Rose beamed as she celebrated the fact that both of her daughters had stepped out of their adolescent lives and into adulthood. The troubled times were over.

Good news found its way into Julia Wilson's life the same Friday. That afternoon, Kim's sister plucked from the mailbox an envelope from Western Washington University. She tore it open and read excitedly. She had been accepted into the small Catholic college. Julia headed straight for the telephone to tell her friends. She even called her mom at work; Western, after all, was the school where her mother had received her bachelor's degree in business. She knew her mother would be pleased. Julia called to say that she would not be home for dinner; she was going out with friends to celebrate.

Bill Wilson worked a full day at Graham Steel in Kirkland, then drove home. He would later pick up his mother-in-law, Julia Mahoney, who wanted to take Kim out to dinner to celebrate her last night in town.

23 On Friday, January 3, David stopped by the Boyd residence to collect Alex. He had been borrowing Marsha's tan VW Rabbit to drive around town, but since that was in the shop, Marsha borrowed her stepfather's black pickup truck. She loaned it to David.

Let in through the basement door, David followed Alex back to his bedroom, where Bob Boyd was playing Nintendo on Alex's computer. Bob and his friends would soon be headed to Sun Villa to bowl during Rock-and-Bowl, a raucous late-night bowling scene in which clusters of adolescents convened to bowl and listen to loud, industrial rock music blasting out of huge black-box speakers.

"You guys going to meet us there?" Bob asked David, who was waiting for Alex to get his trench coat.

"No, we're heading down to Renton, maybe going over to Denny's or Shari's."

"Cool. Later, then," Bob said as he led the group of boys upstairs to his own bedroom.

Alex searched for some cash before walking out to the pickup truck with David. David jumped in behind the wheel and Alex circled the car to the passenger side, got in, and slammed the door. David screeched out of the driveway and turned left onto Bellevue Way Southeast, careening around a curve before jumping onto the Interstate 405 interchange that would take them to Renton, a suburb south of Bellevue.

David and Alex had dropped out of Bellevue's late-night

161

Denny's scene that summer and started hanging out on their own. Increasingly, they were irritated with everyone. Even their friends.

As David steered his way onto I-405 heading south, Alex told David about the promotion he was about to get at Rite-Way Waterproofing.

David talked about his day, which mostly involved sleeping and going down to the mall to talk to Marsha, who was working at RadioShack.

"By the way, Kim's in town," David said as he drove into the parking lot at Shari's and looked for a spot. "Why don't we do the stuff tonight?"

Alex knew what David was talking about, but didn't understand why he was bringing it up now. Why there? Why then?

Alex glanced over at David to see if he had a smirk or a grin on his face, something that would assure him David was joking. But he didn't.

David parked and the boys jumped out of the truck and walked into the restaurant. They didn't need to request a seat in the smoking section. The waitstaff at Shari's was familiar with them and brought them to a booth in the back.

David slipped into the vinyl seat first and Alex followed. David ordered coffee and Alex drank root beer.

As the boys sipped their drinks, they stared at each other intensely.

Alex thought David would drop the subject about killing Kim and they would go on to discuss other things. But David was persistent and determined not to let Alex escape the conversation.

"So let's do it. Tonight." David took a slug of his coffee and cupped a match in his hands as he lit a cigarette.

"I don't particularly want to," Alex said, tapping out a cigarette from his own pack.

"If you don't wanna help, I'll fucking do it myself," David said, his voice edged with impatience.

Alex wasn't biting the guilt bait just yet.

"Come on. We've been talking about this forever. We're best friends. We stick together. Blood brothers, remember?"

Blood brothers. It was all Alex had to hang his hopes on.

"Okay. What do you want me to do?"

"I'll get Kim out of the house and make her come with me to the park. You wait at the water tower behind some bushes until I bring Kim over." David's voice quickened and grew more excited as he laid out the plan. "Then I'll stop. You jump out and put the rope around her neck and garrote her."

Garrote her? Alex was surprised but impressed that David would use such a romantic term to describe a hideous act.

Still not believing his friend was serious, Alex played along. "Okay, fine."

David fished in his pocket and headed out the door to use the pay phone outside the restaurant. He dropped twenty-five cents into the slot, picked up the receiver, and dialed Kim's number.

Minutes later, he came back. "Ready to go?" he asked.

Alex stabbed out his cigarette in the ashtray and got up. An uneasy silence hung in the air between the two friends as they made their way back to Bellevue. Alex still couldn't believe David was serious. He wondered: "We're actually going to kill Kim and her family?"

Just as Alex had a fleeting thought of what would happen if they got caught, David rehashed the plan a final time to make sure each person knew what his role was.

"I'll drop you off at the park, and you wait there while I go get Kim," David said. "Use a rope. I want to make sure it's quiet."

By then, Alex realized David was completely serious.

This was not a joke. This was not David trying to sound tough. This was real.

On the way back to Bellevue, David stopped by Factoria Mall to pick up Marsha from work and take her home.

Marsha, tired from a long day of sales, collapsed into bed and fell asleep. But her repose was interrupted hours later by Mike Anderson. He roused her to ask if she wanted to go to Denny's with him. Tired as she was, Marsha agreed to go along and keep her boyfriend's brother company.

David and Alex hung out at the house for a few minutes and then left to go back to the Boyd residence to gather the materials they would need to carry out the murders. Although it has never been proved, David had probably moved the weapons to Alex's room sometime before that night.

Around 10 P.M., David and Alex started carrying their "props" to the pickup truck, where they stashed the items in the cab section behind the seats.

Christine Sheridan, Ron Boyd's sister, was getting annoyed that David and Alex kept walking in and out of the basement door. She was trying to watch *20/20*, and got so frustrated at the noise the boys were making that she put up a sign on the basement door, asking everyone to use the front door.

Christine looked through the venetian blinds to see what David and Alex were up to. From her window she saw Alex walking with his arm stiff, as if he were holding something long in the sleeve of his trench coat. She watched as the boys moved in and out of the house. *Damn boys*, she thought. *They're up to no good*.

The blood brothers lingered outside near the pickup truck, smoking cigarettes and waiting. They didn't want to move too soon because the Wilsons might still be awake.

About 11 P.M., David glanced at his watch. It was time to go.

* * *

On the way to Water Tower Park, David and Alex rode in silence. They knew what each of their roles would be. Neither needed reminding.

At the park, David pulled into the parking lot and both young men jumped out of the truck. They turned to the left and walked up a gravel trail. About thirty yards into the park, near a tangle of bushes, David stopped.

He pointed to a stand of tall shrubbery and told Alex to stay there until he and Kim came up the trail.

Alex nodded and fingered the rope inside his pocket.

David stared hard into Alex's eyes. "This is it."

Alex watched as David walked back down the trail and out of view. A few moments later, he heard the sound of an engine revving up, and the skid of tires spinning on loose gravel. Then nothing. Alex couldn't believe he was standing there waiting for David to bring him their first murder victim. *This can't be real,* he thought over and over. *This isn't happening.*

About five minutes later, Alex again heard the sound of a car, this time pulling into the Water Tower Park parking lot. Then he heard two car doors slam.

It was just after midnight when Kim and David reached the park. Kim slid out of the truck and got onto the hood, where she sat cross-legged. David stepped out of the driver's side and stood next to Kim, lighting a cigarette.

In the dark, they looked like college sweethearts home for the holidays, spending one last night together before parting. Traffic moaned high over the hills on Interstate 405, and, every now and then a cold breeze whistled through the leaves.

There was no traffic on 23rd Avenue Southwest, the entrance to Water Tower Park, except for a lone car passing by late that Friday, its headlights slashing the pitch-black night.

David and Kim ignored the car and continued taking

drags from their cigarettes. Smoke funneled from their lips in thin white streams and disappeared.

David asked Kim if she wanted to go for a walk.

Kim could never pass up an opportunity for a walk. She jumped off the truck, slapping the dirt from her jeans.

At first, they strolled side by side toward the trails. Then David passed Kim and headed into the park first.

Their feet crunched evenly over the gravel path and Kim took her time. There was no need to rush. She enjoyed the solitude of the park at night, as if the whole place belonged to her.

Alex could hear faint talking and the footsteps drawing nearer. His heart beat wildly with each wet scrape of shoe on gravel. It beat so fast there was ringing in his ears. With each footstep he grew more excited. He held the rope taut between his hands, his muscles fully flexed. *This is real. Oh, fuck, this is real.*

The footsteps came closer and closer until Alex could see two shadowy figures in front of him. David stopped, then glanced quickly toward Alex.

Adrenaline surging, Alex leapt from the bushes. He threw up his hands as if to scare the unsuspecting woman, but then started laughing uproariously.

Kim jumped back and turned to see who it was. Recognizing Alex in the shadows, she tried to calm herself down.

"You scared me," she said, a bit annoyed. But David was there. She would be safe. And in a moment, she started up the path again.

This time, she walked alone.

David cut Alex a look of intense anticipation. *You've gotta do it*, Alex told himself. *You've gotta kill this person. No matter what, do whatever Dave says.*

For a few steps, Kim heard David follow her, but then he was stepping off the path and Alex was moving in.

24 Having given the police their alibis on Wednesday night, David and Alex thought they were in the clear. They went about their days as if nothing had happened. On Saturday afternoon, David and Alex met their friend Joe Kern, a tall, big-boned young man who often crashed at the rental house David shared with his brothers. Joe's younger sister, Jeannie Kern, had had a brief fling with David. The boys talked until late in the afternoon, when David had to leave. Leslie Anderson was making a special belated birthday dinner for Bruce, and she asked all of her boys to come home and celebrate.

Back at his parents' home, David asked his brother Mike to cut his hair. The boys' parents and grandparents had long complained that David's hair was too long, and so finally, that day, David decided to appease them. As the party got under way, Mike stole Leslie's barber kit and hustled David downstairs, where he clipped about five inches off David's head.

David and Alex believed there was absolutely nothing at the crime scenes that could connect them to the murders, so there would be no way they could get caught. What they didn't know was that a tempest was swirling around them. The investigation was picking up. The more detectives learned about the two boys, the more they were convinced that they had something to do with the murders of the Wilson family.

To help move the investigation along, Jeff Gomes called Bob Thompson on Thursday afternoon.

"Hey, when are you going to finish up over there?" Gomes asked, talking on his cell phone. "We really need you."

Thompson, who had been sealed up in the Wilson house busily collecting evidence and processing the complicated crime scene all week, said he would be available that afternoon.

"Would you go over and check out this kid, Alex Baranyi?" Alex had been interviewed by the McBrides the day before, but now Gomes wanted Thompson to reinterview him.

"Okay," Thompson said. "I'll be over as soon as I shut things down here."

Close to 4 P.M., Thompson arrived at the Boyd residence. He had talked to Alex the night before at the Boyd house, and while Alex seemed like a weird kid, Thompson didn't think too much of him. When he knocked on the front door, a stocky, blond-haired, surly-looking boy came to the door.

"I'm Detective Thompson with the Bellevue Police Department. Can I ask you a few questions about Alex Baranyi?" Thompson asked.

"Okay. Sure," the boy said. "Come in."

The boy introduced himself as Bob Boyd and said Alex was renting a room from his parents in the basement of the home. As Bob talked, Thompson thought about the bloody bootprint found on the back of Bill Wilson's T-shirt and his eyes swung down toward Bob's feet. Bob was wearing lug-soled boots.

"Nice boots. Where did you get them?" Thompson asked.

"Oh, I got them over at Volume Shoes, over at Factoria Mall."

"Can I see the bottom of those?"

Kim Wilson

*Photo courtesy of
Putsata Reang*

Bill Wilson

*Photo courtesy of
Putsata Reang*

Rose Wilson

*Photo courtesy of
Putsata Reang*

Julia Wilson

*Photo courtesy of
Putsata Reang*

Abinanti, Mark
Akopyan, Nonna
Anders, Ross
Anderson, David
Andrews, Emily

Angelo, Frank
Anthony, Brand
Aso, Takahide
Baranyi, Alex
Barich, Ross

Alex Baranyi and David Anderson became instant friends after meeting in the 7th grade. Here, in a 1995 yearbook photo from Bellevue High School, David's picture (*left*) falls ironically and symbolically atop Alex's picture.

Photo courtesy of Rick Schweinhart

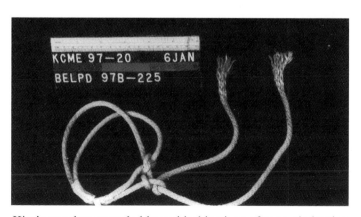

Kim's attacker strangled her with this piece of rope, tied twice around her neck to ensure she would not survive.

Photo courtesy of Bellevue Police Department

A fork in the gravel path at Water Tower Park in Bellevue's Woodridge neighborhood where four boys found the first victim. Kim Wilson's body lay under a cedar tree on the left side of the fork, hidden in thick shrubbery.

Photo courtesy of Bellevue Police Department

The black pickup truck, believed to be the getaway car, belonging to Neil Deacy, the stepfather of Marsha Rash, whom David was dating at the time of the crime. David told police he went for a drive in the truck the night of the murders.

Photo courtesy of Bellevue Police Department

The Wilson home, the morning of January 5, 1997, when the bodies were found. Bill and Rose Wilson spent many weekends remodeling it, and they raised their two daughters, Kim and Julia, there.

Photo courtesy of Bellevue Police Department

David and Alex were regulars at the Sun Villa Lanes, where they spent time drinking coffee and picking up girls.

Photo courtesy of Bellevue Police Department

A cardboard cutout of Mel Gibson with cuts and tears found on a butchering block in Alex Baranyi's bedroom. Alex used it as target practice.

Photo courtesy of Bellevue Police Department

Police found this boot, belonging to David Anderson, in his bedroom during a search after his arrest. It tested positive for the blood of Bill and Julia Wilson.

Photo courtesy of Bellevue Police Department

Police believe the attackers used a blade similar to this one, with a knuckle grip.

Photo courtesy of Bellevue Police Department

This poster was hanging in Alex Baranyi's bedroom, with a quote by Daniel Baldwin: "The good die young. That is why immortality is reserved for the greatest of evils."

Photo courtesy of Bellevue Police Department

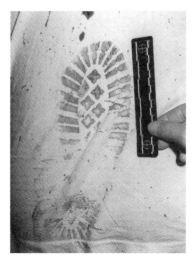

From the hallway, Detective Jeff Gomes could see this bloody bootprint on the back of Bill Wilson's T-shirt when he entered the home to check on the welfare of the family. Alex Baranyi was known to wear black boots with the same distinct diamond-patterned lug sole, as seen here, although his boots were never found.

Photo courtesy of Bellevue Police Department

From left to right: Detective Bob Thompson, King County Prosecutors Jeff Baird and Patty Eakes, and Detective Jeff Gomes at the King County Prosecutor's Office shortly after the guilty verdict was announced in the retrial of David Anderson.

Photo courtesy of Putsata Reang

Pete Connick was aggressive in his calls for objections and mistrials throughout David's retrials, but in the end, a jury would convict his client of murder. He is seen here talking to reporters after the verdict was announced.

Photo courtesy of Putsata Reang

"Yeah, sure," Bob said, lifting up one of his feet so Thompson could check it out.

Thompson's eyes grew wide. The patterns on the soles of Bob's boots looked just like the bootprint on the back of Mr. Wilson's T-shirt.

"I'm thinking, 'This could be our killer right here,' " Thompson recalled.

"Does Alex have these boots?" Thompson asked.

"Yeah, he has a pair exactly like mine. He saw me wearing them one day and asked me where I got them. He wanted a pair just like them."

This raised red flags for Thompson. Alex had told the McBrides on Wednesday night that he had only one pair of shoes—his yellow work boots.

"Do you know where Alex was last Friday night?"

"He was here, down in his bedroom," Bob said.

"Do you know what time it was when you saw him?"

"Yeah, around ten P.M., just before my friends and I left for Rock-and-Bowl. I don't know where he went after that."

"Was anyone else home that night?" Thompson continued.

"Yeah, my aunt was home."

"Who's your aunt?"

"Chris Sheridan."

"Is she home now?"

"Yeah, she's downstairs. She lives across the hall from Alex."

Bob nodded that it was fine for Detective Thompson to go downstairs and talk to his aunt.

Thompson bounded down the steps and knocked at Mrs. Sheridan's bedroom door.

Christine Sheridan, a woman in her late forties and not quite 5-feet tall, came out of her room, wearing blue jeans and a T-shirt. She looked relaxed. Thompson introduced himself, and she was not surprised or alarmed. Sheridan was no stranger to cops knocking on her door. Her own sons, now adults, had been in all manner of trouble and she had grown accustomed to receiving visits from police officers.

"Can I help you?" Sheridan said calmly, her gravelly voice baked from decades of smoking.

"I'm here to ask you a few questions about Alex Baranyi."

"What do you want to know?" she asked.

"Do you know if he was home last Friday night?"

"Well, he was here for a little bit. He and David were here, and they kept slamming the door, walking in and out, making all this noise. But he left around ten o'clock."

Alex left the house? He told the McBrides he and David stayed in his bedroom all night and played Nintendo. Thompson perked up, feeling a shot of adrenaline course through his body at having caught the second in a series of lies Alex would spin to throw investigators off his track.

"How do you know it was ten P.M.?"

"Because *20/20* was coming on. He left with David Anderson."

Thompson thanked Chris Sheridan for her help and gave her his pager number. He asked her to page him as soon as Alex got home from work so he could speak with Alex in person.

His suspicions piqued, Thompson drove back to the BPD to tell Gomes about what he'd just learned.

Around 4:30 P.M. at the Bellevue Police Department, Gomes and Prosecutor Baird were in the conference room going over notes and trying to piece together the latest tips that had come in.

Thompson hurried into the room with his news.

"Baranyi didn't own one pair of boots. He had two, and he had a pair exactly like this guy had, Bob Boyd, who I talked to over at the Boyd house," Thompson said. "And Baranyi wasn't at home that whole time. This woman, Christine

Sheridan, said she saw him leave with David at ten P.M. He lied."

Gomes and Baird looked at each other. "Let's bring him in."

At 6 P.M., Thompson's pager went off. He dialed the number and Chris Sheridan informed him that Alex had just arrived home. Thompson put his trench coat back on and headed out the door with Prosecutor Baird.

When the men arrived at the Boyd home, Alex was in the bathroom taking a shower.

Thompson knocked on the door. "Alex, this is Detective Thompson. I'd like to ask you a few questions."

"Okay. It'll be about five or ten minutes," Alex said.

Thompson and Baird waited in the hallway just outside Alex's room. Alex scrubbed his body nervously. The cops were back. Again. Alex knew there was no way of hiding from them.

He turned off the water and grabbed his towel, taking his time to dry himself. He walked back across the hall to his bedroom, his hair dripping water and a towel cinched tight around his waist.

Alex greeted his guests and smiled politely.

"Come in," he said, motioning for the men to follow him inside his room.

"I'd rather we go down to the police department," Thompson said. "Why don't you get dressed."

Alex nodded his head.

"Oh, okay," he said with cool confidence.

Alex cooperated fully with Thompson and Baird. He asked no questions. He needed no explanations. He knew why they had come.

Meanwhile, Detective Jerry Johnson had picked up David Anderson to bring him to the precinct for more questioning. David, hoping to show he had nothing to hide, obliged.

* * *

Back at police headquarters, Thompson led Alex to a small, windowless interviewing room in the basement. There was a table and several chairs, just one door, and bare walls. Alex took a seat and pulled his chair nearer the table. He was relaxed, sitting comfortably. He looked straight ahead, locking his gaze onto an empty wall.

Thompson sat down in a chair next to Alex. Without saying a word, he moved closer, just inches away from Alex. Looking intent at the young man but failing to get eye contact, Thompson began to speak.

"Okay, Alex. We've got a couple of problems. The first thing is you've got more than one pair of boots. The second thing is that you went out Friday night. You went out somewhere with David Anderson."

Alex turned and looked at Thompson. Suddenly his face tightened up and he sat upright in his chair. His lips and chin began to quiver and his eyes bulged. He would crumble any minute now.

"He looked like a mountain about ready to erupt," Thompson recalled. "Right then, I go, 'This guy did it.' "

Thompson put his hand on Alex's knee to reassure him that it was okay to talk. But Alex shot a cold look at Thompson. Immediately, Thompson pulled his hand back, but remained physically close.

"Come on, Alex, you've gotta get this off your chest. Tell me what happened. What happened at that house?" Thompson said.

It was an interviewing technique that Thompson had used before: ramble on so fast that the interviewee doesn't have a chance to deny anything.

Alex had crossed his arms over his chest, and his legs were crossed at the ankles. He would not budge.

"He was all defenses," Thompson recalled. "That's what I had to break down. I had to get his arms unfolded. He clammed up. There was a wall there I had to take down. I couldn't let him keep the wall. I had to keep chipping away at it."

Thompson rambled on for fifteen or twenty minutes as Alex started to seethe. He had been holding back talking to anyone for nearly a week, and his secret was weighing him down. He was dying to tell somebody, to get it all out, to unburden himself of the responsibility of knowing. He was ready to talk.

"Okay," Alex said. "I want two minutes."

Thompson looked at him, unsure of what was about to happen next.

"No, Alex, we have to take care of this now. This is very serious. You are in serious trouble."

"Give me two minutes," Alex said.

Thompson paused, and looked at Baird.

"Okay. Two minutes only."

Thompson got up and left the room, but Baird stayed behind.

"I really can't stand that guy," Alex said to the prosecutor.

"I know," Baird said. "He's just trying to do his job. He's seen some terrible things."

While Baird stayed with Alex inside the interviewing room, Thompson stood just outside the room with Gomes and Johnson, who had been waiting for their cue to go in. They had been listening in through the partially open door.

Thompson looked at Gomes and gestured for him to enter the room.

"I'm not going to go in," Gomes said. "You keep going. You're onto something here. Don't let me break it."

Thompson nodded his head. He glanced at his watch, and after exactly two minutes, he went back into the room.

Thompson sat down in the chair next to Alex and began rambling again.

"Okay, Alex. Come on. You've gotta tell me what happened in that house. There's family members, you know. They've gotta know. You've gotta talk about it and get it off your chest."

Another fifteen minutes elapsed, most of that time filled with Thompson's probing. Alex was tense, rigid with fear.

"He was just sitting there, gritting his teeth," Thompson would later say.

Finally, Alex dropped his head and shoulders. He began to sob. His face turned bright red and he remained rigid with fear.

"What would happen to me if I confessed?" he asked.

"Well, there's a King County Prosecutor sitting in this room. You should ask him."

Alex turned to look at Baird, waiting for an answer.

"Well, as a juvenile, I can guarantee you would not be a candidate for the death penalty," Baird said. "Beyond that, I don't know. The judge might be a little more lenient with you when it comes time to sentencing."

Baird then tried a different approach.

"Alex, have you ever had this experience where it's as if you're watching yourself do something and the events seem to be unfolding in and of themselves?" Baird asked the young man trembling in front of him.

"Yes," Alex said confidently.

"Where?" Baird asked.

"When I was killing Kim."

At that moment, Thompson and Baird knew for certain they had their man. For the next few hours, Alex confessed in great detail to killing Kim and her family, but now Thompson wanted to record it on tape, and he wanted Gomes to be in the room to hear it, too.

When Alex agreed to rehash details of the crime for Gomes, Thompson read him his Miranda rights. The detectives and the prosecutor offered Alex a lawyer, but he declined. Thompson was not legally required to obtain parental permission as long as Alex was volunteering to confess.

At 8:12 P.M., with Alex's permission, Thompson inserted a blank tape into a recorder on the table and Alex started once again, from the beginning.

On the evening of January 3, Alex explained, he was hanging out with David at the rental house David shared with his two older brothers and another roommate. While David was in the bathroom, Alex said he got Kim Wilson's pager number out of David's address book and dialed the digits. Always prompt about returning her calls, Kim answered the page within a few minutes.

Alex said he persuaded her to meet him at the Chevron gas station down the street from the Boyd residence. Kim told Alex she would be hanging out with Sky Stewart, but she agreed to meet him later.

Alex had not known Kim intimately. In fact, he told Detective Thompson he had seen her less than a dozen times, and it was always with Dave, the only thing they had in common. They were neither good friends nor strangers.

Thompson asked Alex why he had called Kim.

"Nothing in particular," Alex said. "I was bored."

He told Thompson he believed Kim was calling from her parents' home. "I, I, I think she said that that's where she was calling from. We talked for a little while and I asked her if she would meet me at the Chevron I was at in Bellevue. I just wanted to talk to her. We went over to the Woodridge Water Park. It's where I used to hang out and just talk to friends. I've lived there for a while, till I left home. But it was, oh, maybe four or five years, three or four. Maybe from sixth grade until six or seven months ago . . . We—her, David, and I—had been there several times before. Just to walk around and talk."

They weren't smoking drugs or dropping acid, Alex told Thompson.

"I wanted to go there. It was, it was just a familiar place. We could sit, sit around and talk, and walk around and talk . . . We walked around on the trails . . . Just [talked] like, just like stuff that, that we, we had been doing. She told me about her stay at Job Corps, what she did there. Just small talk. I don't remember us arguing. I, I don't remember starting to do it. I remember realizing I was strangling her [with] a rope. It was white, kind of looked like a, a rope you'd have in a sailboat. It was really tough. I don't think it was made out of cloth. I think it was like nylon or something. It wasn't like it was good quality, I don't think. I had it in my pocket. I don't remember why I had left it in there, what I used it for before. And I can tell you it wasn't for strangling somebody."

Alex continued, straightening his back and speaking rapidly.

"I don't, I don't remember starting to do it. I don't, I don't think there was a reason. I just, I realized I, she was on the ground and I was strangling her. And I . . . There's, on the front of the park there is an entrance to the far left that's a trail straight up and then it, it splits off in a, like a T. And we had walked to the right of the T. I think that's where it happened . . . When I, when I realized I was strangling her, I, I remember seeing her face turn blue and I just, I couldn't stop. I don't know why. I just, I felt angry, but I don't know why. [Kim was] lying on the ground, pinned underneath me. She was facedown. I had one knee on her shoulder. I, I didn't know if she was dead or not and I didn't, didn't want her, her coming, coming out of unconsciousness and running to the police. I tied it real tight around her neck. Just like an overhand knot. I dragged her behind some bushes and left her there. And then I used my shoe and then I just scratched out the marks I made, 'cause I could see them even in the dark 'cause they were just deep rivets where her shoes . . . There were, there were rivets where her shoes had dragged. Probably about thirty feet. Maybe more. I'm really bad at judging distances. I took her wallet. And her, and her cigarettes. I took her glasses . . . I, I thought that maybe, since she was at home, that her, her parents might know who she was out with, so I took her car, drove it to her house. No. I took her car and I sat in it for a while and I drove over to her house and sat in it. 'Cause I waited until later at night. 'Cause it, it was probably . . . It, it must have been, it must have been a couple of hours between going into the house and leaving Kim. At least an hour. I didn't park in the driveway and sit there. I parked like up the street and sat. I wasn't watching the house. But I, I knew where it was . . . And I drove into the driveway. I think I parked on the right side of the driveway. I just walked in. I was so scared that . . . her parents knew, but . . . They, they would, they would, they would know who she was out with last. She might have told 'em."

Alex spoke slowly now, methodically, almost as if he were strangling Kim all over again. His speech was stilted, and he repeated words often, as if he were still trying to decide what he wanted to say. His voice wavered between being glum and unemotional to being excited and, at times, flippant. Sometimes the words just stumbled out, piling onto one another like unhinged boxcars.

"I was wearing a pair of sweatpants. Black. I was wearing a black T-shirt and I, there was a black sweater over on top of it. Something, something was written on it. I, I turned it inside out, I think. I was . . . And I was wearing my trench coat. Black. I was wearing a pair of boots. I don't remember what kind they are. I, I think, I think they're called Rugged Outback. I bought them at Payless Shoes . . . I had my knife on me. It's a five-inch fixed blade. It has a knuckle-duster on it. That means that the, it has finger holes and it has the . . . Well, it's, it has, it's, it's like, it's like brass-knuckles type of thing. I went through the front door. It was unlocked. There were no lights on. None that I could see. Just saw there was a room, there was stairs. To the right of the stairs there was a hallway and then a room. Then to the right there was like another room. I think to the left there was like a door, probably to the garage. I went to the right. I went up the flight of stairs. It was the, it was like the TV room. All the lights were off. I took a VCR and a CD changer. I came back later and got it. And then I went up the next flight of stairs. I, I turned to the right. And walked a couple of steps and the dog started barking. There were no lights on. It sounded like it was in the bedroom. I, I went downstairs 'cause I got, I got really scared.

"I heard a man get up out of bed, tell the dog to shut up. I kept going down . . . I went down the next flight of stairs and I went into a door, it was on the right at the bottom of the stairs. I went into like a smaller room. I don't remember what was in it. Then I went into the garage door in the side. All the way in. I think the light was on. The, the dog stopped barking. And I, I guess the guy went back to bed. I assumed he did. 'Cause I didn't hear any walking around upstairs or anything.

"I saw a baseball bat in the corner. It was metal. It was like blue and silver. I went back upstairs."

"Upstairs to the TV room?" Thompson asked.

"Yeah. I went upstairs, up the other stairs. Turned right. And I walked into the bedroom. The, the dog started barking. I hit the woman on the right side of the bed with the baseball bat."

"Okay. And where was the woman?" Thompson asked.

"On the right side of the bed, laying down."

"Sleeping? Or was she lying?" Thompson asked.

"Probably was sleeping."

"So she didn't wake up."

"I don't think so."

"Okay. So just to get it clear, now you, did you go to the

right side of the bed or the left side of the bed?" Thompson asked.

"The right side."

"And you did what?"

"I hit the woman with the baseball bat several times."

"Where?" Thompson wanted to know.

"On the head."

"Okay," Thompson said. "What happened?"

"The man got up."

Alex was getting tired. He had been recounting that brutal night for half an hour and wanted a break. Thompson and Baird agreed it would be a good idea. Alex wanted a smoke. He and Thompson stepped just outside a back doorway to the BPD, where Alex smoked a few cigarettes. During the break, he also ate a hamburger and French fries.

"Okay. We're back on tape and the time now is eight-fifty-four P.M. And where were we when we left off? We were, I think we were . . ."

"I just hit the woman with the baseball bat," Alex snapped impatiently.

"You hit the woman with the baseball bat. Do you know who that woman was?"

"I assume it was Kim's mom."

"Okay. But, as we back up, I think you said that you didn't at the time know that it was a woman?"

"The lights were off," Alex explained.

"But it was the person on which side of the bed?" Thompson repeated his questions, trying to catch inconsistencies in Alex's story.

"The right side."

"Okay. Then what happened? You said that a man got up and started screaming."

"The man on the right side of the bed . . . Or left side of the bed. I'm sorry. The left side of the bed. He got up. He, he started yelling, like, 'What's going on?' And I dropped the

bat and went over to him. I took out my knife and I stabbed
him several times. Upper region of his body. I, I . . . I think I
was trying to aim for his face. He took a swing at me. He
was wearing a T-shirt. And he wasn't wearing any pants. I
found that out after I had gone back to the room and turned
the light on. I stumbled backwards and I went and got the
bat. And when I turned around, he had gone halfway down
the bed, down to the foot of the bed, and he, he was kneeling
down. And I went up to him and I, I just kept hitting him
with the bat till he fell to the floor. He was probably bleeding. I walked out of the room. The hallway light turned on.
Julia came out of her room at the end of the hall. I think
she's, I think she's probably seventeen or eighteen. And I
started coming towards her. And she, she, she fell to the floor
and started crying. She was really scared. She might have
recognized me from school a while back. I dropped the bat a
couple of feet from her and pulled the knife out. And pulled
the knife out of my pocket, kneeled down, and started stabbing her. In the upper chest, neck. She had her arms over her
face, was fending me off. She was crying. I told her I was
sorry. I was sorry that I was killing her.

"I dropped the knife. I picked up the bat and I started hitting her with it. And she grabbed . . . Or I stopped hitting her
for a second . . . 'cause I was getting tired. And she grabbed
the piece of closet organizer, I guess, and held it over her.
She was still alive. And I picked up the bat and I started hitting that, trying to get it away from her, and just grabbed it
and pulled it away from her and started hitting her in the
face with it till she stopped moving. I stabbed at her maybe
seven or eight times, but most of 'em I didn't actually stab
anything. It was, her arms were in front of her and she kept
hitting my, my arms.

"I know I have a cut on my leg that I didn't have the night
before. I'll have to take my pants off. I, it, it looks like a
scratch from a fingernail. The light was off in the room. It

was on in the hallway. I dropped the bat, picked up the knife . . . There was a light switch. I dropped the bat and I picked up the knife. And I went back in the parents' room and turned the light on, saw the guy laying there. And the woman was still in bed. Blood was all over her and she was gurgling. I thought she was still alive. I didn't, didn't want her to suffer, so I stabbed her several times in the face and neck and in the head, 'cause her head was sideways, I think. I think [pointing] towards the window. Yeah. Yeah. I, I think so. And I put the knife in my pocket. Then I went over to the guy and I, I had been wearing a piece of cloth over my hair so that if somebody saw me enter the house, they wouldn't be able to see what kind of hair I was wearing . . . It was, it was, it was, it was a shirt, I think. It had been cut out. I was doing, I had done something with it. Like, like a, a piece of a shirt that was on top of my head. Like covering up my hair. You know, so if somebody saw me from the back walk into the house, they, they wouldn't see what kind of hair I had. So I went over to the guy and I just realized that I had lost that thing that was on my head and I thought it was underneath him. So I grabbed his arm and I hauled him up off the ground and set him behind where he had sat, closer to the window. And I looked around, I looked around for it and I couldn't find it. I eventually came to the conclusion that the dog took it and ran. It was, it was just black, like, like you just cut the front off of a black shirt. I think it's . . . I, I think it still had the, the arms on it, the arm sleeves. Couldn't find it."

Alex explained how he hoisted Bill Wilson to look under his body, setting it down again in a different spot.

"And I didn't find it. And I, I, I scrounged around this pair of pants and I found his wallet and I took his wallet. There was like, there was like three dollars in it. Then I walked back into Julia's room 'cause I thought maybe I dropped it there. And I looked down and she was just staring up, so I closed her eyelids. And then I pulled her farther into her

room. I think I pushed her. I think I grabbed one of her legs
and just pushed her over. I was looking for the shirt that I
dropped. I didn't find it. Can we take a break? Just a real
short one?"

Thompson agreed to let the young man take a quick
break. He led Alex out the back door so Alex could smoke a
cigarette before continuing his confession.

"I, I, I went downstairs into the living room and I took the
VCR. I cut the cables to the VCR [with] the knife. Took the
CD changer. I haven't looked at it since. It's at my house.
I'll, I'll draw you a diagram later to see if you can get it.
[Kim's wallet] would have been in the coat that I threw
away. [Kim's glasses] in the coat. I went, I went out the front
door. I, I took the telephone. It was, it was downstairs in the,
the first room in the house when you walk in the front door,
on the right. I, I took the CD changer, the VCR, and the
phone into the, out, out into the driveway. I put them in the
passenger seat of the car I had driven over there. And I guess
I went home. I had, I had the, the bat with me and the knife
was still in my pocket. I went home. I put the, I, I, I put the
electronic devices in the back room and covered 'em up with
a coat. I went in through the downstairs door. It was . . . I
don't know. I didn't, I didn't look at the clock. I only spent
about half an hour in the house. I guess it was, it was probably after midnight. I, I remember taking the keys but I don't
remember throw . . . I, I had to have thrown them away, because I don't have them anymore. But I don't know where I
threw 'em. I, I walked home. I walked up the street. Uphill.
And I kept going till I got to this one road that I think it . . . I
mean, keep going up that street as far as it'll go until it, it
you'd have to make a left. And if you, and at that intersec-
tion, you look right across and there's Norwood Park, Norwood Pool. And I, I made a right there, down three streets to
a dead-end street.

"I crossed the freeway. It must have been really late at

night because there was, there was like no cars. I just jumped over the fence and walked across the street. And I went down into the woods. There's, it's like, it's like blueberry fields. I'm not really sure what it's called. But I, I've been there before a bunch of times. That's where me and a bunch of my friends used to play Kinabota. It's a . . . You make, you make fake swords out of PVC pipe, wrap it in padding and hold it together with duct tape, and you play sword fight. And I went, I went through there and that ends you up on Bellevue Way. And I walked down Bellevue Way to my house. I, the, the wallets were gone 'cause I didn't have the coat with me. I didn't, I didn't have the knife or the bat. When, when I, when I got home, I didn't, I didn't have anything. I just went to bed.

"I don't remember driving back. As I, I remember, I remember putting the stuff in the Dumpster. I, it was . . . It, it's, it's like a dream you had where it's like everything is really close up. All, all, all I remember seeing was the Dumpster and putting the stuff in. I think it was a parking lot. I remember there being straight white lines. I, I, I just, I'd go down Bellevue Way onto the freeway, then left at the light at the Factoria exit, and . . .

"I woke, I woke up and I remember thinking it was a really, really bad dream. And . . . Probably around noon or one. There probably wouldn't have been anybody there. Ian, Ian, Ian spent the night. Macdougal. Probably in Bob's room. Either that or on the couch upstairs. I don't know. I didn't see him. Bob would have let him in. . . ."

Alex told the detectives exactly where he put the stolen items from the Wilson home.

"It's, it's, it's not really a bedroom. It's just a back room. It, it just has, like, junk and . . . It's right off of the laundry room."

Now the detective and prosecutor wanted to know who Alex's accomplice was.

"Is there any reason you'd be lying to me about all this?"

"No," Alex said evenly.

"Were you by yourself the whole time," Thompson asked.

"Yes."

"Is there a reason you'd lie to me about that?"

"Maybe I was protecting somebody," Alex said.

Thompson pressed Alex to name his accomplice.

"I can't. It's just, I can't. I mean, it's, I can, I can, I can fuck up my life as much as I want, but I, I, I can't. It may be my humbleness and nobleness is all I have left. I'm sorry. I can't."

Because Alex wouldn't divulge any information about his accomplice, Thompson, Gomes, and Baird went on to ask more questions about details of the murders so he could know for sure Alex was in the house at the time of the killings.

"Did you notice whether or not your knife was damaged during this?" Baird asked.

"I think it was bent," Alex said flatly.

Alex then explained his contempt toward Kim.

"She wasn't a very nice person. I thought she was selfish. I just heard she was back in town and I had nothing else to do."

"Didn't you have other friends you could speak with?" Baird asked.

"I guess so. Not really."

"Where was Dave?" Baird wanted to know.

"I think Dave was at home. I think he had just, he had gone home and probably went to bed. I don't, I don't know where Joe was. I think, I think, I think we took him home a while before that . . ."

Alex paused briefly, then spoke again.

"I'll tell you this, though. You're cops and, I mean, I, I don't know if you've ever had to shoot someone before, on duty. But never kill a person. It was, it will tear you apart real good. It really will.

"I, I'm, I was good friends with Marsha. Marsha couldn't do anything like that. She's, she just, she's too nice of a person."

"But Dave could, and you nodded yes," Gomes said.

"I guess. I guess so."

"Was it Dave's or your idea to go to the Wilson home?"

"Mine."

Hoping to get Alex to admit David was his accomplice, Thompson suggested David was in a room down the hall pointing the blame at Alex.

"If Dave's in the other room ratting me out . . . If, if David was in the other room saying that I shot fifty people in Oregon last week, it wouldn't matter. 'Cause he's the only person I've ever liked. Some-sometimes your friends are more important."

"Than your life?" Baird asked.

"Yeah. If you say I have the choice of getting the death penalty or ratting out David for doing something, I'll take death."

Thompson decided to ask other questions, to keep Alex talking. He wanted to know whether Alex hurt Moe, the dog.

"No. No. He . . . When, when I went in the room, I guess he ran out, 'cause when I went in there, the barking stopped. Well, when, when I went back downstairs, the, the front, the front door was like halfway open, so he could have gotten out through the front door.

"The, the knife, when I cut or tried to cut the cable wires to the VCR, I slashed 'em and the knife broke. And I put both pieces in my pocket and then cut them with the other knife."

"Was that the kitchen knife—had the kitchen knife earlier been used in the attack on the people?" Baird asked.

"No," Alex responded.

"But in the house there were a total of three weapons you used?"

"Yeah."

"You took Kim down to the ground. She's facedown on the dirt and you were on top of her. Was your knee between her shoulder blades?" Gomes asked.

"I was on her shoulder."

"And her face turned blue?" Gomes asked.

"Yeah."

"Did she yell?"

"No."

"Did she grab at the rope around her neck with her hands?"

"She didn't. She, she did whenever I first put it around her neck; once she hit the ground, she didn't move her hands at all."

"How many knots did you tie?" Gomes asked.

"I think two. 'Cause I think I, I wrapped it around her neck once, tied it, and wrapped it around again and tied it again. I'm pretty sure that's what I did. Just like, just like a double knot . . . She stopped moving a couple of minutes before that."

"How did you drag her?" Gomes asked.

"By her arms. Her wrists. She's, she was faceup. This, this is where I'm going to have to go into . . . I can't. I can't say the person who helped me. But she, we, we carried her. She didn't touch the ground at all."

"Where did you put her?" Gomes asked.

"Behind . . . Go, going up the . . . In the front, front of the park on the far left-hand side there's a path straight up and it, it forks into a T, one straight ahead and one to the right. Go a little bit to the right, like maybe, I don't know, five feet or so. That's where the, the thick, like, little pine bushes start. That's where she was left.

"The other person kicked her several times. During [the strangling].

"I, I have thought about it, and I, there, there's, there's really no way for me to give you the answers that you really need without betraying the people who trust me. Okay. Um, I can, I can clarify a little more into a little less obscurity. There, there really was no motive as you really define. I, there was no, like, killing jealous or kill, killing because they're going out with another guy or something, or killing because they're going out with another girl. And I told you about that, right? The whole, whole thing with Sarah and Kim going out? I, I don't know that much. I know they went out at one time . . . And it, the, Michael, Mike, Michael had stolen Sarah, stole Sarah away from Kim, and Kim was pretty upset with that. And they, all three of them pretty much lost contact soon after that and really never talked to each other again. I was kind of shocked. I was going out with Sarah when I found out and I had no idea she was bi. It really didn't matter to me. I, I, I cared about her a great deal. I'm, I'm, I'm not a homophobic. I . . . I actually have several gay friends. If, it, it wasn't . . . I mean, yeah, it's like the jealousy thing. It wasn't a real motive. It was . . . I guess the motive would have been just like I told you off the tape when I left the room, it was just getting, getting into a lifestyle that was too stagnant and needed to change. Some, some, a huge, just a huge rock in a puddle."

"So what you're saying is there was no motive. What I understand you to say is there was no motive personal to Kim particularly, but there was a motive to commit a murder," Baird said.

"Yeah."

"And that would change your and the accomplice's lives for the better," Baird said.

"Not necessarily mine. In fact, it was probably, probably figured it to be even worse. I mean, killing somebody isn't a . . . Killing, killing somebody never really ends up with something good. And there is just, there is just that opportunity to experience something truly phenomenal . . . There really, really didn't . . . I mean, Kim, Kim was pretty, it, she was unplanned. It was, it was kind of a spur-of-the-moment kind of thing. It wasn't—"

Thompson interrupted. He wanted to know exactly how long Alex had been contemplating taking someone's life simply for the experience of killing.

"How long have you been thinking about that?" Baird asked.

"Probably years. A long time. The, my, it's . . . Death in itself has always really fascinated me. And I've always been kind of interested in, just in that. I never really contemplated, like, murder until a little while ago. It was, it was like there was no person that I met that made me think about it. It was just like a change on my own. That was, that was pretty much it right there. It's, it wasn't premeditated murder.

"The . . . I mean, I've, I've always thought about this a lot after I've done it. Shooting a gun is a lot different than strangling somebody to death. 'Cause you can, you can shoot somebody in the head from fifty feet away and walk away and barely see a thing. Not feel anything, not hear it, not smell it. It's, it's, it's more profoundly disturbing, I would think, actually killing somebody with like a, a hand-held weapon that's like you have to actually do work rather than pull a trigger. I mean, I don't, I, I don't, I don't know how people like . . . I don't know. You, you read stuff like about like the old Italian Mafia, how they could like strangle somebody to death. Like strangle like five or six people in a week and still live with yourself. I mean, it's . . . I could, I could see like the person in a gang shooting somebody and not really feeling remorse about it but being like excited and stuff. That's 'cause it's like you get to tell all your friends you shot somebody and you really don't feel, and you, you weren't close to the person when they died.

"When, when I, when I killed those people, I thought to myself, it's just a job. It's just something that you have to do. That, that's a bad word, 'cause I, I didn't, I didn't have to do it. But it was . . . I thought to myself, it's, it's just a job. Just like jackhammering out a chunk of concrete. You don't want to do it, but you do it anyway because it's there. But, and whenever you do it, it . . . whenever I did it, at least, it was, I pretty much acted just like a machine. I didn't, I didn't feel anything. I just did it. Waited, waited until I was sure the person was dead, and moved on. Directly afterwards you hit like a wall of your own self-consciousness, of humanity. And you realize you've just killed somebody. And you can, you can, you can smell the fact that . . .

"The, you, the, the, the smell is definitely the worst thing. The, your, your sight . . . You, you can disbelieve what your eyes see a lot better than you can anything else. Your, the sound of a bat hitting a human being's skull will forever haunt you. I, I, I, I, I've heard, I've heard stuff in my sleep that just, that sound, and I've woken up to it and it's been my alarm clock. The, the smell is by far the worst, though. It, human beings generally will . . . A, a scent is one of the most powerful forms of, of, you can, you can smell the smell of chocolate chip cookies and think back for years to like my . . . Well, as my mom said, I mean, if she smelled chocolate chip cookies cooking in the oven, she thought back thirty years to when her grandmother was making chocolate chip cookies in Pittsburgh. But the . . . I can't even imagine when you guys got there. The smell was so overwhelming in that house. It, it was just horrible. And every now and then I'll, I will just, I'll, it'll, it will just come back to me and I'll remember what it smelled like. Then I remember what I did and really regret it.

"The human skull is a lot harder than I ever imagined it would be."

"Why did you, why did you hit their heads?" Thompson asked.

"Well, the, I, a, a baseball bat . . . I mean, it, it would take one hell of a beating to beat somebody's body to death.

"When the . . . Hitting somebody with a baseball bat in the face, they're, if you hit them directly in the face, the nose will give way. You, it's . . . I, I would be, I would be honestly surprised if you told me that their skulls have been cracked. I mean, the, the . . ."

"They were cracked," Baird said sternly.

"They were?" Alex asked curiously. "But the . . . I mean, I, I was expecting something along the lines of like hitting a couple of times, weakening it, and then it just caving in. And it doesn't. It stays pretty much in that form . . ."

Gomes tried to steer Alex back to his original train of thought.

"How does it feel to plunge a knife into a human body?" he asked.

"Yeah. I was just about to get to that. That's, that's an even worse feeling. A knife will go right through your temple with no problem at all. When, when you stab somebody, I, oh, I'll, I'll use a metaphor of, of waterproofing, just 'cause that, that's the best way I can possibly describe it. Whenever you dig a hole, that's like, there's, there's a bunch of water around the dirt. And you dig a hole and then the water just fills up from the bottom up. That's pretty much what happens. I mean, I, I stabbed that woman in the neck. And when I pulled the knife out, you could see a hole for a second and then it filled. It filled up with blood.

"I'm sure you've probably, you've probably had like a real special woman in your life. Then it's like maybe she dumps you to go out with some other guy and you just think to yourself, 'God, I really want to kill that bastard.' But there is, there is not one goddamned thing on this earth that could ever make me kill a person. There is, there is nothing."

Gomes had worked hard to get to this point—to a suspect who was spilling his story—and now wanted Alex to name his accomplice. Gomes was so close to solving the case if Alex would just say the name.

"I guess, what you're asking me to do is rationalize which is better, to fuck over an entire family or fuck over one person . . . Or fuck over your friend," Alex said.

"Your friendship has ended," Gomes responded. "Your life, as you know it today, has changed forever. For a long, long time, a long, long period of time, your life has changed dramatically. That friend you're so interested in protecting . . ."

"Is going to mean nothing in a moment," Alex said. "It's nothing right now. If you, if you guys have the other person in the room, in another room doing the same thing to him right now, why does it matter that I tell you? Do you just want to see me say it and do the right thing? . . . I feel, down to my gut, logically thinking, truthful as anything, that if I say his name, it's the wrong thing to do. No matter how many people are suffering, no matter how much you, how many more years I'll be in a goddamned penitentiary.

"If, if I, if I totally admit the part about having a partner, what else is going to happen to me than if I don't? So what you guys are basically saying is that I, I'm just going to have to live with the fact that I didn't do the right . . ."

"Would it be easier to write it down?" Thompson asked.

"I'm sorry. I really am."

Gomes sighed. He knew that was all the information he would be able to get for now.

"I appreciate the efforts you've gone to, to try to adhere to the principles. Still, tell us as much of the truth as you can. And if there's anything else you can tell us about it that would, that would help," Baird said.

"All right. You better give me your phone number. 'Cause one, one day I'm, you're going to get a call from me and I'm going to tell you. I, I promise you that."

As Alex finished talking around midnight, Thompson was high-fiving people in his mind. High-fiving Gomes, Johnson, Baird, Eakes, his bosses, his family. There was much to be celebrated. But working to get the confession out of Alex was so draining that when Thompson finally finished and came out to take a break, he didn't have the energy to high-five Gomes and Johnson, who were standing outside the door with arms raised and, for the first time in days, wearing wide smiles.

The emotional strain of listening to a young man boast in intimate detail about killing four people proved taxing to Baird, too. As everyone else celebrated, Baird was quiet, almost numb to the excitement around him. It was as if he had just walked out of a movie theater, having sat through one of the most disturbing horror flicks imaginable.

As Alex Jr. was starting to spill his story to Thompson, Gomes, and Baird, in another room of the Bellevue Police Department that night, David Anderson wasn't saying a word.

Prosecutor Eakes and Detective Jerry Johnson hoped they could get David to talk. Unlike Thompson and Baird, who confronted Alex immediately about inconsistencies in his alibi, Johnson and Eakes eased into their interview with David. The forty-five-minute interview was filled mostly with small talk. David spoke about family, high school, how he spent his days.

This detective-prosecutor tag team had also brought David in to talk about his own inconsistencies with his alibi. On Wednesday night, David had told the McBrides that he had been with Alex all of last Friday night playing Super-Nintendo. But when questioned again that Thursday, he told detectives that he was really driving around all night in his girlfriend, Marsha Rash's, pickup truck.

Johnson and Eakes wanted to know why he'd lied.

"To protect Alex," David said evenly. He denied having anything to do with the murders. David was growing increasingly angry that Johnson and Eakes didn't believe him and continued their interrogation.

As Johnson asked specific questions about the night of the Wilson murders, David threw out crumbs of information. He admitted he was at the park that Friday night but refused to say anything further. He immediately clammed up.

"Look, I didn't do it," he snapped.

Johnson and Eakes knew they would have to work hard at getting David to talk. He would be tough to crack. Unlike Alex, who clearly wanted to get the weight off his chest, David held everything in, including his emotions. So Johnson tried a different tactic. If David wasn't willing to talk to both of them together, maybe he would talk to Eakes alone. Johnson left the room briefly and went down the hall to talk to Gomes.

Patty, alone with David, shifted in her seat.

David sensed her unease, and, acting as if they were old friends, he put a hand on her knee to reassure her.

"How are you doing with all of this?" David asked.

A chill coursed through Eakes' veins just long enough before Johnson returned. She hadn't gotten very far. David still wouldn't budge.

This time, Eakes left the room so Johnson could have a crack at talking to David alone. Gomes and Baird walked down the hall during a break with Alex to see how Eakes and Johnson were doing with their suspect. Eakes explained that David wasn't budging. Together, they came up with a plan: Gomes and Baird would storm into the room and confront David, scare him into talking.

With that, they swung open the door of the interrogation room where Johnson was sitting with David and began their surprise attack.

"You're a murderer," Gomes said, staring straight into David's eyes. "You killed those people."

Baird started yelling profanities. "You're a lucky mother-fucker you're not eighteen, or you would have faced the death penalty," he barked, standing just a few feet away from David. "You did it, and we'll prove you did it." Then Baird told the smug young man he could go home at any time.

David was stunned at the sudden intrusion. His eyes widened, and he clenched his jaw, but still he said nothing. However, he was clearly getting upset. His eyes seemed to say it all; they were dark and blank, Gomes would later recall. To him, they were the eyes of a cold-blooded killer. "Just using the profanity just outraged him," Gomes would later recall.

David wasn't the only one caught off guard by Gomes and Baird's interruption. As they began screaming at David, Johnson looked up at them as if to say, *What the hell are you guys doing?* Later, he would tell Gomes he'd been close to getting David to open up, and that sudden, aggressive intrusion might have destroyed Johnson's rapport.

"I kind of lost my temper with David," Baird would later say, admitting, "It was stupid of me to do this."

David finally asked for a lawyer. At that point, there was nothing more the detectives or prosecutors could do. They had to let him go.

"Probably the hardest thing I ever had to do was to make that decision [to let David go] knowing in your heart but still not convinced by physical evidence," Gomes would later say. "He had something to do with this, but the law restricted you."

What was frustrating to Gomes was not only to see a suspected killer walk out the door, but to know he was getting a ride home from a cop. "We should have just kicked him out," Gomes said.

He didn't worry that David would try to skip town. He was more worried that he might try to hurt someone else.

"I was thinking, 'Is he gonna kill again?' "

Eakes watched as David walked out the door, followed by Johnson, who gave him a ride home.

But there was nothing they could do but wait for some hard physical evidence to surface that would link David directly to one or both of the crime scenes.

Later that night, after he was dropped off at the rental house, David decided to call Alex's parents to let them know where their son was. At around 10 P.M., Alex Sr. and Mary Beth received the call.

"Kevin is in trouble," David said, his voice calm and monotone.

"Have you heard from him?" Alex Sr. demanded.

"I don't know how to tell you this," David said. "Kevin has been arrested. He's been taken away by police."

Alex Sr. pressed David for more details, but David referred the Baranyis to the police.

Disbelieving David, Alex Sr. dialed the number to the Boyd residence. He spoke with Valerie Boyd, who had not yet learned of Alex Jr.'s arrest. The Boyds hadn't bothered contacting Alex Jr.'s parents because they figured he would be back later that night, since he had returned home after police picked him up and took him to the station the night before. The only thing Valerie Boyd could tell Alex Sr. was that police had come by the house and taken Alex away.

"Fuck! I can't believe it," Alex Sr. barked into the phone.

He got the confirmation he needed regarding the status of his son when, later that night, a police officer phoned the Baranyi house to tell them Alex Jr. had been arrested on suspicion of killing the Wilson family. He would be locked up overnight at the King County Juvenile Detention Center. Patricia Baranyi was to be contacted the next morning.

Rather than contact police that night to try to clear things up, to vouch for Alex Jr. and insist that it was all a mistake, that police had the wrong person, Alex Sr. got out of bed and started drinking coffee. He and his wife stayed awake the rest of the night, confused, scared, and uncertain as to what to do next. His son had just admitted to murdering four people, and he wanted nothing to do with it.

At around 2 A.M., the phone rang again at the Baranyi house. David called again. Alex Sr. demanded to know any information David had.

"When's he coming back?" Alex Sr. asked.

"It's going to be a long time before he gets out," David said, his voice still calm. "I just want to let you know I'm really, really sorry."

On Friday afternoon, Detective Gomes and Patty Eakes had their first crack at talking to Sarah Lamp. They already had Alex in custody, and they hoped Sarah could provide some information that might incriminate David.

Marsha Rash agreed to drive Sarah to the BPD, but before her interview with Gomes and Eakes, she had dropped acid. Marsha told Gomes Sarah did this because the only way she could deal with the cops was while being high.

As Sarah sat in Gomes' office answering questions, he noticed she was wearing combat-style boots with the same sole patterns as those at the crime scene. Gomes took photos, and he would later regret not taking the boots altogether to get them checked for blood spatters. He had not ruled out the possibility that more than two people were in the Wilson home and involved with the murders.

Sarah spoke quickly as she responded to questions, her words stumbling out and crashing into one another. At times she made no sense. She was anxious and nervous. Realizing she was high on acid, Gomes knew there was no way to rein her in and get any good information from her. When asked where she was the Friday night of the murders, Sarah wavered in her answers. First, she claimed to be sleeping all night, since she wasn't working. Then she said she was working. Another time she said she was up all night talking to her roommate.

By the end of the hour-long session, Sarah's story was a twisted web of lies and conflicting statements that, combined with the type of shoes she wore, made her look like a possible third suspect. She was clearly trying to protect her buddies. Gomes was convinced she knew a lot more than she was willing to divulge.

When she left the BPD, Gomes asked Sarah not to stray too far. The police would be contacting her again.

Early Friday morning, January 10, the Baranyis watched the TV news with horror. Their son was associated with the violent deaths of a family in their own neighborhood. Shocked and in denial, Alex Sr. and Mary Beth stayed home that day, behind locked doors with the curtains drawn. When they finally left the house, they sped out of the driveway to avoid the TV and newspaper reporters who had already started crawling up and down their street.

It wasn't until the next morning, at around 8 A.M. Saturday, that Alex Sr. and Mary Beth drove down to the Bellevue Police Station.

Gomes happened to be in the office when the Baranyis arrived, and while it was a surprise visit, he invited them in to talk. The couple was shaken up by the quadruple slayings, and by the fact that their son had confessed to them. But their concern appeared to Gomes to be more for themselves than for Alex Jr. He had been the only one arrested so far in connection with the killings, and they feared another killer was on the loose and would target them next.

As he spoke, Alex Sr. remained oddly detached from his son, as if Alex Jr. were merely a kid he happened to know but had absolutely no relation to. He never asked how his son was doing, or what evidence the cops had to keep him in custody. He was simply worried about his and his wife's safety.

"You know, I love him, but I feel that Kevin is capable, he has the anger," Alex Sr. said, his East Coast accent strained with worry. "My feeling is that he couldn't have taken out four people by himself."

Alex Sr. wanted reassurance from Gomes that he and his wife would be safe, since they presumed there was at least one other person out there responsible for the murders. But it was reassurance Gomes couldn't give, because he couldn't say for sure who that other person was.

Gomes asked the Baranyis for more information about their son and their son's lifestyle.

"He was so abusive to us," Alex Sr. said, his voice now calm. "He'd been threatening to leave our home. I kept saying, 'We can't control him.' "

The Baranyis told Gomes that their son had only one friend—David Anderson. Mary Beth said Alex Jr. had always been a loner until he met David. Alex Sr. explained how they became bosom buddies at Chinook Middle School, but felt David was a bad influence on their son. "They went fuckin' around all night," Alex Sr. said. "We separated them. You know, no more overnights."

Then Gomes wanted to know about Alex Jr.'s interest in swords and violent TV shows and video games. It was a topic Alex Sr. didn't take seriously. He knew his son had a bizarre fascination with fantasy games and medieval paraphernalia, but he couldn't imagine that interest would motivate him to kill. Alex Sr. laughed as he thought about his son's violent tendencies.

"He had a couch down there sliced up. It scared the shit out of me," Alex Sr. said.

Gomes wondered why it took so long for Alex Sr. to come

forward and talk to police about his son. He didn't believe that this man sitting in front of him, more worried about himself and his wife, really loved his son.

"That was bullshit," Gomes would later say about Alex Sr. "How can you love your son and then turn around and say he's a murderer?"

For four days after Alex's arrest, David walked around Bellevue as cool and controlled as ever. But what he didn't know was that in a laboratory at the Washington State Patrol Crime Lab in downtown Seattle, forensic experts were working around the clock to match a piece of rope found in the black pickup truck, which David admitted he was driving the night of the murders, with the ligature found around Kim Wilson's neck.

On Monday afternoon, Lieutenant Ed Mott cornered Gomes in the basement of the BPD to tell him the good news. Kim Duddy, a forensic expert at the lab, had completed the mind-numbing task of counting more than 1,000 threads in each piece of rope under a microscope. Visually, the ropes matched.

After consulting with the prosecutors, Gomes learned that that was enough physical evidence to place David under probable cause and arrest him. The detective was ecstatic. For the first time in a long time, he could finally breathe easier. The waiting was over.

The next day—Tuesday—detectives devised a plan on how to go after David. Officer Molly McBride had been in contact with Marsha Rash, and, hoping to check out all angles of her and David's stories, McBride requested a work order on her VW Rabbit.

BPD detectives figured that if they asked Marsha to come down to the police department, David would probably come along with her.

They were right.

That afternoon, as Lieutenant Ed Mott was leading a community meeting to answer questions and allay fears of some 300 Bellevue residents who attended, Marsha and David showed up at the BPD. While Marsha ran inside to drop off documents for Detective McBride, Officer Tom Wray headed out to the parking lot and found David sitting in Marsha's car. He arrested him on the spot.

Wray read David his Miranda rights as he was led into the building. But David invoked his right not to comment. Maybe he knew he was not yet clear of trouble, because earlier that afternoon, before accompanying Marsha to the BPD, he had already retained an attorney.

Gomes and Baird learned of the arrest while driving across Lake Washington on the floating bridge back toward Bellevue. They had just left Seattle, where they had interviewed Sarah Lamp for a second time. This time she was more coherent, but not any more helpful than when Gomes first interviewed her. She waffled on her own alibi on the night of January 3, 1997. At first, she said she was working, but then recanted and said she was at home sleeping.

When Gomes called in to the office that afternoon, he got the news. "David's been arrested!" he repeated into the phone. He got off his cell phone and looked at Baird. Both men were beaming as they gave each other high fives. The hunt for the killers was finally over. However, the work was not. Now came the hard task of building a case against these two young men.

PART THREE

The Trial

25 Spring in Bellevue blazes with color—the leaves begin to redden with life and the apple blossoms burst open like popcorn along the branches. It is also flooding season for the Northwest, when the temperatures rise just high enough to melt the snowcaps off nearby mountain ranges, gushing into streams and rivers that quickly overflow. Other than that, there really is no telling winter from spring; it still rains, and it's still cold outside.

In the spring of 1998, as the students at Bellevue High School were starting their last semester, their two peers—Alex Baranyi and David Anderson—sat in the King County Jail, waiting for their day in court. They had been confined nearly a year and a half by then, as their separate attorneys worked to develop their cases for a joint trial set for the fall.

In the Woodridge neighborhood, the yellow crime-scene tape had long since disappeared from the Wilson home. The house was padlocked and still in police custody as detectives continued to search for more clues that would connect David and Alex to the crime scene.

Inside their offices on the eastern edge of downtown Seattle, Alex Baranyi's defense attorneys, Kathy Lynn and Mark Flora, were trying to figure out just how to defend their client; they knew they had no valid defense. They couldn't say he wasn't at the Wilson residence, because he had already confessed, in great detail, not only to being there but to actively participating in the slayings. The only strategy that might save him from a long prison term would be to use the insanity plea, but the judge denied them that request. They were left with only one approach: to try to downplay Alex's role and involvement in the murders.

A judge had already decided to try the pair together, which meant Alex's attorneys had one small advantage—they could physically point a finger at David and blame him for the murders.

David's attorneys, Michael Kolker and Stephan Illa, took a vastly different approach by claiming their client was nowhere near the Wilson home at the time of the murders. Instead, he was driving around in a truck he borrowed from his girlfriend.

But the prosecutors had enough physical and circumstantial evidence to link both Alex and David to the crime scenes, and believed they had enough to convince a jury the boys were both guilty as charged.

Much of 1998 elapsed with little media coverage on the Wilson quadruple homicides. As police continued to search the homes of the Wilson family and the Boyds, as well as the house where David lived, newspapers reported on their findings, which offered a closer glimpse into David's and Alex's lifestyles. There was also little legal haggling between the prosecutors and the defense attorneys on the case.

Kathy Lynn and Mark Flora were digging deep into their client's past—interviewing Alex's mother and father and their friends, and poring over dozens of pages of poetry and drawings found in his bedroom after his arrest—to scrape together a portrait of Alex that might help explain why he had snapped. As it happened, the picture that developed was of a pathetic, misunderstood young man, consumed by loneliness and constant despair.

Meanwhile, David's attorneys, Kolker and Illa, scrambled to collect evidence and witnesses who would show the jury their client had nothing to do with the murders of the Wilson family. They mined court documents and reinterviewed the prosecution's witnesses, aggressively pursuing a defense strategy that would suggest to the jury that the prosecution was trying to convict David merely because he was friends with Alex. Guilt by association, Kolker would insist, is neither a valid nor a fair reason to convict.

Bruce and Leslie Anderson showed up faithfully to each pretrial hearing, but no one from Alex's family attended the proceedings. Neither family had the money to post the $5 million bail set for each of the teenagers, although David's brothers joked about how they could bust David out.

By summer, the lawyers were meeting frequently in court to discuss and debate numerous pretrial motions, mostly initiated by Kolker.

Kolker, a spry attorney with curly salt-and-pepper hair who was adept at making his client appear like the harmless boy next door, had represented accused criminals for some two decades. He realized his work as a defense lawyer would not make him popular, but he always upheld the ideals of an individual's rights, not the least of which was the right to a fair trial.

In July, Kolker asked Judge Bobbe Bridge, a petite, sensible middle-aged woman, to waive his client from giving hair and handwriting samples, arguing these would impinge on David's right to privacy. The prosecutors had asked for the hair sample to compare David's DNA to that of blood samples taken from the crime scene. They also wanted a writing sample to figure out whether David had indeed signed the promissory note to Kim Wilson, agreeing to repay her money.

But Judge Bridge denied both of Kolker's motions. She ruled that requesting such information would not be intrusive, and added that the prosecutors' requests were not unreasonable.

In another pretrial hearing, Kolker asked the judge for a

change of venue, arguing that the media hype around the case would make it difficult to find an unbiased jury pool in the Seattle area. He produced a stack of newspaper and magazine clippings as thick as a phone book to prove his point: the Wilson murder case had received extensive media attention. But Judge Bridge did not agree, insisting that in an area the size of King County, attorneys should be able to find jurors who were not familiar with the case.

Later that summer, Judge Bridge announced that she would no longer be handling the Wilson homicide case because of other court responsibilities and commitments; instead, King County Superior Court Judge Michael Spearman would take over. Soft-spoken and reserved yet accessible, Spearman would see the trial to its end.

With a new judge on board, Kolker continued filing a series of motions on behalf of his client, who remained locked up on the eleventh floor—the floor for the most dangerous offenders—at the King County Jail, a block from the courthouse. In September, as the start of the trial was approaching, Kolker asked Judge Spearman that David be tried separately from Alex—a request Judge Bridge had already denied once. Kolker's main concern was that information—namely, Alex's confession, which the prosecutors planned to present—would unfairly incriminate David. What was more, by having the young men sitting together in the courtroom, the prosecutors would unfairly use a guilt-by-association tactic to link David to the crime.

But it would be difficult enough for relatives of the Wilson family to sit through one emotionally charged trial, much less have to endure two, prosecutors argued. Two trials would also come at a great cost, in both money and time.

Judge Spearman sided with the prosecutors; to appease Kolker, he ordered that Alex's confession be edited to exclude comments about David and any reference to an accomplice. That meant Alex's confession would read as if he acted alone, and the prosecutors were wary of giving the wrong impression to jurors. In the end, they decided to leave the confession out of court. Kolker thanked the judge for that small victory, well aware of how many other battles there would be to come.

Summer passed with less frequent and more sporadic pretrial wrangling as both the defense and the prosecution were hard at work, preparing for opening statements, scheduled for October 6.

As it happened, Kolker ended up getting what he had previously asked for and was denied—a separate trial for his client. The wheels of the joint trial for David and Alex had been set in motion with the jury selection process beginning September 22; a jury had been impaneled in two weeks. But on October 1, just as attorneys were continuing to pare down the jury, proceedings were interrupted when a court messenger briskly delivered a note to Judge Spearman's clerk. The Supreme Court decision on State vs. Ellis had come down that morning, which relaxed the rules on using a diminished capacity defense. The Pierce County, Washington, case involved Joey Ellis, accused of murdering his mother and half sister. This defense strategy is rarely used. It hinges on a claim that because the defendant is mentally ill, he or she will be unable to premeditate any crimes. Attorneys use the defense as a last-ditch effort to win an acquittal, or a conviction on a lesser charge.

This defense technique has been used a limited number of times in the past twenty years because of tight restrictions. Under it, testimony about emotions including anger, hatred, jealousy, and fear is banned, and expert witnesses are required to explain precisely how a mental disorder affects the defendant during the crime.

It's a do-or-die gamble in the minds of many defense attorneys, especially when a defendant has already confessed to the crime. Attorneys know that jurors are less willing to show mercy for a defendant who readily admits he took part in the crime. Nonetheless, Alex's attorneys grasped at the chance to use the defense. It was better than nothing, which was all they had.

In a pretrial hearing earlier that summer, Judge Spearman had rejected Alex's mental-illness claim and refused to allow his attorneys to present expert testimony from a psychologist who evaluated him in jail and found he suffered from manic depression. The defense had planned on calling San Diego psychologist Dr. Karen Froming to testify that Alex suffered from the mental disorder, and therefore, he could not have premeditated the murders. She would claim that he was so caught up in fantasy role-playing games that he was incapable of distinguishing fantasy from reality when he decided to kill the Wilsons. But the Supreme Court decision now provided the impetus for Judge Spearman to reconsider admissibility of the expert testimony.

The high court ruling set off a new round of motions for both David's and Alex's attorneys. Defense counsel for Alex asked the judge for permission to use the diminished capacity defense and Dr. Froming's testimony. They also asked to delay the trial, since they would be switching gears and could use some time to gather more information. David's attorneys, meanwhile, once again asked the judge to separate the trials, and the prosecutors moved to admit Alex's confession in its entirety.

On October 7, after a pretrial hearing in which Froming provided a preview of what she planned to say in court, Spearman made one of the most important decisions in the case by allowing her testimony to be admitted in the trial. Consequently, he granted Kolker's request to separate the trials so that David would not be incriminated in Froming's testimony, which overtly directs blame on him. The decision was a boon both for the state and for the defense. The prosecutors could now use Alex's confession in its entirety without worrying that it would prejudice David's chance for a fair trial; and Alex's attorneys could use Froming's testimony, which would presumably help show he was mentally ill during the crimes and therefore unable to premeditate the murders.

While the decision was another victory for Kolker, he now lobbied for his client to be tried first, worried that any further delays in the trial would allow more media coverage to influence jurors. Alex's attorneys, meanwhile, pleaded with the judge to present their case second, as they would need more time to pull together a new diminished-capacity defense strategy. But Alex's trial was expected to last only a month, while David's was expected to last twice as long, and a jury had already been impaneled and was waiting. To avoid prolonging the present jury's time on the case, Spearman decided to try Alex first. With that, he ordered Mark Flora and Kathy Lynn to be ready for opening statements the following week. David would have to wait for his friend to be tried before he got his own day in court.

Patty Eakes and Jeff Baird were prepared for either trial to begin. Spearman's decision to start with Alex proved beneficial to them in the end. They knew they had an airtight case against Alex, and if they could convict him, it might be easier to later convince a jury that Alex had had help from none other than his best friend, David Anderson.

David and Alex now would be facing their respective trials alone.

On Monday morning, October 12, more than two dozen people had arrived early on the ninth floor of the King County Courthouse. They were eager to get a good seat in Judge Michael Spearman's courtroom, and for a majority of them, to get their first glimpse of one of the two local teenage boys who stood accused of Bellevue's worst homicides ever. Alex was led down a hallway crowded with TV and newspaper reporters. He made no comment as he proceeded briskly into the courtroom, flanked by two police officers. On the first day of his trial, he dressed in his usual dark style: black Levi's Dockers, a turquoise button-down shirt, and black leather dress shoes. Despite his attorneys' efforts to make him look like a normal, innocent kid, Alex appeared uncomfortable in formal clothes, awkward in his new, polished look.

Outside, brown leaves crackled underfoot like parchment as pedestrians scrambled across busy streets. The streets and air were moist with dew, but it was not raining that crisp day. A light wind rushed across Puget Sound and through the downtown streets, sending a chill down the spines of pedestrians. But inside, on the ninth floor of the King County Courthouse, the heat was turned on and spectators waiting for the trial to begin removed their winter coats and gloves.

Judge Spearman's courtroom had quickly filled up with about 100 people, and still many more people tried to push through the door. Court watchers, media representatives, and friends and family of both the victims and the accused settled into the tight rows. The front row, reserved for the media, was so jammed with local and national reporters that some had to wait outside in the hallway. Behind them, relatives and friends of the Wilson family took up an entire row, sitting somberly shoulder to shoulder as they waited for the proceedings to begin. Behind them, in the row reserved for Alex's family, only his mother and her two brothers, Tom and Gary, sat, spaced apart. Patricia Baranyi was clad in a dark dress, her thick, flowing, long blond hair covering her slouching shoulders. Tom Stephan, wearing a suit and trench coat, might have been mistaken for an attorney, while Gary Stephan arrived in blue jeans and a light cotton jacket. In the back of the courtroom, Michael Kolker, David's attorney, sat amid the court watchers. As Judge Spearman emerged from his chambers, the crowd stood just long enough for the jury of seven women and eight men to file out of the jury room and take their seats. By the end of the trial, the court would eliminate three alternate jurors, leaving twelve who would have to decide whether Alex Baranyi had been lost to a fantasy world and lacking the mental capacity to know what he was doing when he killed the Wilsons; or whether he was simply a morally bankrupt, cold-blooded murderer who had killed for the thrill of it.

After instructing the jury on how the trial would proceed, Judge Spearman turned to Prosecutor Patty Eakes and asked that the jurors also direct their attention to her. The trial was beginning, and though it would last less than one month, for those who sat through its entirety, the span of time would prove to be one of the longest and most brutal of their lives.

Patty Eakes, dressed in a sharp black suit and flowing silk scarf, rose to deliver the opening remarks. Her first order of business was to familiarize the jury with the people involved in the case, starting with the young defendant sitting before them, whom she would attempt to portray as a monster without feeling, without remorse.

"Alex Baranyi saw murder as an opportunity. It was an opportunity, in his words, to experience something 'truly phenomenal,' " Eakes said, her voice sailing smoothly across the packed courtroom. "It was an opportunity for him to fulfill a lifelong ambition. You see, Alex Baranyi wanted to experience death. He wanted to experience murder firsthand. He wanted to experience it in an up close and personal way."

So, instead of using a gun, he used his hands, Eakes said. He used knives. He used bats. This was going to be the biggest experience of his life, Eakes explained, so he wanted to make sure he engaged his senses. "He wanted to hear the sounds of a baseball bat as it crushed a human skull. He wanted to watch the face of the victim as he pulled a rope around her neck and strangled her to death. He wanted to know what it was like to take a knife and plunge it into flesh. He wanted the experience of watching each and every one of his victims die.

"Why would he kill?" Eakes asked. "Alex Baranyi will tell you there was not a traditional motive for this crime. He didn't kill out of jealousy. He didn't kill for money. He didn't kill to exact revenge. Alex Baranyi will tell you he killed simply for the thrill of killing itself."

To help the jury understand the seriousness of Alex's alleged crime, Eakes briefly digressed to the definition of premeditation, and why the word was crucial in presenting this case. Premeditation means thinking or plotting before acting, she explained. It doesn't have to be a year or three months or three days. It can be as imminent as minutes before acting. Alex Baranyi did more than just premeditate the murders, Eakes explained. He *planned* it two years in advance, and executed that plan with his best friend, David Anderson.

While this was Alex Baranyi's trial, Eakes knew it was important to connect Alex and David so there would be no question among the jurors that Alex did not kill four people alone, and that his accomplice was none other than his best friend. It made sense, and Eakes wanted the jury to see that. Eakes then offered a glimpse into the lives of Alex and David, how they were inseparable friends and how their lives paralleled in so many ways. They had much in common: playing violent video and fantasy games, collecting swords and knives, and dressing in black. "But what no one really appreciated, what few people recognized, is that they had one other interest in common, and that was murder."

Eakes captivated the audience with the first several minutes of an articulate, well-planned speech. With their full attention, Eakes now wanted the jury to get to know the victims. Showing 8½-by-11 portraits of each victim, the prosecutor then segued to the Wilsons, painting a picture of a typical middle-class, suburban American family. Both Bill and Rose had backgrounds in finance and were avid University of Washington Huskies fans, Eakes explained. Julia was the youngest, and she worked part-time after school in a prominent Bellevue law firm. Finally, Eakes introduced Kim. She graduated in 1995 and by the summer of '96, she decided to join AmeriCorps.

Kim was at home in Bellevue enjoying the holiday break with her family the month before they were slain.

"I think it's safe to say that none of the Wilsons had any idea that they were picked to die," Eakes said. "None of them had any idea that the Christmas of 1996 would be their last."

Kim was spending her last hours at home visiting with old friends. The Friday night of her death, she spent time with at least three close friends before one of them dropped her off just after 11 P.M.—the last time anyone except her killers saw her alive.

Kim had a lot of friends, Eakes explained. She counted David Anderson among them. But what she didn't know was that David and Alex hated her. They hated her so much they had planned to kill her and her family.

Blindly, Kim trusted David. She trusted him enough to accompany him to Woodridge's Water Tower Park that fatal Friday night when Alex came out of the bushes and strangled her to death.

Eakes took her time in recounting the sheer brutality of the crimes. She wanted to make sure the jury knew just how gratuitous and unnecessary the massacre was. In grisly detail, she recounted what happened at Water Tower Park, and later at the Wilson home that horrific night of January 3.

"There were no survivors. There were no witnesses," Eakes said. "The entire Wilson family was gone. Dead. And they thought that they had committed the perfect crime."

Although David and Alex were careful not to leave fingerprints and they got rid of their clothes and hid the murder weapons, they made at least two critical mistakes, Eakes said. The first mistake was that their alibis were easily disputed by their friends and people who saw them that night, and the second was that, as careful as they were, they did not get rid of all the blood. Alex was smart enough to dispose of his shoes, Eakes explained, but for some reason, he kept the shoelaces. On those shoelaces, experts found tiny droplets of Bill Wilson's blood. David kept his shoes, probably because the bloodstains were not visible to the naked eye, Eakes said. But the blood and brain matter of Bill and Julia Wilson had smeared on them. Those two major mistakes led to the suspects' undoing.

Nonetheless, Alex got what he wanted, Eakes recounted.

"Alex Baranyi had succeeded. He had experienced death firsthand, in a personal way . . . And [he] shared that experience with four people: Kim Wilson, Rose Wilson, Bill Wilson, and Julia Wilson."

After an hour, when Eakes had finished her remarks, Kathy Lynn, the defense counsel, stood up and approached the jury.

Lynn worked hard to paint a very different—in fact, a completely opposite—picture of Alex. To counterpoint the inhumanity Eakes had created around Alex, Lynn tried to show the jurors a more human side to her client. She wanted the jury to know the lost, lonely, angry child Alex had always been. A child who craved friendship so much that when he finally found a companion in David Anderson, he would do *anything*—even murder someone—to keep the friendship intact.

Lynn, a full-figured, no-nonsense woman with short blond, wavy hair, spoke at the same deliberate pace as she walked. She made her points directly and succinctly. A graduate of the well-reputed Gonzaga University, Lynn had worked in private practice for two years before applying for a job with the King County Prosecutor's Office. She might have found herself on the opposite side of the courtroom, prosecuting Alex rather than defending him, had it not been for car problems. As fate would have it, her car broke down on the way to the interview for a job as a prosecutor. The interview was never rescheduled, and in 1989, she subsequently took a job as a public defender with the Society of Counsel Representing Accused Persons.

Although she had known Mark Flora, her co-counsel, years before 1997, it wasn't until the Wilson homicides that they had their first opportunity to work together.

Flora, a short, curly-haired, and bespectacled middle-aged man, had fought hard for fifteen years defending clients tangled up in all sorts of felonies from drug cases to homicides. He graduated from the University of Washington Law School in 1983, and took his first job six months later working for the city of Renton, litigating misdemeanor DUI cases. As with all of the attorneys involved in the Wilson case, this would be Flora's biggest and most important case ever. And Lynn and Flora knew they had their work cut out for them.

Approaching the jury in the same polite fashion as Eakes had, Lynn began describing Alex as a loner, a kid who wanted to fit in and who would do anything to be part of a group, and so he latched onto David Anderson. Because of David, Alex had friends. Because of David, he had self-esteem. But because of David, he was also sitting in the courtroom now, on trial for murder. Alex simply followed David, Lynn explained. He worshiped David and was loyal to the end.

Lynn asked the jury to keep an open mind as it heard evidence in the case against their client. She said the jury would eventually meet Dr. Karen Froming, a clinical psychologist who had evaluated Alex. One of the questions Froming had set out to answer was whether Alex was mentally incapacitated at the time of the killings. According to Froming, Alex suffered from a bipolar affective disorder, which manifests itself in manic depression. Two critical factors—biological and psychological—cause the disorder, Lynn explained. Alex came from a family with a history of depression. His mother suffered from depression. But it was Alex's environment that also contributed to his psychological suffering. His mother abandoned him at age eight and he was left to live with his father. And recently, just a few months before the murders, his father kicked him out of the house because Alex wanted to work rather than go to school.

But there were other things that impaired Alex's ability to form intent, Lynn explained, one of which was his obsession with fantasy role-playing games.

"Alex and others including David Anderson and other friends, played this fantasy game called Kinabota. They take PVC piping, they take padding and duct tape and make all kinds of fake swords. They go out into fields in the Bellevue area and have mock battles. It was one of Alex's favorite things to do . . . The question is, at what point was Alex in a fantasy world versus reality?" Lynn suggested it was at that point, when fantasy collided with reality, that Alex slipped over the edge and into murder. "The fantasy games were taking over more and more of his life," she said.

Those games, and Alex's close relationship with David Anderson, are what brought him to this place, Lynn suggested. She offered jurors the same scenarios that Eakes had given in her opening statements regarding Alex's friendship with David. "Alex's sole friend was David Anderson. That was where he got his self-esteem and that's who he followed." She added, "Alex is loyal to a fault, to his detriment. Even today, he is not pointing a finger at David."

Lynn then offered the jury examples of inconsistencies in Alex's own taped confession which she believed would prove his delusional state of mind during the attack. But she failed to bring up the fact that Alex himself admitted to the detectives who interviewed him, and later to another psychologist who evaluated him, that he lied throughout the entire confession.

"We're not disputing that Alex wasn't there," Lynn said. "The question is his state of mind, and the second question is what was his role."

Not surprisingly, Lynn pinned the blame on David. "David was the one behind the impetus to kill the family," she said. And Alex—poor, lonely Alex, who merely followed along because he wanted a friend—was David's fall guy.

If Lynn and Flora succeeded in getting the jurors to focus on these two things, and to see their perspective, they might have a chance to win a lesser sentence for their client.

As a final request, Lynn again asked the jury to listen carefully to all of the evidence before deliberating. "It is essential that you do not rush to judgment. It would be easy to do that after you've heard the state's case, how horrible and senseless these murders were. But in order to give the system a fair shake, to give Alex and the system a fair trial, keep an open mind."

That afternoon, Prosecutor Jeff Baird presented the state's first witnesses. In his folksy, easygoing yet assertive approach, he addressed the jury often, encouraging witnesses to speak up so the jury could hear. He was hospitable, offering witnesses water and tissues. Just a few inches over 5 feet tall, Baird wore the same black suit to court each day—a stark contrast to his trial partner, Eakes, who donned delicate silk scarves and whose various sophisticated suits suggested a well-stocked wardrobe. Baird, who was blessed with a resonant voice, moved across the courtroom as if it were a stage. At times, he would stand close to the bar, where he would be within a few feet of the witness; other times, he preferred to stand far back behind the jury box, encouraging witnesses to speak up, as he was doing now with his first witness, Detective Jeff Gomes.

Dressed in a suit and tie, Gomes appeared professional and personable. Baird had called the Bellevue cop to the stand for one thing only: to introduce him to the jury, and to let them know he would maintain a constant presence throughout the trial. The strategy was clear: to show the jury the detective's deep commitment and interest in the case. It was important for the jury to like Gomes. To get to know him. To trust him. And ultimately, to believe that he, Jeffrey Adam Gomes, had conducted a comprehensive and successful investigation that culminated in the arrest of the young man sitting before the jurors—a young man Gomes firmly believed was partially responsible for killing the Wilsons.

After Gomes' brief introduction, the state's next witness was escorted into the courtroom in a wheelchair. Wearing black pants and shoes, and a black sweater with a holiday theme, Julia Mahoney was helped to her feet by Detective Jerry Johnson as she balanced herself on her walking stick and slowly made her way to the front of the courtroom. Her dark attire and the frailty of her movements suggested old age, but more than that: a victim hardly recovered from the sudden death of her only daughter and her daughter's family. The short, gray-haired woman spoke softly, her voice constrained with self-control. That day was the first chance she had to look her family's suspected killer in the eyes, and she wasted no time sending off her first round of darting stares. She fixed a hard glare on Alex Baranyi for a short, piercing, uninterrupted moment. Alex paid no attention, seemingly untouched by the tension around him.

Baird eased into his direct examination by asking Mrs. Mahoney to talk a little bit about her family. She discussed her daughter's and son-in-law's jobs, and her granddaughters' activities. Kim, she explained, was in the AmeriCorps program and faithfully wrote to her grandmother from San Diego, where she was stationed.

But as Baird zeroed in on the night of Friday, January 3, 1997, Mrs. Mahoney's voice tensed up. She had wanted to do this, to testify on her daughter's behalf. But that meant drawing on nightmarish memories anyone would want to forget. The last time she spoke with her daughter was that Friday night when she had gone out to dinner with Rose, Bill, and Kim, she told the jury. That Saturday, she had tried to call Rose all day. She and her son, Gerald, began to worry about where the family might have gone.

"We couldn't understand why they wouldn't pick up the phone," Mrs. Mahoney said, her voice cracking. "We almost decided to go over there to see what the heck was going on. We didn't, thank God for that."

Trying to keep her composure, Mrs. Mahoney seemed to stare absently into space as if numbed by recall as she answered Baird's next question, a question she had answered so many times before: When did she learn of her family's fate?

"Not until I was watching the Sunday night news and I saw the house on the television and I just froze." Mrs. Mahoney continued to recount how a family friend picked her up to go to the Wilson home, where she was met with a confusing scene of police cars and ambulances. She knew then that something terrible had happened to her family and she was completely helpless.

There was nothing the defense could do to take the emotional sting out of Mrs. Mahoney's testimony, and so they simply waived their opportunity to cross-examine her.

Judge Spearman called for a recess, and that afternoon, the jury heard from the last two witnesses for the day: Kim's friends Erin Gauntlett and Sky Stewart—the last friends to see the young woman alive. They both said Kim was in good spirits that night, excited about her life. There was nothing in her mood that suggested she was worried or afraid of anything.

On Tuesday, October 13, the jury heard from several more lay witnesses: a friend of Kim's who remembered her talking about an outstanding debt she intended to collect from David; a neighbor of the Wilsons who reportedly heard shouting coming from the Wilsons' front porch at around 11 P.M., and finally, that afternoon, Marsha Rash, David's exgirlfriend.

Rash would be an important witness because she was able to corroborate Alex's confession with a single conversation she had had with him at the King County Jail shortly after his arrest.

Dressed in blue jeans and a purple Huskies sweatshirt, with her hair cut short and dyed black, Rash nervously approached the witness stand and took her oath. Eakes started off by asking her to talk about how she met Alex and to explain the relationship between her ex-boyfriend and Alex.

In a soft, barely audible voice, Rash answered all of Eakes' questions without hesitation. She told the same story that everyone who knew the duo had. David and Alex were close friends, Rash said. But they fought frequently, sometimes not speaking to each other for days. David sometimes got tired of Alex's moodiness, Rash explained, but for the most part, they remained tight.

Alex, she said, was intelligent, funny, a good friend. But there was only one problem. "He didn't get along with people very well. He's not a people person."

Rash portrayed Alex as a young man who succeeded in hiding under a veil of normalcy, but who lived on the dark side, who had murder in him. After his arrest, she didn't want to believe the media when it was reported that Alex had confessed to police. So she decided to go to the source directly and hear it from him.

Just a month after Alex confessed, she and her friend Jeannie Kern showed up at the jail to see him, Rash told the jury. "He seemed fine," she said. "He wasn't upset."

It seemed odd that after being accused of killing four people, Alex could be so calm and casual, as if he had already resigned himself to a life in prison.

"I asked him if David had been there, and he said, 'No,' but he nodded at the same time," Rash went on to tell the court.

Rash testified that she asked Alex if he killed the Wilsons, and Alex admitted he did, telling her that he "got carried away" when he was killing the younger daughter and accidentally stabbed himself in the leg. As he talked specifically about the attack, he became more upbeat, Rash said. He grew fidgety in his chair.

"I said, 'Well, then you got what you deserve.' And he said, 'Yes.' "

The courtroom remained silent for a brief moment, stunned at Alex's apparent lack of remorse. The jury had been briefed in opening statements that Alex had already confessed to the police, but here he was bragging to his own friends that he killed the Wilsons.

In cross-examination, Mark Flora drew Rash away from Alex's involvement in the murders and focused instead on his involvement in fantasy role-playing games. Specifically, the attorney wanted to know about a character named Slicer Thunderclap who seemed to inhabit Alex's body and mind. Marsha appeared to know quite a bit about this character. The goal of this demigod was to rule the world, Marsha explained. Slicer Thunderclap's true love was a fictional character named Rose, she explained.

The defense counsel's strategy was to try to use each witness they could to show that their client suffered from mental illness and therefore could not have premeditated the murders. So with Rash, as with other witnesses to come, the lawyers would focus on Alex's supposed mental instability. Flora questioned Rash about Alex's mood swings, which she said fluctuated between "extreme highs and extreme lows, where he'd be kind of scatterbrained at times." During his highs, Alex would be fun-loving and humorous, a blast to be around, but in his lows, he was depressed and avoided people.

Flora asked how close David and Alex were.

"Alex loved David. David loved Alex," Rash said. Not in a romantic sense, she insisted, but clearly, the two friends would do anything for each other.

On redirect, Eakes broke apart Flora's early groundwork in showing his client's mental state by asking Rash whether Alex stayed in his Slicer Thunderclap role all the time, to which she replied a resounding "No." Eakes also asked whether Alex had a hard time distinguishing fantasy from reality. Again Rash answered with a resounding "No." With that, Eakes had no more questions and Rash quietly left the courtroom.

During the remainder of the afternoon, the court heard from Bob Boyd, now sixteen years old, who testified that he and Alex wore black boots with the same diamond-sole pattern as that found at the crime scene. Alex's boots were never found, but it was determined that the boots Bob said Alex owned matched the pattern of the bloody shoeprint found in the Wilson home. Bob's aunt, Chris Sheridan, also took the stand, as did Ricky Nelson, a Woodridge resident who said he saw two people sitting on a dark-colored pickup truck parked in Water Tower Park at around 12:20 A.M. that Saturday morning. (Alex had already admitted to the police he was in Marsha's stepfather's black pickup truck the night of the murders.)

That afternoon, Ron Boyd, Bob's father, was the last to take the witness stand. As he was questioned by Baird, Boyd told the jury how his son became enamored with David and

Alex and "worshiped everything they did. [David] was like a messiah." David had lived with the Boyds briefly that fall before moving out because he couldn't pay the $50 rent, Ron explained. Besides that, he had drug problems that were beginning to rub off on Bob. Ron described Alex as a hard worker and a good kid, honest and helpful around the house. Alex couldn't hurt a fly, he seemed to suggest.

But prosecutors would attempt to show he was a man with murder on his mind. Later that day, they called Dr. Richard Harruff to the stand to begin the grim task of presenting the autopsy findings to the jury. The Wilson relatives sobbed quietly as they joined the jurors in looking at explicit photographs of bruises on the body of Kim, and wide gashes and swelling on the bodies of Bill and Rose. Days later, they would finally see and hear about the injuries inflicted on Julia. The Wilson relatives had been briefed before the trial ever started about the horrific pictures that would be displayed, and still they decided to remain in court during the medical examiner's testimony. A couple of the family members abruptly left during some parts of the testimony, unable to hold back emotions. Harruff showed the jury a part of Wilson's skull with a piece of metal, believed to have come from Alex's knife, still sticking in it. During a graphic discussion of the autopsy, one juror clutched her hands to her chest. But there was to be even more grim testimony from Harruff.

Over the next several days, the jury would hear from a host of other witnesses with little or no cross-examination by the defense. Among those to testify were Ed Sheridan—a heavyset blond man in his late twenties—who lived with his mother, Christine Sheridan, across from Alex in the Boyds' basement, and who watched as Alex left the house that night with something long in his coat sleeve; forensic expert Kim Duddy, who testified that the rope found in the truck David was driving, and which Alex admitted he had been in on the night of the murders, matched the piece of rope around Kim Wilson's neck; Police Officer John Jesson, who found a pair of shoelaces in Alex's trash can in his bedroom with the blood of Bill Wilson on them; the McBrides, who first questioned Alex about his whereabouts on the night of the murders; and Detective Bob Thompson, who discovered a piece of torn black T-shirt in Julia Wilson's bedroom. (In his confession, Alex told Thompson he lost his black headpiece and went back into the bedrooms after killing the Wilsons to look for it.)

Piece by piece, the prosecution was building its case against Alex Baranyi, using an eclectic mix of witnesses, some more articulate than others. So far, the witnesses had provided a portrait of Alex and David as bored, rebellious adolescents, but now the prosecutors wanted the jury to see how these two restless suburban teenagers had begun plotting a murder.

On Monday, October 20, a slight young woman with dirty blond hair took the witness stand. She stated her name, Sarah Elizabeth Kennedy Lamp, and, pointing at Alex Baranyi, identified the defendant as her friend. Alex smiled fondly at Lamp and shivered slightly as he watched her take the stand, as if, seeing her for the first time in more than a year, he was falling madly in love with her once again. Lamp, a twenty-year-old woman about 5 feet 4 inches, had her long blond hair braided in the back of her head. She wore black pants, a black jacket, a white blouse, and small black shoes.

A high school dropout who moved to Alaska within months after the murders, Lamp was not an easy witness to find and interview. Even after learning that two of her friends were suspected of killing the Wilsons, she did not come to police; instead, police had to find her. Once authorities contacted and interviewed her, she was unwilling to provide information that would point the finger at David and

Alex. She was protecting them, and possibly even herself, because she knew about the murder plan long before it was executed and did absolutely nothing to stop it.

During her testimony, Lamp reluctantly answered Eakes' questions, pausing often as if calculating her words, trying not to say anything that would incriminate her friends. She contradicted herself often and seemed to have difficulty re-membering dates and details of events. The end result, which was both good and bad for the prosecution, was her damaged credibility as a witness. On the one hand, Lamp's testimony would show she had something to hide. But on the other hand, jurors would have a hard time deciphering what was true and what was false.

Lamp explained how she met David and Alex while she was volunteering to clean up Camp Seal on Vashon Island—one of several islands in Puget Sound—with her on-again, off-again boyfriend, Mike Anderson, David's older brother.

Lamp said she and Alex quickly became friends, and then they dated briefly.

"We never did more than hold hands," she said. "It was so not happening." She added that Alex "most definitely" felt stronger about her than she did about him. "He would tell me that he loved me and wanted me to be his girlfriend."

When the couple broke up, Lamp explained how Alex wrote her letters suggesting he was going to commit suicide. But Lamp chose not to contact him, figuring he just needed to cool off, and refusing to believe he would actually harm himself.

To disprove the defense's theory, Eakes asked whether Lamp thought Alex was mentally ill.

"No, not the person I knew back then," Lamp said quietly.

Then Lamp explained how she met Kim through Mike Anderson. The two women became close friends, hanging out together at Denny's, going to movies, and taking long walks. Sarah described how the four of them—she, Kim,

David, and Alex—spent time together at the all-night restaurant. There, they talked about movies, work, and how much they hated school.

But the conversations during those times when Kim wasn't around were what most interested Eakes. Specifically, the prosecutor wanted to know about the conversations Lamp had had with David and Alex about murder. Lamp admitted she had about a dozen such conversations with the two boys at Denny's. "Originally, the conversations never involved anyone getting hurt," Lamp said. The threesome talked about crimes to make profit, such as burglary or robbery. They were interested only in making a quick buck. But then, over time, the group added a new, more titillating dimension to the discussions—murder.

"Kim and her family weren't so much the targets, but they had three or four cars and valuables in their home," Lamp testified. "I never remember it being personal or vindictive, but since they never leave, you'd have to kill them."

Lamp spoke nonchalantly and matter-of-factly, as if murder plans were discussed all the time. No big deal. "My belief is they were conversations. They were never going to happen."

Eakes wanted to show just how serious the suspects were, and pressed Lamp to talk about how the discussion progressed into details about murder weapons. In earlier sworn statements she gave to police, Lamp said that Alex and David discussed using knives and swords and baseball bats as weapons—which were indeed the actual murder weapons. But on the witness stand, Lamp said the group discussed using only a lamp or other object nearby if the family being robbed should wake up and find the intruder in their home. Eakes was too shrewd to suggest Lamp was lying, but she firmly believed Sarah knew more than she was willing to admit on the stand. So, Eakes let her hang herself on her own previous statements made to police by referring to and quoting parts of the statements, then holding Lamp to those.

As the testimony continued, Lamp told the jury how she and Kim drifted apart following a major fallout Kim had had with David. Kim learned through him that he and Alex were planning to commit a crime. Worried that they would wind up in jail, Kim confronted the boys, which fueled their hatred for her. Lamp sided with Alex and David, almost blaming Kim for the murders because she was "nosy."

"People were mad she was sticking her nose into other people's business," Sarah said finally.

In cross-examination, Alex's attorneys again turned the tide to focus the discussion on Alex's supposed mental disorder. Flora presented Lamp with the two letters Alex had written her and signed "Slicer Thunderclap." The letters suggested Alex was contemplating suicide and were nothing more than a rumination of Alex's tortured and obsessive thoughts about wanting Lamp to be his girlfriend. Lynn and Flora hoped to show how their client was influenced by a fantasy world and depression. That, they argued, explained why he would sign his letters "ST"—the initials of his role-playing character.

As Sarah read the letters, Alex's face turned red, showing embarassment that his private letters to a woman he was obsessed with were surfacing in front of complete strangers and there was nothing he could do about it. He continued to stare down at his notepad, raising his head only briefly to snatch a glimpse of Sarah.

But it was a far stretch. In redirect, Eakes pointed out, through Lamp, that the envelopes which the letters arrived in were addressed from none other than "Alex Baranyi."

The second week into the trial, prosecutors knew they needed to show that Alex Baranyi was not depressed during the murders. In fact, his life seemed to be going quite well, as recently as the day of his arrest for the murders. They needed someone to point that out, and they found the perfect witness in one of Alex's former employers.

On October 21, Janice Jeffries, a petite woman with brunette hair and a reserved demeanor, approached the witness stand. She was a fifteen-year employee of, and worked as a secretary and general office manager at, Rite-Way Waterproofing, where Alex and David had worked in the fall of 1996.

On Thursday, January 9, six days after the killings and the day Alex was arrested, he arrived at work to learn he had just been promoted and would receive a raise, Jeffries testified. In her mind, the promotion was well deserved. She described Alex as a model employee—punctual and thorough. He was respectful and polite, greeting Jeffries in the mornings with an enthusiastic "Good morning."

Not only was he a good employee, he seemed to be a good kid. Before being hired, Alex passed a drug test, Jeffries said. She didn't think he ever drank.

"He was quiet, a very nice young man, like you would want your son to be," Jeffries said.

That's why news of his arrest stunned her.

"I thought they arrested the wrong person."

Prosecutors wrapped up the day by putting Gomes back on the stand. The detective read from notebooks recovered from Alex's room during search warrants. The white sheets were a compilation of notes on crime and punishment, from how to get out of getting caught while shoplifting, to the best places to pickpocket.

The following day, Officer John Jesson took the stand to tell the jury he had found a telephone, CD player, and VCR, covered with dried blood, hidden under a coat in a storage room down the hall from Alex's bedroom at the Boyd residence. Alex's fingerprints, made in Bill Wilson's blood, had smeared on the VCR. The cop also found shoelaces in the trash can in Alex's room which tested positive for Bill Wilson's blood.

Later, Gomes returned to the stand to introduce various belongings the police took from Alex's bedroom during a search warrant, including books on crime and punishment, an *Excaliber* magazine, and various writings.

Dr. Harruff was also recalled to the stand, presenting more autopsy photographs, this time of Julia Wilson. He explained how she was the only one who had defense wounds; her arm was broken, and her hands and feet were cut and bruised. Dr. Harruff testified that she was stabbed three times in her left eye—an injury that completely destroyed the globe—though she was already dead. Jury members averted their eyes away from the graphic pictures after initial glimpses, and focused instead on Harruff as he spoke.

Up until that point, the trial had been uncontentious, with small dramatic moments. Alex's attorneys sat by with few objections as prosecutors put forth their case. However, that afternoon, in a terse confrontation with the judge, Kathy Lynn and Mark Flora would raise the possibility that they would seek a second trial.

After prosecutors indicated they would soon complete their case, Judge Spearman asked Lynn and Flora to be prepared to present their star witness, Dr. Karen Froming, the following Monday. Flora insisted he needed more time. He told the judge that he felt rushed into trial after Spearman had denied Flora's earlier request for David to be tried first so he and Lynn could have more time to fully prepare their case.

Flora insisted that Froming would not be able to come into court until Wednesday, October 29. Spearman, who wanted to keep the trial running smoothly without any further delays, said if that were the case, he would consider excluding her testimony. That fueled a heated response from Flora.

"We told you in plain English we were not ready," Flora said. "Your Honor is buying a second trial for Mr. Baranyi, if you haven't done so already."

Clearly upset at Flora's outburst, Spearman adjourned the court for the day and promptly summoned the attorneys into his chambers, where they further discussed the matter. Spearman warned Flora he didn't want to see another outburst like that again. In the end, Spearman made a compromise that both the prosecution and the defense agreed upon: Froming would testify on Tuesday.

So far, the jurors heard nothing from Alex, but they watched him during various witness testimonies. At times, he seemed thoroughly interested in court proceedings and testimony, but most of the time he wrote letters and doodled on a notepad, appearing bored and disinterested. During Dr. Harruff's testimony on the autopsies, Alex craned his neck to get a better view of photographs of the injuries he had inflicted. These were displayed on a TV screen and poster boards.

Without the jury present, he interacted not only with his own attorneys but with those around him. One day he sat down in a huff, angry over a mug shot in the *Seattle Times*. He turned to Mark Flora and asked, "Is my nose really that big?" Also during the trial, he seemed to keep up a running commentary on Eakes' fashion sensibilities. For the most part, he liked her outfits. But one day he asked Eakes why she didn't wear open-toed shoes, to which Eakes replied, "It's winter; open toes are out."

It seemed as if the seriousness of Alex's crimes was beyond him. It was clear that Alex was somewhat detached during the slayings; and he was detached even now as he sat quietly in the courtroom each day, his life being dissected before his eyes in front of complete strangers who were sure to be critical of his courtroom behavior.

After almost two solid weeks of the prosecution presenting a well-rounded blend of lay and professional witnesses, the jury would finally hear from the accused, perhaps the single most important testimony of the entire case. Even though Alex would never take the stand in his trial, prosecutors planned to present the next best thing, his entire taped confession.

On October 22, the prosecution wheeled in a tape player they placed in front of the jury and inserted the first of four hour-long tapes of Alex's confession. Each jury member was given earphones to better hear Alex as he described to police the sights, sounds, and smells of murder.

In his confession, Alex's voice fluctated from an almost robotic and unemotional monotone to a more excited, frantic pace as he gave chilling and intimate details of how he attacked each member of the Wilson family. He described the experience of killing in such detail that the jury was left stunned and traumatized.

As Alex recounted how he murdered Kim, his voice began to crack.

"I realize I was on the ground, and I realize I was strangling her," Alex said, breathless as if he were reliving the attack in his mind. "I didn't know if she was dead or not." He started to sniffle.

Then the jury heard Alex tell Bob Thompson about entering the Wilson home, and after stabbing and beating to death her parents, he went after Julia.

"Julia came out of her room at the end of the hall," Alex said, his voice speeding up. "She was really scared . . . I dropped the bat a couple of feet from her. I started stabbing at her. She had her arms over her face, she was fending me off."

Alex's voice continued to crack as he talked about his attack on the Wilson's younger daughter.

"I was sorry that I was killing her," he said, breathless and crying.

Judge Spearman called for several breaks during the lengthy and brutal confession. The jurors clearly needed it. As Alex recounted his last attack on Julia, one juror, a middle-aged woman with long brunette hair, started to cry. Some of the other jurors blinked hard, looks of horror etched on their faces. Some shook their heads, and others gripped their chairs so hard their fists turned red. It was as if they were sitting through a horror film, and what they were hearing was beyond their worst nightmares. Unlike when viewing a film, where images would be connected to words, the jurors had no pictures to look at, but only their own imaginations to fill in the blanks.

Alex continued to talk about the events that unfolded that night and the role he played in the murders. By the end, he still refused to name his accomplice, despite the detectives' pleas.

At 2 P.M., prosecutors pushed the stop button and rested their case. The confession was the most compelling piece of evidence in the entire case. It was the eyewitness account by the young man who committed the crime. Spearman declared a recess until Tuesday, allowing the defense one extra day to prepare its case.

26 On Monday morning, October 27, just before the defense called its first witness to the stand, and without the jury present, Judge Spearman informed the court of Alex's request for a new trial. He insisted that his attorneys arm-twisted him into going along with a diminished capacity defense when that was not what he wanted. Alex asked the judge in a written statement to grant him a new trial, at which time he would potentially represent himself.

In an articulate letter to Spearman, Alex indicated he was "dead set" against using the diminshed capacity defense.

"I just have little faith that defense could be used in a court of law," Alex said. "They say you should choose your battles, and it looks like this is going to be my Waterloo."

Alex went on to say, "I realize to change our defense now would be at the least, futile, and at the most, utterly disastrous. I'd like a chance to have a new trial. I'd like a chance to defend myself as I see fit."

Kathy Lynn and Mark Flora had nothing to add to their client's request. All along, they saw a mistrial in the works, and were not surprised or hurt that Alex would plead ineffective counsel in his request for a new trial.

But Judge Spearman, appearing sympathetic but firm, denied the request.

"He did indeed make a choice," Spearman said. "Examining the alternatives, he is unlikely to be successful."

Spearman also said that Alex had made his request for a new trial too late in the process; he should have asked for a new trial long before the prosecution had presented its evidence and rested its case.

Having resolved the only pretrial motion on the schedule that day, Judge Spearman ordered a short break, after which the defense called to the stand its first witness. Valerie Boyd testified little more than that, in her opinion, David seemed to be the leader over Alex. Officer Jesson then took the stand. He had searched Alex's room and the defense wanted to know what he found. Among other things, Jesson discovered a charcoal-gray hooded wool cape, several Kinabota swords, and various drawings and writings. From a notebook, Jesson read the first page: "This is a warning to you who are reading this journal. You have just opened a door into the shadowy world that is my mind."

Alex was mentally ill, his attorneys tried to say, and they suggested his own writings proved it.

Then the tone of the day shifted dramatically when the defense's third witness sashayed into the courtroom wearing a dramatic black-lace dress, black nail polish, black combat boots, and dark makeup. Her name was Jeannie Kern and she said she and Alex had once been good friends. She was also friends with David.

"I kinda sorta dated him," Kern said, tittering as she looked around the room, fidgeting in her seat.

Kern said that David and Alex did in fact enjoy participating in role-playing games and jousting with their fake swords. She was a colorful witness, lively and chatty as if she were answering questions on a TV game show rather than at a murder trial.

Kern described Alex as a "normal, average guy"—a good friend who was fun to hang out with. Kern hoped her testimony would show Alex as a happy, harmless teenager. He wouldn't hurt a fly, she said.

But by the time Baird launched into his cross-examination of her, she had slouched back into her chair and crossed her arms. Baird's intense questioning slowly deflated her.

Baird confronted Kern with a sworn statement she made to Bellevue Police Officers in a Denny's parking lot a few days after the murders, when she gave a much different picture of her friend. Asked if she considered Alex to be violent, Kern emphatically denied it. So Baird requested she read parts of her statement she had voluntarily given to the police after the murders.

"You said he was using violent language, didn't you?"

Realizing Baird had picked up on her lie, she answered quietly, "Yeah."

Baird continued to press Kern for more details about her statement.

"You told the police Alex Baranyi said he hated the human race and he hates people?"

Slinking further into her seat, Kern scowled at Baird before she answered.

"Some people just don't get along with other people," she said. "A lot of people get on his nerves. He's not a people person."

By the time Baird finished his cross-examination, Kern had been reduced to a surly teenager, angry that she was put on the spot. She bolted up from her chair and, starting to cry, stomped out of the courtroom.

After prosecutors presented Alex's taped confession as their last and most important piece of evidence, there was only one line of defense for Lynn and Flora.

On Tuesday morning, October 28, the defense called its final witness to the stand, Dr. Karen Froming. Her testimony would last an entire day, spilling over into the following morning, as she talked about Alex's family and fantasy lives, and, according to her, his mental disorders. Her testimony would be an intense lesson in neuropsychology, but also, in the end, a lesson on the importance of owning up to one's mistakes.

Dr. Froming, a middle-aged, calm woman with short black hair that had a conspicuous shock of white on one side, approached the stand wearing a turquoise shirt and a long skirt. Her extensive list of credentials included her testimony in a pretrial hearing in the notorious case of unabomber Theodore Kaczynski to determine whether Kaczynski was sane enough to stand trial. In an ironic twist of fate, her own life had, in the past, been touched by murder—one of her college friends was murdered by Seattle's serial killer Ted Bundy.

On the stand, a confident and poised Dr. Froming told the jurors she had spent more than twenty-five hours interviewing Alex in six different meetings. In her evaluation, Froming concluded that Alex suffered from a manic-depressive disorder, partly because he was abandoned by his parents during two separate instances, and also because of biological factors: both sides of his parents' families had a history of depression.

Using charts and graphs, Froming painted a picture of a lost, lonely boy who came from a dysfunctional family. Although he had a caring, doting mother, he was forced to live with his father from age eight.

"His memories of her are positive. She's warm, supportive," Froming said of Patricia Baranyi. "His father, on the other hand, was one of the most hostile, demeaning people I've ever interviewed. Here we have this child who's been abandoned by the mother he idolizes. Here he's put with a male role model who put him down. When Alex Sr. remarried, it was clear to me that both of them were just as happy to have Alex out of the house."

Froming described to the jury Alex Jr.'s constant struggle to make friends even into his early teens, until the day he met David Anderson. Alex's parents, while they didn't particularly like David, were glad to see their son finally forming a friendship. They described David as "devious and manipulative, but they were so happy their son had a friend. They didn't want to disrupt that," Froming told the jury.

When Alex met David, his entire world seemed to shift in a positive direction.

"If you were a part of David's circle, you had a bigger circle of friends," Froming said. "[They] were almost groupies to David. To abandon or break away from this relationship would be psychologically damaging. He would do whatever it took to keep the relationship."

Continuing her testimony, Dr. Froming indicated she had administered several different types of tests to determine whether Alex had any neurological problems. One of those tests was the famous Rorschach inkblot exercise. The doctor had asked Alex to describe what he saw as she held up a card with inkblots on it.

Alex spun a story about a boy named Bill and his sister, Julia, unable to get home after encountering a gnome. The story was laced with themes of depression and loss as the gnome turns Julia into a violin, and, in the end, Bill, who misses his sister and longs for her, uses the violin to beat the gnome.

Ironically, Alex used the names of two of the victims in the real-life story he was involved with, but Froming failed to point that out to jurors—something that prosecutors would pick up on and use against her later during an intense cross-examination.

Even Alex's own attorneys failed to comment on why he chose the names Bill and Julia in the story. Instead, Flora asked about another test Froming conducted on Alex. The MMPI is a lengthy personality test involving a series of questions that help psychologists get into the minds of criminals. Answers to the questionnaire are scored and charted

on a graph with subscales. Froming said that Alex scored
high on depression, social dysfunctions, and family problems. One of the subscales also noted was ASP (which
stands for antisocial practices), but during her testimony,
Froming misspoke. Instead of testifying that Alex had rated
highly for antisocial practices, she said he had high aspirations. It was a mistake that prosecutors keyed in on, and one
that would later come back to haunt her.

Given his apparent mental disorders, Flora now asked the
doctor to talk about how that played into his life. The manic
depression seemed to manifest itself in Alex's robust fantasy
life, a life which was structured around the TV show *Highlander* and fantasy video and role-playing games, Froming
said. She spoke at length about Alex's fantasy life and suggested he was deep into that make-believe world when he
killed the Wilsons. If the jury accepted her theory, there
would be a chance at an acquittal, or a conviction on a
charge of murder in the second degree, which carries a sentence of twenty to forty years.

While her jailhouse interviews with him appeared to be
complete and thorough, she forgot one major thing—to ask
about the crime. Alex eventually volunteered information on
his own, admitting to Froming that he killed Kim Wilson
and then went to the Wilson home to finish off the family.
But that part of the interview never made it into Froming's
notes. During direct examination, she explained to the jury
that she stopped taking notes because she was traumatized,
and because she wanted to maintain eye contact, and therefore a good rapport, with Alex.

Froming finished her testimony by saying she believed
Alex was unable to have premeditated the death of Kimberly
Wilson, but she was unclear whether or not he had intended
to kill Bill, Rose, and Julia Wilson. She reiterated her opinion that Alex was simply following David's direction when

he killed the Wilsons. "I think in his heart it was his reliance on this relationship and how much it meant to him, and that the other very significant part is the fantasy life that is built up around having this loyal, bonded relationship, this blood brother you would do anything for."

In just moments, Baird, tenacious and highly skilled in cross-examining, destroyed the case of mental incapacity that Flora had built during hours of testimony with Froming. Through a series of glaring mistakes, inconsistencies, and unanswered questions, Froming had laid the groundwork for her own demise as an expert witness. Baird connected her lengthy deposition, jailhouse interviews, and her own recent testimony to show a tangle of information and opinions that clearly contradicted one another.

That Froming was too distraught to take notes as Alex recounted the horrific attack was unlikely, Baird suggested to jurors. A more plausible scenario was that Froming didn't take notes during Alex's recollection of the crime because they would have shown his intent. During the jailhouse interviews, Alex told Froming that he and David planned to kill Kim Wilson when she was home during the holiday break. He also recounted how he killed Kim Wilson and then, at the Wilson home, went looking for Julia to kill her, too.

Over the next several hours, by asking a series of pointed questions, Baird blasted Froming's theory that Alex was mentally incapacitated and didn't know what he was doing during the murders.

Froming claimed that Alex showed no signs of premeditation when he talked to her about the crimes. In fact, Alex was so deep into his fantasy world that he thought the murders were merely a game. But Baird easily disproved that in a rapid exchange of question-and-answer.

"He knew what he was doing when he killed Kim Wilson, correct?" Baird asked.

"He did not actively perceive," Froming said.

"Do you think he was tying up a boat at a dock or do you think he was wrapping a rope around a woman's neck?"

"He knew he was tying a rope around a woman's neck, correct."

"And he knew it was wrong, correct?"

"That's correct," Froming admitted.

"All right, now, when he killed William Wilson, he knew what he was doing, correct?"

"He claims he didn't kill William Wilson."

"He acknowledges he attacked Mr. Wilson with a knife, correct?" Baird asked, growing impatient.

"That's correct."

"And you're familiar with the fact that Mr. Wilson's spinal cord was severed and his throat was slashed—you know that, don't you?"

"Yes," Froming said.

"All right. When he did that to Mr. Wilson, he knew what he was doing, correct?"

"Correct."

"He didn't think he was carving a pumpkin?"

"That's correct."

"And he knew that what he was doing was wrong, correct?"

"Correct."

"Now, when he stuck his knife in Mrs. Wilson's head in an effort to stop her from gurgling, he knew what he was doing, correct?"

"Yes."

"And when he went off hunting for Julia, he knew what he was doing?"

"Yes."

"And he knew it was wrong?"

"Yes."

The point was simple: Froming had insisted that Alex

could not have premeditated the murders of the Wilson family because he was not mentally with it, but all along during the attack, she agreed that Alex clearly knew what he was doing. Even if Alex didn't know what he was doing while he attacked the family, there was more than enough evidence and testimony from other witnesses—namely, Sarah Lamp—to show premeditation.

Baird paused briefly, took a sip of water, reloaded, and continued his cross-examination. This time, he pointed out the major flaw in Froming's evaluation of Alex using the MMPI. Baird confronted her with her mistake in stating the ASP abbreviation stood for high aspirations rather than high antisocial practices. Baird asked Froming when she noticed the mistake and why she didn't correct herself later, when she discovered she had made it, or why she didn't at least inform the defense attorneys. Her answer simply was, "I forgot."

By late afternoon on Wednesday, Baird indicated he would need a little more time to question Froming. But by that point, Lynn and Flora were boiling over with anger. In their eyes, Baird had launched an unnecessarily massive assault on their key witness. Clearly irritated, the defense attorneys argued that Froming had already spent two days testifying, and she had to return to her work in California. Spearman suggested the attorneys wait and see what happened by the end of the day, and if Baird needed more time, Froming would have to return on Thursday morning. If not, the defense counsel might have to forgo their right to redirect. With that, he called for the usual fifteen-minute afternoon recess, during which Flora bolted out of his chair and headed toward Baird. "We'll waive our right to redirect so you can ask your stupid questions," Flora said, his face red.

Surprised at the sudden outburst, Baird cut a stern look at Flora and responded, "Get a grip, Counsel."

After everyone returned from the break, Baird took his

time in continuing his cross-examination of Froming. It was
no surprise that he failed to finish by 4 P.M.—the end of the
court day. Froming would have to come back one more day
to face Baird.

The following morning, on October 30, Baird took one
last shot at a wary and frustrated Froming while continuing
to damage her credibililty during cross-examination. He created a hypothetical situation which drove home the point to
the jury that Froming, who occasionally taught psychology
courses, was not to be trusted. She made mistakes and didn't
come clean with them. She contradicted herself in her testimony and in her evaluations of Alex and couldn't explain
why. Baird, in the end, would finally hold her responsible
for her own words.

Baird posed the scenario: "Now, if one of your students
came up to you and said, 'I've got a question. I've been hired
by the defense in an aggravated murder case where the client
has been accused of killing four people and the defense attorneys want to evaluate whether or not he has a mental defense and premeditated the crimes, and I have had an
opportunity to interview him, and I know I'll have to testify
and have to write reports as well,' would you say to this person, 'Well, my advice to you would be go ahead and interview him, but whatever you do, don't ask him anything at all
about the crime . . . ' Would you give him that advice?"

"No," Froming said. "I wouldn't advise him of that."

"But that's what you did?"

"That's correct."

"All right, now, if this person came back to you and said,
'I really made a mistake. I did what you said and I didn't ask
any questions about the crime. I got subjected to cross-examination and I'm going to have to go back and interview . . . ' would you say, 'Whatever you do, ask about the
crime but don't take any notes'?" Baird asked.

"I wouldn't advise him, no," Froming responded warily.

"If one of your students or colleagues said, 'I've got a problem. I've testified in an aggravated murder case. I made a mistake interpreting the MMPI, it's kind of a silly mistake. I saw a peak [representing a high score] on the content scale, I called it aspiration instead of antisocial practices . . . ' would you advise the person, 'The best thing to do is not say anything'?"

"No."

Then, finally, Baird put the finishing touches on a very compelling, and often tense, cross-examination.

"The MMPI is composed of five hundred questions. Number Two-two-three is, 'I very much like hunting,' correct?" Baird asked.

"I don't know. I don't have the manual," Froming said.

"There's two answers, true or false, and Mr. Baranyi said, 'True.' "

"Okay," Froming said, clearly defeated.

"Nothing further."

That day, the prosecution called to the stand Dr. Robert Wheeler, its rebuttal witness—the last person to testify in Alex's murder trial. In the end, when it came down to deciding whether or not Alex was mentally incapacitated at the time of the crime, it would be one psychologist's word against the other's.

On Friday, October 31, Dr. Wheeler, a tall, slim man with dark hair and a beard, approached the witness stand to be sworn in. Like Froming, he also boasted a dizzying résumé of experience and qualifications as a mental health expert.

He had administered the same tests on Alex as Froming had, but his results were markedly different. Wheeler told the jury he believed Alex suffered from a personality disorder marked by aggression, impulsiveness, and lack of empathy. But he knew what he was doing before, during, and after the murders, Wheeler testified.

"He was clearly weighing, reasoning, and deliberating,"

Wheeler said, informing the jury that Alex had told him: "I obviously knew we were going to kill them."

Dr. Wheeler succeeded in disproving Dr. Froming's theory that Alex was so caught up in role-playing games that he was mentally absent when he killed the Wilsons. Alex knew what he was doing and he focused on his mission, Wheeler said.

That Alex used the name Slicer Thunderclap wasn't so much because he believed he was this character as because he wanted to impress his friends, Wheeler explained. It was just a character, and Alex knew he was not a demigod.

The defense asked a few obligatory questions during cross-examination to reintroduce the idea that David was Alex's only friend, but then the lawyers called it quits. Their star witness had been effectively broken down, first by Baird, then by Wheeler.

On Tuesday, November 3, the second and last time Judge Michael Spearman's courtroom would be packed to capacity in this trial, Jeff Baird and later Mark Flora rose to deliver their separate closing arguments. Their comments were similar insofar as both attorneys asked that the jury focus on Alex's mind during the crime. But their opinions diverged from there.

Hoping to win the respect of the jurors, Baird sympathized with their exhaustion and acknowledged their efforts to follow court procedures and the judge's admonishments not to read the paper or watch TV or discuss the case with anybody, even each other.

"Members of the jury, you've heard some terrible things," Baird said in a soft yet assertive voice. "You've seen terrible things. You've been recalled to witness the events of a nightmare which are worse than any of your nightmares, and you've been forced to witness them in silence, suffer the most terrible things in silence. Soon . . . you'll be able to go back to the other jurors and contemplate the terrible things you've seen. And among the terrible things you must contemplate, you must face one more time, is a human mind, a mind with no disorder except one of personality. A mind that on that night felt no empathy, felt no qualms about what he was doing. A mind utterly without mercy."

Baird pleaded with the jury not to make a decision based on sympathy for Alex, but instead, to use reason. No one made Alex kill the Wilsons, Baird argued.

"It's somehow an attractive thought to think the devil made him do it," Baird said, referring to the defense's theory that Alex was simply following David's lead during the murders.

"Now, Mr. Anderson is not on trial. Mr. Anderson's time will come, just as surely as Mr. Anderson's lawyer sat here through some of the proceedings, Mr. Anderson's time will come," Baird said, pointing to Michael Kolker sitting in the back row. "But this is Mr. Baranyi's time. There's something tempting about the idea that he was under the control of someone else. It was outside him. It's an absurd idea, but there's a certain temptation to think he was under the control of someone else the same way that an inanimate toy was under remote control or some kind of remote-control device. And it's absurd because what would this device look like in this case? Did it have three levers: one that said, 'Strangle,' one that said, 'Bludgeon,' one that said, 'Stab'?"

Sympathy, Baird emphatically declared, is not a defense.

As he paced up and down the jury box, Baird acknowledged this was a complicated crime that would leave jurors with many questions, not the least of which was, "Why?"

"Why on earth would two young men from our community cut and beat and stab four people? Why?" Baird asked. "Some kind of morbid curiosity? A mind with complete indifference to anybody's life other than their own? I don't know."

Then Baird turned his remarks to Alex.

"The defendant in this case has certain unalienable rights. He's entitled to a fair trial. He's entitled to a presumption of innocence. He's had all those things, but he's not entitled to a defense," Baird said. "Some folks are just plain guilty."

Baird then reminded the jury of various testimonies from witnesses who portayed Alex as a smart, sane, independent, and pathetic if misunderstood loner who wanted to experience the ultimate thrill of murder. And because of his selfishness, an entire family was dead.

The prosecutor also took one last opportunity to chip away at Dr. Froming's testimony, suggesting that the defense's star witness did more to help the prosecution than the defense. Froming's faulty testimony ended up proving rather than disproving premeditation.

Then, as if to pay homage to the Wilsons one last time before the trial ended, to show the court one last time that these were human beings slaughtered by an inhumane young man, Baird displayed the portraits of each family member which Eakes had first presented in her opening remarks.

"Soon enough, you're going to have to go back and look at how he left them. But it seems to me that you have the right and the victims have the right to see how they were in life. Because if they'd been snuffed out in a traffic accident, they would be remembered as real people. But that's not the way you remember them. You remember them as horribly disfigured people who suffered horrible crimes."

Baird propped each picture up on a TV cart for the jurors to get one more look at Bill, Rose, Kim, and Julia Wilson, each smiling brightly in his or her respective photo. "That's the way they were in life. That's the way they deserve to be remembered until you go back and look at how Alex left them."

Baird wrapped up his closing arguments in about two hours and sat down so Mark Flora could have the jury's attention. By then, the jury was so mesmerized by Baird's incredibly compelling and personal comments that it would take an expert presenter—and an equally persuasive counterargument—to bring the jurors back to center. Flora was far less articulate than Baird, but equally emphatic in his approach.

Flora used barely half an hour to make his closing statements. Referring often to handwritten notes, he began by admitting to the jury that Alex did a stupid thing.

"I submit to you that it's crazy. It's one of the most idiotic, pointless, unfathomable things we can imagine," Flora said.

During the trial, much was made of Alex's high IQ, but Flora asked the jurors not to think that simply because he was intelligent, he was capable of planning the murders.

"You know, from your common sense, he can be extremely bright and extremely nuts," Flora said.

Flora wanted the jury to focus on Alex and the circumstances that had brought him to this courtroom for committing murder—his bad childhood, his dependence on David, his birth into a family that suffered from mental illness.

"Certainly I'm not asking you to think this case is about forgiveness, but what I'm asking you to do is understand. I'm asking you to understand and appreciate the terror and the horror in the Wilson house on the night of the third. We have to go beyond that and try to understand how Mr. Baranyi came to be here on trial. Mr. Baird, a little while ago, made mention of the same issue I talked about, the 'Why?' question."

That answer, while still not totally clear, was wrapped around Alex's manic depression, and his willingness to do anything for his one true friend, David Anderson. Without those things—especially without David's influence—Alex wouldn't be here, Flora said.

On Wednesday, November 4, the jury was finally handed the case and they made quick work of it. After only three and a half hours of deliberation, they found Alex guilty on all four charges of aggravated first-degree murder.

Alex said nothing but smiled at his attorneys before and after the verdict was announced.

"We are obviously very pleased with the verdict, but unfortunately for the family, the case is not concluded," Patty Eakes told reporters. "We're halfway where we need to be."

The trial over, the court went into recess for the holiday season. But everyone would have to return one last time to find out how long Alex would be behind bars.

On January 9, 1999, several days after the second anniversary of the Wilson homicides, Alex Baranyi, chained at the ankles and cuffed at the wrists, walked into Judge Michael Spearman's courtroom to be sentenced. As usual, relatives of the Wilson family took their place behind reporters. A few members of the jury also appeared to hear the sentence.

Baird asked for life without the possibility of parole as he described Alex's crime as "somewhere between murder and genocide."

Flora asked for mercy. He pointed out that Alex's mother and uncles had been present during the entire trial, but were unable to make it to the sentencing because of the long delay between the time the verdict was announced and now.

Judge Spearman finally asked Alex if he had anything to say.

"No," Alex said calmly. "I don't think so."

Spearman explained to Alex that while he believed Alex was capable of doing good things, he was unable to use discretion in sentencing. The evidence overwhelmingly pointed to Alex's guilt. Spearman, his voice cracking, imposed four consecutive terms of life imprisonment without the possibility of parole.

Alex showed no emotion as he signed court documents. As jail officers walked him out of the courtroom and through a hallway of reporters waiting for him, he said only, "I'm ready to get out of the King County Jail."

Within a month, Alex would be moved to a state penitentiary. It would mark a final separation from his blood brother, David, who was still sitting in the King County Jail, waiting for a chance to win back his freedom.

27 During pretrial hearings, David Anderson's lead defense attorney, Michael Kolker, made one last attempt to get a change of venue for his client, arguing that media coverage of the case was so extensive it would be difficult to find an impartial jury in King County. As Judge Bridge had previously done, Judge Spearman denied the motion, but said he might reconsider after the jury selection process started. But that wasn't going to be necessary; among the roughly 1.6 million residents of the county, there were still many who had not heard about the Wilson murders, much less about the juvenile defendants. To weed out prejudiced jurors, the prosecutors and defense attorneys randomly selected prospects among the group and targeted questions to them. The primary questions asked of each person was how much, if anything, he or she had heard about the case, and whether he or she had any connection to the case or anyone involved that might impact the person's opinions. Finally, the attorneys wanted to know whether the prospects had any reason at all to prevent them from making a fair decision at the end of the trial. Everyone who was questioned confidently replied to each answer: "No." On January 21, after two weeks of quizzing a pool of 101 prospective jurors, the attorneys finally selected sixteen among them—ten men and six women—who all swore they would be fair and impartial jurors. Among them, four alternates would be chosen at random in the end and would not be allowed to deliberate.

On Monday morning, January 25, 1999, the ninth floor of the King County Courthouse bustled with the same level of activity outside Judge Michael Spearman's courtroom as it had three months earlier during Alex Baranyi's murder trial. The hallways whirled with commotion as camera crews jockeyed for a good position to get a compelling shot of the second suspect in the Wilson murders.

Just a few weeks after the second anniversary of the Wilson family's deaths, a confident and self-possessed David Anderson was led by two police officers into Judge Spearman's packed courtroom, smiling at his parents before one of the officers took off his handcuffs so he could slide into a seat between his attorneys. But before sitting down, he shook each of his attorneys' hands with a firm grip—a ritual that would occur each day of the trial, and which would help him appear to the court as a young man with good manners. David looked disarming in his choirboy attire of black slacks, a white button-down oxford shirt, and shiny black dress shoes.

Inside the courtroom, the faces in the first two rows— members of the press and relatives of the Wilsons, Bill's sister, Rose's brothers, their in-laws and close family friends—remained the same as in Alex's trial. But unlike in Alex's case, the third row—reserved for family members of the defendant—was packed. David's parents had good company most days of the trial as they sat sandwiched between relatives and friends. During the trial, Leslie Anderson poured her stress and sadness into stitching, working faithfully on an embroidery of the Twenty-third Psalm, the Psalm of David. The hopeful message of the Psalm seemed to be the only thing to calm her nerves, the last line of which reads: "Surely goodness and mercy shall follow me all the days of my life, and I shall dwell in the house of the Lord forever." Bruce Anderson would occasionally bring a stadium seat to provide cushioning on the hard, cold wooden bench. It was as if he were coming to watch a game, there to cheer on his son in a match that involved perhaps the highest stake imaginable—his son's freedom.

Michael Kolker, still leading the defense team, worked closely with his co-counsel, Stephan Illa. Standing just over six feet tall, he towered over everyone else in the courtroom when he wasn't slouching. When he spoke, he often nodded his head and scrunched his eyebrows, joining his fingertips to form a small steeple that he used to point him in a certain direction as he paced up and down the jury row, pensive and engaged. He would prove to be relentless and sharp while cross-examining witnesses, complementing Kolker's aggressive style.

The defense team's strategy in proving their client's innocence was bold, to say the least. They would claim that the night of the Wilson murders, David was driving around in his girlfriend's stepfather's pickup truck. This would be difficult to prove, since Marsha Rash had previously admitted to police that very little gas had been used by the time David returned the vehicle to her. However, what the defense had going for it was a lack of substantial physical evidence—such as fingerprints or footprints—that would directly link David to the crime scenes. Forensic experts did find blood on David's boots, taken from his bedroom during a search, that matched up with blood from two of the victims, but no shoeprints of those particular boots were ever found in the Wilson home.

Nonetheless, the prosecution—once again powered by Jeff Baird and Patty Eakes—felt confident about its case against David Anderson. The prosecutors walked briskly and purposefully into the courtroom each morning, ready to do battle. Alex's trial was a slam dunk for the young attorneys, given his confession both to police and later to friends after the slayings. But David's trial would prove much more challenging, since he didn't confess and vehemently denied being anywhere near the murder scenes the night of the crime. The prosecutors had no luck convincing Alex to rat on his best friend in exchange for a potential lesser sentence. He figured no matter how much his consecutive life terms were lessened, he would probably still be locked up until he died. And he didn't want the label of being a jailhouse snitch, fearing he would be a target once again for bullies. While the prosecutors had no confession from David, they did have enough pieces of the puzzle to place him at the crime scene—his boots, which were a very strong piece of physical evidence, an abundance of circumstantial evidence, and David's own boasts to friends and girlfriends about wanting to commit a major crime before he turned eighteen.

Eakes, who was skilled at laying down the groundwork for her case, once again provided the opening remarks as she had done in Alex's trial, leaving Baird, who had a knack for tying pieces of testimonies and evidence together at the end of a trial, to give the closing arguments. She arrived in court with a computer printout of her opening statements but she glanced down only occasionally at the neat white sheets to stay on track. Baird needed no notes at all to guide him through his closing arguments. Though different in style, both prosecutors were effective.

Obviously well rehearsed, Eakes approached the jury with confidence. Dressed in a black suit and white blouse, Eakes reiterated how the murders had occurred, and how David was a key player in the crime. She set the tone for the trial by first talking about David's relationship with Kim Wilson.

"David Anderson hated Kim Wilson," Eakes announced. "His hatred for Kim Wilson engulfed him. His hatred consumed him and his hatred possessed him. He had no good reason to hate Kim Wilson and he certainly had no good reason to kill Kim Wilson and her entire family."

However, Eakes added, David did have his own reasons for wanting Kim dead. She was a nuisance to him, an unwelcome annoyance that seemed to remain a constant presence in his life. David felt superior over people, and it was a feeling of superiority that engulfed him and made him look down on others, especially Kim.

"In David Anderson's eyes, Kim Wilson was unworthy of him. He considered her beneath him. She wasn't part of the cool crowd. In his eyes, she was overweight . . . a nerd . . . a loser."

Nonetheless, David allowed Kim to associate with him, Eakes said. In return, he expected to be compensated, so he allowed Kim to buy him meals, pay for movies, lend him money, and give him cigarettes. In David's mind, he owed Kim nothing for these things. In fact, he felt she owed him. "Kim Wilson owed him for the pleasure of his occasional company. He made her pay with her life."

Eakes went on to explain how the two dated in junior high school, how Kim fell for David because she thought he was cute and fun. When they broke up, they remained friends, and Kim continued to buy David food and lend him money. But after a while, Kim stood up for herself, Eakes said. She calculated how much money she had loaned him over the course of time and asked David to repay her.

He was insulted, furious that Kim would dare ask for her money back, Eakes reported. He began to loathe her even more. "David Anderson's hatred for Kim Wilson grew over time, like a cancer. It became an obsession."

And so, to extinguish that hatred, he planned to get rid of her. While other teenagers his age were thinking about the prom, David was thinking about murder, Eakes said. Not only did he want Kim exterminated, but he wanted everything close to her gone. But he couldn't kill an entire family alone, so he started tossing around the idea with some friends, to see who among them would be open to joining him. Ultimately, he chose his best friend, Alex Baranyi, as an accomplice and scapegoat, Eakes explained. David knew Alex would do anything for him, and so if police ever became suspicious of him, he could easily blame Alex.

Eakes then described the early bond between David and Kim from childhood up through high school, and how that bond shifted and changed over time. First, they were friends in grade school. Then they dated during the summers in junior high school. Finally, once both were attending the same high school, Kim became a sisterly figure to David, taking him under her wing. Kim never suspected at all that her "little brother" was planning to kill her.

As she did in Alex's trial, Eakes then talked about the victims of David's burning hatred—the Wilson family. As she described the murder scene at the Wilson home, it became clear that the attacker was full of rage: blood in the master bedroom was sprayed onto every wall, and the injuries to Julia especially were unmistakenly gratuitous; she was stabbed three times in her left eye after she had already died.

David made three major mistakes that led to his undoing, Eakes said. The first was that he couldn't resist bragging to friends about his plan to commit murder, at least a couple of years before the crime. The second was that he assumed Alex Baranyi would take the blame for it, but evidence suggested two people attacked the Wilsons. The third was that he failed to get rid of his boots smeared with blood drops that matched the blood of Julia and Bill Wilson.

"That was his worst mistake," Eakes said. David did a good job getting rid of the clothes and the murder weapons, but he kept his boots. "And now David Anderson sits here today, perhaps incapable of even understanding his flawless plan failed."

As Eakes took her seat, Michael Kolker hurried to face the jury as if to stave off any spare moment in which thoughts of guilt could creep into the jurors' minds. He seemed in a frenzy to find a way to break down the blame Eakes had placed on his client. He spoke in short, emphatic sentences, capping them with a resounding "Period" and pausing between transitions to look at his handwritten notes and gather his thoughts. Rather than presenting evidence of innocence, Kolker instead focused his opening remarks on the state's strategy of guilt by association, which he argued was invalid.

"Ladies and gentlemen, David Anderson has never killed anybody in his entire life," Kolker began. "It is true that David and Alex were friends. That looks bad for David because we know Alex is guilty."

As David blamed his best friend for the murders, so, too, did Kolker. "Alex murdered this family on January 3, 1997. It is important to remember David and Alex were not roommates." Three items that were taken from the Wilson home and tested positive for Bill Wilson's blood were found in a storage room near Alex's bedroom at the Boyd house, Kolker said. Forensic experts also found a handprint made in blood on the items. "There was not one of the items in David Anderson's house, because David didn't do it. The only fingerprints police found were Alex Baranyi's fingerprints." He then added, "What Alex did to those people was brutal. He stabbed and beat those people to death."

Kolker continued offering more and more evidence against Alex, turning the focus away from his client. Kolker said the jury could expect to see horrible crime-scene and autopsy photographs during the trial. "These same photos will demonstrate David did not do it. He wasn't there. Alex did it alone."

Before the state even had a chance to put its first witness on the stand and present evidence against David, Kolker already mentioned a part of the state's lineup and how witness testimony and evidence the state planned to produce would attest to David's innocence.

It was true that David admitted driving Marsha Rash's stepfather's pickup truck the night of the murders, but prosecutors were unable to find physical evidence of the crime inside the vehicle.

"Terry McAdam, he examined this truck for blood. He will tell you on the floor mat he found a small stain that tested positive for blood. They found biological material. They specifically excluded every one of the Wilson family [members]. There were no hairs from David Anderson in the Wilson home. There were no hairs in the truck. There is not one fingerprint in the Wilson home, period."

The Wilson home was covered with more than 160 bloody shoeprints, but none of them matched the leather boots taken from David's bedroom. The only evidence found—the VCR, CD player, and phone—was taken from Alex's room, not David's.

"The only evidence they have against David Anderson is guilt by association."

But it wasn't entirely true. While Kolker delivered a provocative opening statement, he failed to mention that a pair of David's boots taken from his closet had Julia's bloodstains on them. "The only thing that proves is those shoes were in the house," Kolker told the jury. "It doesn't prove David Anderson was wearing those shoes," he said, suggesting the attacker had borrowed his shoes.

In closing, Kolker suggested David's boasts about murder were nothing more than idle bantering to his friends. "When he was a kid, David talked about committing a murder, but none of them took him seriously because he wasn't." Those friends, Kolker added, were part of what has been called the Denny's crowd. Kolker proceeded to list, by name, members of that crowd, of which David was a part. The group members dyed their hair and wore black clothing, dark makeup, and fangs. They also liked playing fantasy role-playing games, and computer fantasy games like Dungeons and Dragons, Vampire the Masquerade, and Rifts.

"Members of this group engaged in talk of committing a crime. All it was was talk. They were bored, alienated teenagers. They played these kinds of games, talked about these things."

One of David's friends in the Denny's crowd was Kim Wilson. Similar to Eakes' opening remarks, Kolker's also spoke of the friendship between David and Kim, but provided a much different slant. "David had only good things to say about Kim Wilson," Kolker recounted. And like any friend, Kim Wilson helped David when he was in trouble. He ran away from home at one point, and Kim took him out to eat. David signed a promissory note agreeing to pay Kim back, though he wasn't happy about it, Kolker added. But it was nothing he was too upset about. Nothing that would compel him to murder.

That afternoon, on the first day of trial, the state put on the stand the same lineup of witnesses as in Alex's trial. Julia Mahoney once again spoke of the shock she experienced after learning her family was murdered; Jeff Gomes spoke briefly about the layout of the crime scenes; Erin Gauntlett and Sky Stewart talked about the last time they saw their friend.

The next two days would be more of the same witnesses who testified for the state in Alex's trial. On the afternoon of January 26, Jeff Gomes, dressed in his usual formal attire, took the stand to detail how he came across the bloody bodies of the Wilson family on a routine visit to the home to give the family the news that Kim had died.

As he took this new jury through the events of that day in January 1997, starting at Water Tower Park, where he saw

Kim's body, he spoke again with precision and poise. For two years, Gomes had lived and breathed the Wilson homicide case, and for the most part, he did not let the tragedy get to him. But on that day, his thick shell cracked. As he spoke about searching the home and stumbling upon the bodies, his voice gave way to the emotional trauma he had felt.

"There was blood everywhere around the body," Gomes told the jury, talking about Julia. "I didn't even have to touch her. I knew she was dead."

Gomes briefly lost his composure while describing how he exited the house out of the same sliding glass door and told Eakes and the medical examiners what he saw. His eyes welled with tears. Eakes paused momentarily as Gomes reached for a handkerchief and gently dabbed his eyes, proceeding to tell jurors how he then led the prosecutor and the medical examiners back into the home so they could see for themselves the carnage inside.

Detective John McBride finished off that day's court testimonies and started the following morning's witness testimony by describing to the jurors David's reaction when questioned about the murders, how he had seemed bored, unemotional, and unengaged, which was odd considering someone he counted as a friend had just been murdered. David was polite and cooperative, which led McBride and his wife to believe he had nothing to do with the crime.

That morning, two new witnesses took the stand—Danielle Berry and Amryn Decker, David's ex-girlfriends whom he specifically talked to about committing murder.

Berry was first. She was an effective witness, somewhat bubbly but quick to respond and compliant. Wearing a blue shirt with black pants, black combat-type shoes, and glasses, the blond-haired young woman appeared studious, with an educational background that matched the image; she told jurors she was a premed major at the University of Washington.

Patty Eakes questioned the nineteen-year-old about her relationship with David, which was short-lived and filled with the normal teenage dating activities like talking on the phone each night, taking walks, going to movies, and hanging out at the mall. One of David's favorite places to take walks with his girlfriends was Water Tower Park, Berry said, which "he knew like the back of his hand."

After allowing Berry to talk about her activities with David, and then about David's relationship with Alex, Eakes directed her questioning to a time, several years earlier, when both she and David were fifteen years old.

"Can you tell the jury, did David Anderson ever talk to you about committing a murder?" Eakes asked.

"Yes, he did, many times," Berry said.

"Did he say things to you about committing a murder in general without naming a specific victim?"

"Yes, he did. When I was hanging around him and dating him, he talked many times about that. He specifically said he had done research and he was going to commit a murder before he turned eighteen. I think eight or nine times [he told me]. He casually mentioned he knew the laws and knew how to get around them."

"What did he think would happen to him if he committed a murder, in terms of the legal repercussions before he turned eighteen?" Eakes asked.

"Being that he would have been a minor . . . he would get a lesser sentence."

"He thought he would be tried as a juvenile?"

"Yes."

Eakes wanted to know how Berry reacted to her then boyfriend's candid discussion about wanting to commit a murder.

"Obviously, I was quite frightened. I didn't really know

people had discussions like that. I was frightened and scared and perplexed by the whole situation," she said.

David, who had been taking notes during Berry's testimony, stopped writing and gripped his pen hard, his hand turning red as he appeared to scowl at his ex-girlfriend.

"Did he tell you why it was he wanted to kill somebody?"

"Um, he said he wanted to experience the power of killing someone in his own hands . . . He was unhappy with the situation he was in and he wanted to experience some change in his life," Berry said. "He talked in detail. He said it was going to be very violent. He said it was going to be a very special murder and he wanted his victims to feel pain. He wanted them to experience the pain he felt all his life."

The weapons he procured were a metal baseball bat and knives, Berry said. "He had played baseball and was skilled. He said he was going to use a metal baseball bat and he had a large collection of knives and he said he was skilled at [baseball] and would show off his skill."

Berry told the jury she was disturbed about the conversations and would try to change the topic each time David brought it up. But she chose not to tell anyone because she didn't want to believe he was actually serious.

Eakes wrapped up her questioning by asking Berry about the Gothic subculture and whether David was part of that community. Berry explained the term and said David wasn't necessarily a Goth, but that he wore black clothes because the color was easy to match.

On cross-examination, the defense tried to show the witness's personal motive for testifying against David. Kolker immediately asked how and why her relationship with David ended. He suggested it was because she found out David was dating her best friend at the time, Amryn Decker. Even after Berry denied that was the case, Kolker continued to badger her to admit it was true.

Eakes objected to Kolker's aggressive pursuit of the

state's witness, angry that Kolker kept cutting Berry off in the middle of her sentences. Judge Spearman sustained the objection, and Kolker toned down his cross-examination.

Berry had already told jurors that she was frightened when David started talking about murder, but she continued to date him—something that Kolker picked up on and ran with. He wanted to show the jury she was full of contradictions.

"Did you break up with him after the first time he told you [about the murder plan]?" Kolker asked.

"No, I did not."

"Did you break up with him after the second time?"

"No."

"You didn't think it was necessary to tell anybody?"

"No."

With that, Kolker thanked the witness and confidently walked back to his seat.

That afternoon, jurors heard from Amryn Decker, who told essentially the same story that Danielle Berry had of David discussing his plans to commit a major crime. Heather Herberg, a former Woodridge resident who knew David, also took the stand, and told the court David approached her one day while she was playing at the park and said he was planning to murder a family. Then, as the afternoon came to a close, Ed Sheridan and his mother, Christine, told jurors about the odd behavior of both David and Alex, who kept walking in and out of the Boyd house on the night of the murders.

During the trial, as witnesses spoke candidly of David's life and the plans he had made, the defendant sat quietly in his chair, making eye contact with no one, except for a glimpse or a glare at various witnesses. Every now and again, he turned to look back at the gallery to see who had come to support him. He whispered often into the ears of his attorneys, seemingly urgent whispers sometimes accompanied by the shaking of his head. The content of those whispers was unknown until the fourth day of the trial, when David spoke up.

In a closed-door meeting with the judge and his attorneys, David said he wanted to fire Michael Kolker, who he believed was not providing a good defense and was ignoring his suggestions on how to cross-examine various witnesses.

But Spearman was not convinced that Kolker was acting unprofessionally or performing poorly. Spearman denied the request in open court.

"I have seen no indications his performance has been deficient in any way," he said. Spearman worried that bringing in a new attorney at this point would only delay the trial much longer than necessary. "Things can be tense when you're in trial," he said, looking at both Kolker and David. "Try to get along with each other a little better."

For the rest of the trial, David continued to shake hands with Kolker, but the tension remained between them.

That afternoon, Ron Boyd and his son Bob took the stand to answer a series of questions put by Baird which locked David into a time frame. Bob told the jurors he had been playing Nintendo games with several friends in Alex's room the night of the murders, and he watched David and Alex leave the house at around 10:30 P.M. Bob's testimony was crucial to the prosecution in order to show that David had lied to detectives when he said he was playing video games with Alex all night in Alex's bedroom, and to show that he could not be accounted for during the time frame when the Wilsons were murdered. Ron Boyd, who worked a graveyard shift as a truck driver and so stayed up late, said he didn't see Alex come home until around 3:30 A.M. Saturday morning. He was accompanied by none other than David Anderson. The best friends left the Boyd residence together, and they returned together. It would be nearly impossible for

David's attorneys to somehow get him out of that time frame.

On Monday, February 2, as David's trial entered its second week, prosecutors used his own words to incriminate him. The prosecution called Marsha Rash, David's ex-girlfriend whom he was dating at the time of the murders, to the witness stand as a way of introducing a damning handwritten note she found while going through boxes at home. Although vague in its meaning, the note suggested David intended to harm Kim Wilson. Rash took the note to police. On a sheet of notebook paper, possibly a journal entry that David apparently wrote sometime in 1995, he talked about his fear of his own friend Alex Baranyi: "I have every cause to fear him as much as he should fear me, but we are the best of friends—or so he pretends," David wrote. Jurors followed along on a poster-size blowup of the note. "Possibly he is trying to do the same thing to me as I will do to Kim."

Despite the implication that David would harm Kim, Kolker was quick to point out that the note was written long before the murders, and it was much too vague to conclude that David planned to kill her.

That day, prosecutors also called to the witness stand a DNA expert who testified that blood found on David's boots, taken from his bedroom, matched that of Julia and Bill Wilson.

Jurors also heard from Ricky Nelson, a Woodridge resident who drove past Water Tower Park at around midnight the night of the murders and saw a black pickup truck with a young woman sitting on the hood and a young man next to her. While the prosecutors had no concrete evidence that those two people were in fact David and Kim, it seemed likely that that was the case. And if so, that would lock David into an even tighter time frame: He left the Boyd house with Alex at around 10:30 P.M., was seen at Water Tower Park at midnight, and was back at the Boyd house at around 3:30 A.M. the following day. Piece by piece, the prosecution was retracing David's tracks that night so the jury could see the fragments of the story fit together logically and sequentially, and they would have to conclude that David was guilty.

The following day proved to be one of the most dramatic days in David Anderson's trial. On February 3, Prosecutor Patty Eakes called to the stand expert witness Terry McAdam, of the state's crime lab, who would testify to the bloodbath found in the Wilson home. However, he told the jury he found no blood in the pickup truck David was driving that night.

This forced Eakes to pursue a different approach to this witness's testimony regarding blood evidence. Eakes asked McAdam about a recently tried case in which two men killed a South Park couple and their dog in 1996 and the getaway car did not have blood in it. However, one man had the dog's blood on his clothes, and the men were convicted based on analysis of the dog's DNA, which was a legal first.

Clearly angry about McAdam's testimony, Kolker leapt out of his chair and snapped at the prosecution's expert witness. "Could another explanation be that the person didn't have any blood on them?" Kolker asked. "Have you ever heard the expression 'presumption of innocence,' Mr. McAdam?"

The outburst prompted Spearman to call for a break, at which time the jury was ushered out of the courtroom. Kolker immediately asked for a mistrial, suggesting Eakes had improperly questioned her witness.

"Any other results in any other case are totally irrelevant to this case," he said. "It is an attempt by the prosecution to explain why [McAdam] found no evidence and use that as evidence against [Anderson]."

But Spearman refused to end the trial, adding that it would become an important issue if the case were to ever go to appeal. Instead, he called the jurors back and asked them to disregard the mention of a verdict in the case McAdam had referred to.

After McAdam was excused, the prosecution introduced Dr. Richard Harruff, who would begin his lengthy and detailed testimony on the wounds inflicted onto each member of the Wilson family.

On Thursday, February 5, a surly Michael Anderson took the stand to tell the jurors that yes, his younger brother had signed a promissory note to repay Kim Wilson $350, but it was not something David was overly upset about. Michael Anderson was an unwilling witness from the start, refusing to submit to a pretrial interview with the prosecutors until Judge Spearman ordered him to do so a couple of weeks before the trial began.

On the night of the murders, he told the jury, he was out dancing with some friends and returned home after midnight. Shortly thereafter, he went into Marsha Rash's room to wake her up to see if she was interested in accompanying him to Denny's. Rash got dressed and the pair hung out for several hours, drinking coffee and smoking. By the time they returned, around 5:30 A.M., David was home, but already in a deep slumber.

In the third week of the trial, the prosecution presented one more witness, who would provide a detailed description of at least two conversations he had had with David in which David explicitly spoke of his intent to murder.

Mike Dickinson entered the courtroom dressed in the professional attire of a suit and tie and shiny shoes. Dickinson was a polite, ordinary young man, slight and clean-cut. He started his sentences with phrases such as, "I do believe that . . ." He told the jurors he met David Anderson in middle school and quickly became friends with him. But Alex considered him nothing more than a tagalong, someone whom he would have to compete with for attention from

David. The two remained friends through the eighth grade and into the early part of high school. Now Dickinson was nineteen years old, working at a sporting-goods store in downtown Bellevue.

Prosecutor Jeff Baird allowed for only a short introduction, then got down to business. In asking Dickinson to describe when he first heard about the murders, and then who he thought might be involved and why, Baird drew out detailed and chilling responses from the dark-haired young man that left the jurors stunned.

Dickinson told the jurors during Christmas of 1995, he was spending the night with David when David first brought up his plot to kill a family. David told Dickinson a group of people were in on the plan; the murder weapons had already been procured and were being stashed underneath his bed. Dickinson told how, at David's prompting, he reached under the bed and pulled out a black nylon pouch with several knives, including a butcher knife and paring knives.

"Did David Anderson go on to say how these knives would be used by him and his accomplice or accomplices?" Baird asked.

"They would be used on any major arteries, neck, heart, whatever," Dickinson said.

"Did he ask you to join him?"

"Yes, and I said no. I was invited and I turned it down."

Dickinson went on to say David admitted killing people before, which Dickinson believed was a lie. David had also asked Dickinson not to tell anyone about the plan, specifically Alex Baranyi, which he agreed to.

Then Baird wanted to know whether at that time Kim was still friends with David. Dickinson said Kim regarded David as a good friend, but that feeling was not mutual.

"Did you hear Mr. Anderson make comments about Kim Wilson?"

"Just that she irritated him. She rubbed him the wrong way."

"Did he tell why Kim irritated him or rubbed him the wrong way?"

"He was irritated by her weight. I'm not sure why."

Dickinson then described the second time David brought up the murder plan.

"I do believe I was at Ground Zero," Dickinson said. He and David were playing pool at the favorite downtown Bellevue teen nightclub when David approached him.

"He mentioned they were on the list. They were on the list to be taken out of families that could be taken out," Dickinson said.

While Dickinson was an effective witness, Kolker, in a short exchange with him, raised a specter of doubt as to the witness's credibility.

"He told you he had already committed fifteen murders?"

"Yes," Dickinson said. "I assumed it was not the truth."

"He was telling you this in a sarcastic sort of way?"

"Yes."

"After he told you this, you did, in fact, spend the night?" Kolker asked.

"Yes."

"You weren't afraid of him?"

"No."

The point was well taken. If David were serious about killing a family, wouldn't Dickinson be scared of spending the night? But on redirect, Baird gained back whatever ground he might have lost to Kolker during cross-examination.

Kolker finished his cross-examination by asking Dickinson about the pretend sword-fighting game called Kinabota, which David was known to play. The game involved using fake swords and costumes; Dickinson said he occasionally played along. In bringing up the game, Kolker seemed to suggest that the weapons David kept under his bed were nothing more than props for it. But Baird would have a chance to clarify that in redirect.

"Mr. Dickinson, you said you were not afraid to spend the night at David Anderson's house even after he made these statements to you. Is that because he didn't threaten to kill you and your family?" Baird asked.

"No," Dickinson said. "He's my friend. I saw no reason why I would be threatened."

"Now, when you looked under the bed at his suggestion, you did not find Kinabota swords under the bed, did you?"

"I think those were in the closet."

"But he didn't direct you to the closet where the fake swords were, did he?"

"No, he did not."

Baird made it clear to the jurors that David was not playing live-action role-playing games when he revealed his plans for murder to Dickinson. He knew what he was doing. He had stashed weapons—*real* weapons—under his bed. He was planning and calculating every part of the scheme, and he would carry it out with surprising precision.

28 Each day, at the end of court, Judge Michael Spearman smiled at the jurors in appreciation and reminded them of several basic admonitions to abide by as jury members. These included not talking to anyone about the case, including their spouses, co-workers, and each other, not reading newspapers or watching the news, and reporting anything they overheard which had anything to do with David Anderson's murder trial. The rules are set in place to ensure that the jurors remain unbiased about the case and that the defendant has a fair trial. Serving on a jury—especially on a major murder case that will inevitably take up substantial time and emotional energy—can often be one of the hardest public tasks. The rule concerning not talking about the case is especially difficult; it's an extraordinary act in isolation and discipline. When faced with compelling information or stories, people naturally want to talk. But for a juror, even the slightest mention of the case at hand could warrant removal from the jury box.

On Tuesday, February 17, that very scenario played out in Spearman's courtroom. During the previous week, after several jurors had completed a jigsaw puzzle in the jury room, the group began brainstorming for a title. Juror No. 4, a young woman who appeared attentive during trial, suggested using the title "He's Guilty." Bothered and embarrassed by what she had said, she later came forward with the information and underwent a barrage of questioning from

270

both the judge and the attorneys. The juror insisted that she had not decided David was a murderer; she had simply made a joke. As expected, Kolker asked that the woman be removed from the jury panel; the prosecutors didn't argue with the request. While the comment was made in jest, it was enough for Spearman to dismiss the woman.

"I don't have any doubt she made a careless comment and it truly didn't reflect her state of mind at the time," Spearman said, adding, "Sometimes the appearance of fairness is just as important as fairness itself."

Spearman thanked the woman for informing the court about her comment and for her service during the previous three weeks. The juror rushed out of the courtroom, her face flushed, clearly upset at the decision to remove her. And while it was not a major decision in the case, it would demonstrate Spearman's conservative nature in erring on the side of caution to make sure David received as fair a trial as possible.

With the woman's dismissal, fourteen jurors remained (one had previously been dismissed because of an illness). Each of the remaining jury members was questioned individually as to whether or not he or she had heard the comment; only one had, and she'd dismissed the comment.

Spearman called for a recess, after which the courtroom, without the jury present, heard preliminary testimony from who was quite likely the surliest witness on the case.

Tony Bolton, a career criminal with a reputation as a jailhouse informer, was serving a two-year term for possession of stolen property and stealing a car. He shuffled into the courtroom, his ankles in chains and his wrists in cuffs. Dressed in red jail pajamas, the short, dark-haired man with a mustache took his oath and then slouched back in his seat, glaring at David as he waited to be questioned.

He was to testify that David confessed to him in jail that

he killed Kim Wilson and was present while his friend killed the remaining three members of the Wilson family. But the defense requested that Spearman bar that testimony from court, suggesting Bolton was being compensated to testify for the state. To prove its case, the defense argued Bolton had testified on several other occasions in exchange for a lesser sentence, or cash. In one case in Snohomish County, north of Seattle, Bolton earned a lesser sentence after he testified against a defendant.

But the prosecution emphatically denied making any deals with Bolton. Rather, it said he had come forward on his own.

"He's been offered nothing," Prosecutor Eakes said. "And we've made it clear to him on more than one occasion that we don't intend to offer him anything."

Kolker aggressively questioned Bolton about his criminal past and his alleged deals with a prosecutor in neighboring Pierce County on at least one case in which he provided jailhouse information to police. Unmistakably annoyed by Kolker's badgering, Bolton spiked his responses with "Like I told you . . ." and "Weren't you listening?" When asked about getting compensated for basically snitching on fellow inmates, Bolton snapped at Kolker, "I'm not getting anything. I'm doing this because the guy's a creep."

Judge Spearman rejected the defense's request to prevent Bolton from testifying, saying there was no evidence thus far to prove the prosecutors had made any such deals with Bolton. Bolton was scheduled to testify later in the trial, but ultimately, the prosecutors weren't sure whether the jury would believe him; they elected not to put him on the stand.

The following day, the state's case culminated with testimony from Ross Gardner, a Georgia-based crime-scene analyst who was considered one of the best in his field. He wore a suit and spoke with a faint down-home Southern drawl, punctuating his sentences with "Yes, sir," and "Absolutely, sir." Gardner had expertise at analyzing blood spatter to indicate in what direction the attack occurred, and, perhaps more important, just how many people were involved in the attack. Gardner painstakingly measured a substantial sample of blood drops throughout the room, on the walls, on the furniture, on clothes. He documented approximately how high or low each drop had landed, and the size of those drops. That information was then transferred into a computer database program that calculates with geometric accuracy exactly in which direction the attack occurred, who died first, and how many people were involved in each attack. It would be a lengthy, daylong education in blood-spatter analysis that, because of its complicated nature, would require closer scrutiny than the state's prior expert-witness testimony.

Kolker had maintained all along that Alex Baranyi alone killed the Wilson family. But he failed to explain exactly how David's shoes ended up with the blood of both Julia and Bill Wilson. Now he would be faced with having to prove Gardner's highly technical theory was wrong.

According to his analyses, Gardner concluded that Rose Wilson was attacked first as she lay sleeping in bed. The back of Bill Wilson's T-shirt was stained with his wife's blood, which suggests he was still lying in bed with his back turned to her while she was attacked. Bill apparently got up and was subsequently attacked with the knife, Gardner testified. He tried to escape from the killers and made it to the foot of the bed, where Gardner says he was simultaneously beaten and stabbed from two distinct directions.

To help the jury visualize the attack on Bill Wilson, Gardner asked Prosecutor Baird and Detective Jeff Gomes to help him demonstrate. Baird got down on his hands and knees while Gomes stood in one spot and Gardner stood in the other. Gardner used a pointing stick in place of a bat, and Gomes was armed with a wooden ruler. The jurors got up to get a closer look and also focused on a computer screen which depicted a man on his hands and knees with vertical planes protruding from him that indicated the directions of blood spatter.

Gardner had also tested David Anderson's boots and testified those shoes were only a few feet away from Julia as she was coughing up blood.

There was little the defense could do to break down the scientific data that strongly suggested two people were in the Wilson home. Nonetheless, they wasted no opportunity in cross-examining witnesses.

After some three and a half hours of testimony, Baird finally finished his questioning, and Stephan Illa rose to ask some of his own questions. He wanted the jury to know an important point—that Gardner had never been inside the Wilson home, and was basing his analysis on crime-scene photographs and a crime-scene video detectives had made. Not only had Gardner never stepped foot inside the Wilson home, he'd been hired more than a year after the murders.

Illa also tried to suggest that because Gardner was hired by the state—which he repeatedly referred to as "the government" during cross-examination—Gardner would provide test results that proved favorable for the prosecution. Finally, Illa brought up the fact that Gardner had never been a witness for the defense, suggesting that he had a bias and possibly a personal agenda.

"In all the times you have testified, you have never testified on behalf of someone accused of a crime, like Mr. Anderson?"

"As an expert, no, sir," Gardner said.

"That's all I have, thank you."

"Yes, sir."

The judge asked Baird if he had any redirect questions. As usual, Baird quickly followed up to set the record straight.

"Yes, the *government* has a few questions," Baird said

with a faint smirk on his face. The response drew chuckles out of several jurors and court spectators.

It was true: Gardner had never testified on behalf of a defendant, Baird conceded. However, he had been previously summoned by defense attorneys to examine blood in preparation of other trials. In fact, when Gardner first started his consulting practice, about 60 percent of his business came from defense attorneys, Baird told the jurors. But for whatever reason, he was never actually called to testify.

"Does it make any difference in your actual analyses or the methods you employ whether you're hired by a defense attorney or prosecutor?" Baird asked.

"No, sir, not at all."

On Monday, February 23, David Anderson arrived in court wearing corduroy pants and a sweater vest over a cotton shirt. He sported a buzz cut, which made him look as if he were in some sort of boot-camp training. That morning, the prosecution took a swipe at the defense's theory that Alex Baranyi single-handedly attacked the Wilsons by asking its last witness, Jeff Gomes, absurd questions about Alex's feet.

First, Baird asked Gomes to describe Alex's build. Then Baird asked specifically about Alex's feet.

"Is there any doubt in your mind Mr. Baranyi had two arms and two feet?" Baird asked.

"No."

The defense's theory was irrational because it was obvious two different pairs of shoes were in the home—the ones that made the diamond-patterned print on Bill Wilson's T-shirt, and David's blood-spattered boots.

Baird thanked Gomes and then rested the state's case.

Immediately after Gomes left the stand, Michael Kolker brought in the defense's first witness, Lynn McIntyre, a forensic scientist for the Washington State Patrol Crime Lab. McIntyre was hired by the defense to analyze bags full of items taken by police from David Anderson's bedroom and the rental home he shared with his brothers, including baseball bats, knives, and clothing. None of the items had blood on them, she testified.

But that didn't necessarily prove anything, because the murder weapons and the clothes worn at the crime scene were never found. Those items could have been burned, stashed, or dumped somewhere.

Kolker next called Troy Anderson to take the stand. The second oldest Anderson son made light of the fact that his younger brother liked collecting swords; he did, too, he told the jurors. It was no big deal.

"I have a very nice interest in knives," he said. "It's a collection. I find them very nice to look at. It's not like I take 'em out and see what kind of damage they can do."

Hoping to establish the possibility that the Wilson killer borrowed David's shoes the night of the crime, Kolker asked Anderson whether the best friends borrowed each other's clothes. On occasion, David wore Alex's shoes, Troy Anderson said. But he never said whether Alex wore David's shoes. And it would have been unlikely, since Alex's feet were much larger than David's.

Next, Jeannie Kern took the stand. She was nineteen now and pregnant, dressed more conservatively yet casually in blue jeans and a sweater, rather than in her now-infamous attire of a black-lace dress and combat boots. But she still wore dark eyeliner and her hair was dyed black. She was to testify that her brother, Joe Kern, received a phone call from David the night of the murders. But just as Kolker worked his way up to that point, the prosecution objected on grounds of hearsay. Judge Spearman sustained the objection and Kolker ended his questioning.

The jury finally heard from Laurie Buehler, who continued to cast David in a favorable light, and by the end of the afternoon, the defense had wrapped up its case.

* * *

On Tuesday morning, February 23, a little more than four weeks after the trial of David Anderson began, attorneys were ready to give their closing arguments. Once again, the hallway outside Judge Michael Spearman's courtroom became the center of attention at the courthouse as reporters waited for the suspected killer to appear. At the opposite end of the hall, David's family stood huddled together, refusing to talk to any reporters. Bruce Anderson glared at any reporter who passed by to get a drink of water from a faucet near where the relatives had gathered.

Jeff Baird, dressed in the same black, pinstriped suit he had been wearing every day of the trial, delivered a compelling and resonant speech. He started by talking about David's youngest victim.

"Julia. That was the worst of it, wasn't it. That's where Mr. Anderson finally stopped. That's where he left us, with Julia," Baird said. "We'll follow a path Mr. Anderson chose for us when he took a path directly through the lives of the Wilsons, as he destroyed them one by one."

During Baird's speech, relatives and friends of the Wilson family wept and hugged each other. They had sat through two intense and tedious murder trials and they were exhausted, now only wanting the second suspect in their family's murder case to be brought to justice.

Baird went on to summarize the unanswered questions still remaining at the end of the trial: Did David Anderson kill Kim Wilson? Why did David and Alex take Kim's glasses and wallet? How did Julia and Bill's blood get onto David's boots? Was there a conceivable possibility that David was innocent?

"The truth is that the defendant is guilty beyond a reasonable doubt."

Baird then echoed Eakes' opening statement by talking about hate, and how David's hatred for Kim sparked a homicidal impulse that resulted in a rampage. "You know more about hatred that you ever hoped to know," he said.

The presecutor asked that the jurors use common sense when making their decision. He reminded them how Claire Hearn had testified that Kim was leery of Alex. Evidence suggests she wasn't forced to go to Water Tower Park that night. It made sense that David lured her there. And she was so comfortable with him that night that she smoked a cigarette while walking with him through the trails. Detective Jerry Johnson found that cigarette butt with her saliva near where her body lay under the cedar tree. "There's no way Kim Wilson would have walked up to a dark, secluded park with Alex Baranyi," Baird said. He added, "She was in the presence of someone she trusted, someone she thought was a friend, and that was a fatal mistake."

As he continued to draw on the previous two weeks' testimony, the jury seemed mesmerized, with pensive looks on their faces. He brought up important evidence and key testimonies, the most bizarre of which, he said, was that of Sarah Lamp. Lamp had told jurors that she, David, and Alex discussed killing only if they were forced to during a burglary. But that seemed odd to Baird. Why would anyone kill someone over a few insignificant possessions like a VCR or a telephone? After the Wilson murders, she neglected to come forward with crucial information about David and Alex. Baird also pointed out how Lamp had described her discussions with David and Alex about murder in a nonchalant manner.

Finally, the prosecutor talked about the gratuitous wounds to the bodies of Bill, Rose, and, especially, Julia. "Someone went through the trouble, after her throat was slashed, of taking a small knife and stabbing her in the left eye," he said.

Clearly, the killers were enjoying their work. And the facts spoke for themselves, Baird suggested.

"We know that he's guilty. Guilty of killing Bill, Rose, and Kim, and finally, of Julia."

Michael Kolker wanted to remind the jury that the sole suspect in the Wilson homicide case had already been convicted. "The prosecutors' case depends on you being so shocked, so horrified, and so scared by what Alex Baranyi did that you either won't realize or won't care that they have no evidence David Anderson was there," Kolker said.

He said that the evidence and the witness testimony the state had provided in its case only proved his client was innocent. "They don't have evidence. They have a lack of evidence plus an explanation," Kolker said, referring to Terry McAdam's testimony, in which McAdam tried to explain why no blood was found in the black pickup truck David was driving the night of the crime. "Clothes were never found, possibly because he wasn't there, so there would be no bloody clothes," Kolker said.

Turning to David's boots, Kolker made the leap that if David's boots were in the Wilson home with all the blood spilled, there would have been shoeprints left by those boots. It was one of many mysteries that would remain unanswered.

"You may hate David Anderson," Kolker finally said. "It's okay. He hasn't done much in his life for you to like him. A lot of people will be happy if you find David guilty. It is not your job to make people feel better."

It was 1:30 P.M. Judge Spearman advised the jurors to return to the jury room and begin their deliberations. Two alternates were excused, leaving a final jury of eight men and four women to decide David Anderson's fate.

After two and a half hours of deliberation on that Tuesday, February 24, the jury had not reached a decision. For the next few days, the jury would continue to struggle to come to an agreement. As time wore on, it became clear the jury was in a deadlock. Finally, by Friday, the jury foreman sent out the first word since deliberations had begun. He wrote a note to the judge indicating he and his fellow jurors were deadlocked. But Spearman urged the jurors to try again to reach a verdict.

Members of the media and the Anderson family kept a close vigil on the ninth floor of the King County Courthouse, bringing books to read and pacing up and down the hallways. Baird and Eakes watched matinees at a new cinema in downtown Seattle to avoid obsessing over how the jury was deliberating. After a while, the young prosecutors' hope for a conviction began to flag. In general, a quick return on a verdict points to a conviction, and the longer it takes for a jury to complete deliberation, the more likely the jurors will return a verdict of innocence, an acquittal, or a hung jury.

A stunning eight days had elapsed before the agonizing was over. Spearman's courtroom brimmed with people once again on Thursday, March 4, as the jury reconvened. Baird and Eakes knew whatever the judge had to say couldn't be good. After everyone settled into their seats, Spearman announced a hung jury. David would have to face a new trial.

Instantly, word got out that a single juror—Lanette Inmann of Kirkland, Washington, who allegedly bore a grudge against the police and the judicial system—had stonewalled her fellow jurors since the deliberations had begun, reportedly refusing to convict David because she had undergone an acrimonious divorce with her ex-husband, a cop.

In a closed-door interview with the jurors after the mistrial, jurors told the prosecutor Inmann refused to convict David Anderson because she had a personal mistrust of police.

"She sabotaged the case," Baird said, a comment widely reported in the press. He was frustrated that this woman with what he saw as an obvious agenda had somehow slipped through the cracks and made it onto the jury.

Kolker said Baird's criticism was a cheap shot and accused the prosecutors of blaming the juror for their own failure to successfully prove David guilty.

While Inmann indicated during jury selection that she had been married to a policeman, she failed to say, after being asked, that she harbored biases that would affect her opinion in this case. Because that was simply a lie by omission, there was little the prosecutors could do after the mistrial had already been announced.

In the jury room, evidence of the tremendous effort the jurors had made to convince Inmann that David was guilty beyond a reasonable doubt was strewn everywhere—400 pieces of evidence including notes, diagrams, and drawings covered the tables and walls. But the eleven jurors who agreed David was guilty were unable to get the woman to change her mind.

Kolker gloated after the announcement, calling the deadlocked jury a victory.

Despite that "victory," David Anderson fired the attorney a week and a half after the hung jury was announced. David cited irreconcilable differences between him and Kolker as the reason for wanting a new attorney to represent him in his new trial.

The deadlock only hardened the prosecutors' resolve to work harder on—and to be much more careful about—whom they picked during the jury selection process. David would remain in prison as the prosecutors prepared to try him a second time.

David's case took one more twist later that summer, as attorneys were preparing to start a new trial on September 10. Lanette Inmann, the holdout juror, announced that she was suing the King County Prosecutor's Office and Jeff Baird for defamation and emotional distress, which she claimed she endured after she refused to convict David.

In the $350,000 lawsuit, filed in court on September 3, Inmann claimed that Baird damaged her reputation by accusing her of "sabotaging" the case. However, nothing was to come of the suit.

Baird was on vacation at the time, and Patty Eakes had recently returned from a monthlong vacation when the news reached them. They told reporters they were too busy preparing for the new trial to be bothered by this latest development. Clearly, the suit was an act of retribution, and the prosecutors refused to let it distract them.

29 Unlike Judge Michael Spearman's, Judge Jeffrey Ramsdell's legal background was that of a prosecutor. He became a King County Superior Court judge in 1997 after three years of working as a prosecutor for the county's criminal division a decade earlier. Ramsdell proved to be an amicable and patient judge who allowed each side to have its say, however long or short. Since this was the second trial of a young man who stood accused of murder, he made sure to be extra conservative, taking the time he needed to decide matters rather than rushing to judgment. As everyone who attended the trial would soon discover, nothing was to be rushed during this new trial.

Ramsdell was already familiar with the Wilson homicide case before the duty to preside over the retrial fell into his lap. His courtroom is directly across the hall from that of Judge Spearman, and during Alex Baranyi's trial and David Anderson's first trial, Spearman occasionally conferred with him on various legal matters. Judges always have a desire for trials to run smoothly and efficiently. But Ramsdell was about to discover that that would not be the case in David's retrial; there would be too much contention between the prosecutors and defense attorneys for this trial to stay on schedule.

In late September, a jury pool of 106 was chosen to undergo the individual jury selection procedure. At the request of the prosecutors, Ramsdell allowed them to poll each

member of the pool separately—a process that lasted two
weeks. But it was a crucial procedure to Baird and Eakes,
who were still reeling from the hung jury. In the end, eight
women and eight men were impaneled and sworn in as jurors, and of them, four would eventually be picked as alternates and excused from the deliberation process. While most
were middle aged, their racial and professional backgrounds
were diverse. They included an African-American man and
a Latina woman. They also varied in their professions. One
juror was a Boeing engineer, another a grade school teacher,
and yet another was retired.

Both sides were confident with their picks and the trial
was ready to begin. On a cold, wet Monday morning, October 11, the same faces that streamed into Judge Spearman's
courtroom a year earlier for the first trial in the Wilson
homicide case were back again, for the third time. The cast
of characters on the witness stand would be largely the
same, too. The biggest difference between the first two trials
and this retrial would be the startling new testimony from
several of the same witnesses. The one witness the state
hoped to call was sitting in his jail cell at the Clallam Bay
Correctional Center outside Olympia, Washington, beginning his life-sentence term. Baird, Eakes, and Gomes had
traveled to the prison just weeks before David's trial started,
hoping to persuade Alex to testify. However, they were to be
disappointed: there was no advantage for him, and Alex also
worried about being branded a jailhouse snitch if he were to
testify against his best friend. Snitches always become the
targets of other inmates, and Alex didn't want to wear that
badge. The state pressed on, knowing it had a compelling
case against David, with or without Alex's testimony. There
were rumors, too, that David might take the stand, but as in
his first trial, David's attorneys had to practically throw
themselves in front of him in order to prevent that from happening.

Early on in the process, it became apparent that David's second trial would be about long delay tactics and interruptions, and later, it would be about egos.

The initial delay of the trial came on the first day, when David's sober-speaking defense attorney, Pete Connick, opened up by requesting a change of venue, arguing that eight of the sixteen impaneled jurors had read newspaper articles about the Wilson murder case, and only two claimed to have never heard about it. The judge had denied a previous change-of-venue motion made in September, and now he denied this one, too. He was satisfied that those jurors who indicated they had read newspaper accounts would be fair jurors, as they also said they had only vague memories of what they'd read.

Pete Connick, a heavy, round-faced man who shuffled across the courtroom, set the tone for how aggressive the defense would be in holding the prosecutors accountable for their actions. Connick had a reputation for several things—his expertise in the area of DNA analysis and his courtroom strategy of delaying the process at every conceivable juncture. To that end, he was zealous when it came to objecting, and, some would argue, overzealous. In a rare move in any trial, Connick raised objections during Eakes' opening remarks. Even more stunning was the number of times he did so—*at least nineteen.*

More than with just objections, the trial would be fraught with motions for mistrial—fourteen by the trial's end—and allegations of attorney misconduct, which the lawyers lobbed like grenades at each other.

David watched the courtroom drama at times with great interest, and at other times with obvious boredom. He was a tenacious notetaker, thumbing through exhibits and keeping tabs on what had or had not been formally admitted as evidence in the trial. Each day he sat poised, as if attending a job interview, and usually kept his head down, only occasionally facing the jury. As in the previous trial, he entered the courtroom each day and shook the hand of Attorney Stephan Illa. It was a small gesture that seemed to say, *I'm a polite, respectable young man, not a killer.*

On the first day of the retrial, David wore a black-and-white knit sweater over a freshly ironed white oxford shirt, black slacks, and the same polished black dress shoes he wore during the first trial. He had an Army-style crew cut. Nearly three years without sunlight made his skin look paler than ever.

As usual, Leslie and Bruce Anderson were present, as was a slim young man with short, dishwater-blond hair who was about David's age. He was a church friend who wrote letters to David since his arrest, and who had kept a constant presence at his first trial. They sat close together at the end of an entire row, and when a group of more than a dozen high school students tried to sit in their row, Bruce Anderson refused to budge until court clerk Richard Crumley quietly approached him and asked him to make room.

"Why should we? This is for family," Bruce barked. He wanted his space, a buffer between his family and the rest of the world. Reluctantly, Leslie moved about a foot to the right, and Bruce shifted slightly to accommodate two students.

The courtroom was packed with media, court watchers, family and friends of the victims and the defendant, and young cub attorneys eager to hear the opening remarks.

As in David's last trial, Patty Eakes delivered the opening statements for the state. Wearing a crisp black suit with a full-length jacket, an orchid-colored, button-down blouse, and a pearl necklace and earrings, she exuded the same professionalism as in the previous two trials. In her two-hour statement, Eakes covered familiar ground. She first talked about David Anderson's plan to kill, and then she went into the lives of the Wilsons and how they were tragically, sense-lessly murdered while David Anderson gloated.

"All of David Anderson's murderous ambitions finally found their target," Eakes said. "Their target was Kim Wilson."

Eakes explained to this new jury how David had put his murder plan into action, luring Kim to a park, killing her, then killing her family.

"We may not know exactly how he got Kim Wilson to go to Water Tower Park, but you'll learn she did go there, and Water Tower Park, as I told you, is a very small park. It's a park David Anderson knew like the back of his hand. It's a stomping ground."

That was literally true in Kim's murder. Eakes would suggest to the jury that David stomped on Kim, breaking bones in her rib cage while Alex strangled her to death.

"David Anderson thought he had succeeded. David Anderson knew he had left no witnesses. Evidence will show David Anderson destroyed all the evidence which would link him to the murders. He believed he committed the perfect crime. But he was wrong. He had been careful, but not careful enough; he had been clever, but not quite clever enough. He made some mistakes and his mistakes are part of the evidence you will hear about in this case."

Once again, Eakes delivered dramatic opening state-ments, spiked with energy and emotion. At 11:20 A.M., she thanked the jury and left the stage for Pete Connick to enter. But he had already made himself known to the jury during Eakes' opening remarks. It's rare for objections to be made by either side during opening statements, but Connick may have set a record by injecting nineteen into hers. He walked a fine line between being overly persistent and making a nui-sance of himself.

Whatever first impression—good or bad—he might have

given with all of his interruptions, he would try to make a more important impression as he rose to give his client's version of events leading up to the murders and why his client was innocent.

"Ladies and gentlemen of the jury, I want to state at the outset that we're here today because David Anderson is not guilty of the crimes for which he is charged. That's the question, that's the issue," Connick said, looking at some jurors square in the eye. "My remarks mean nothing [nor] do the remarks of the state. So all the inflammatory imagery that Ms. Eakes or the government wants to raise to put you in the spirit of convicting David Anderson should not influence you. It's not the government that convicts, it's you. You must do it by way of evidence."

Connick's style was vastly different from Eakes'. He was a simple man, with a simple approach: present the case as clearly and concisely as possible without the drama. Rather than bothering with theatrics, he stayed calm and unemotional. His opening remarks were pointed, even if the deliverance was somewhat monotone. But there was another major, more subtle difference between Eakes and Connick—Eakes paid attention to the way in which she spoke, using proper grammar and syntax, and showing deference to the jury, her fellow colleagues, and Judge Ramsdell. Connick often misused prepositions and would start a sentence, stop, and then start an entirely new sentence. He often appeared to be stumbling over his thoughts, constantly blurting out, "Uh . . ." before he spoke. It was odd that an attorney, highly educated and well versed in his practice, would use such poor grammar, but Connick proceeded, perhaps unaware of his own strange syntax. Jurors and court watchers alike would soon discover his gruff, off-putting mannerisms. Connick did not have the same sense of diction and didn't bother with courtroom propriety. He showed little respect for anyone in the courtroom, addressing Judge Ramsdell with an abrupt "Judge," rather than using the more polite "Your Honor." On occasion, when he got angry enough, he would point his finger at the prosecutors and the judge.

Despite that, he proved to be a tenacious trial lawyer. Connick was trying to prepare the jury for what he considered meaningless testimony from the state's witnesses.

"The government's case is based on a lot of speculation. A lot of it is going to be the idle banter of a bunch of adolescents, not just David Anderson, but a group of adolescents."

There would be physical evidence, too, that Connick urged the jurors to scrutinize.

"Now, these boots found at David Anderson's is the one piece of physical evidence that the state claims convicts David Anderson, but that's not what their experts say. That's not what they're going to argue. It's their interpretation of the physical evidence that gives them problems in this case," Connick said.

He told the jury that forensic experts examined several bags of David's clothing and other items found in his bedroom. Connick suggested to the jury that it was preposterous that David would keep his boots.

"He held on to these one pair of boots. There's something very strange about these pair of boots. They're trying to identify who was wearing them at the crime scene. Other physical evidence will show it was not David Anderson."

One might wonder, if it was not David Anderson, then who wore the boots found in his bedroom, stained with the blood of two victims? Who would be so senseless as to wear David's boots during a multiple murder and then place them back in his room? It was also yet to be seen whether Connick would ever provide a name, or just leave that question to linger unanswered.

In anticipation of what he considered to be the state's attempt to find David guilty by association with Alex, the defense told the jury that that was not the case at all, that David and Alex were not the best of friends, as the prosecutors would have them believe.

"The government asserts that they were connected at the hip, basically, and one didn't do anything without the other. We will challenge that suggestion. Alex would actually become upset with David and resent him for taking girlfriends that he focused on, and I should comment a bit about this because this isn't your normal 'I have a crush on you' type of [attachment]. This is a bizarre, almost psychotic focus where Alex Baranyi believed that he is some type of Goth god, a person named Slicer Thunderclap, and that he has some Gothic girlfriend."

Finally, Connick suggested that other teenagers who were a part of David's constellation of friends might be just as guilty as David.

"When they interviewed these kids, let's call them the Eastside Denny's crowd, many of these kids were investigated. So you had boots taken from Bob Boyd. You even had boots taken from Prosecutor Patty Eakes, because when she went through the scene, she went running into the scene rather than allowing the homicide detectives to get in. Fingerprints were taken from Sarah Lamp; a knife was taken from Joe Kern because it was believed to have blood on it and [that was believed to be the murder weapon.] The evidence will show that these people will be as guilty as David Anderson. If one was guilty by association, one was guilty of adolescent banter. The government will ask you to make a conviction based upon . . . speculation. I believe, however, that the physical evidence will lead you to the correct verdict of not guilty for David Anderson. Thank you."

Connick's opening remarks took about a half hour, ending just before noon. Compelling as both arguments were, the real drama of the day would not unfold until after the lunch break.

* * *

As in Alex Baranyi's trial and David's first trial, Jeff Gomes was one of the first witnesses to take the stand, simply to be introduced to the jurors. He was to be recalled several times throughout the trial. Erin Gauntlett, Kim's friend who had visited her the night of the murders, was again the state's second witness. Soon after her direct testimony, the lawyers broke into their first skirmish.

Gauntlett, who was now attending college in Idaho, took the stand in David's previous trial to tell the jury about the Friday night she spent walking around Woodridge with Kim—the last time Gauntlett would see her alive. Her testimony served to place a time frame around Kim's death. But during cross-examination, the defense took a different approach, apparently ignoring the issue of time frames. Stephan Illa was more interested in Kim's relationships.

"The state during their opening statements alluded to the fact that there might be some sort of romantic attraction between Kim Wilson and David Anderson. Is that something you talked about that night?" Illa asked.

"No," Gauntlett replied.

"Did she ever tell you she was romantically interested in David Anderson?

"No."

"Well, who was she interested in?"

"At the time, I don't know. We didn't talk about that."

"How about before that time?"

"She dated a gentleman named Bill for a few years in high school and that's about all I know," Gauntlett said, clearly becoming agitated with Illa's questioning.

"Was there anyone else she was romantically interested in other than Bill that you knew about?" Illa asked, trying to coax a different response from her.

Gauntlett paused, as if she didn't want to answer the question. She reluctantly gave in.

"Um, she was interested in a girl named Sarah at one time."

Illa proceeded to delve into Kim's relationship with Sarah.

"Did she go out with a girl named Sarah?" Illa asked, his voice condescending.

The prosecutors were outraged. Illa had stepped way over the bounds of his cross-examination by diving into a topic that was off-limits: Kim's sexual orientation.

"I'm going to object," Baird interjected.

Uncertain of where Illa was going, Judge Ramsdell overruled the objection and asked Gauntlett to answer the question.

"I know that she was romantically involved with Sarah for a while."

Illa thanked the witness and Gauntlett got up to walk out of the courtroom, looking at members of the Wilson family as if to say, *I'm so sorry.*

But Baird refused to allow the defense to get away with blatantly breaking a previous court ruling.

"Mr. Illa stood up and brazenly questioned this witness about Kim Wilson's attraction for women, something which was prohibited by a prior court's ruling," Baird said, after a summary of how the defense had just gotten away with crossing the line. "I was stunned when I saw what was happening, what was being elicited. But I think the question that followed the witness's disclosure clearly indicated that that was exactly what Mr. Illa was shooting for."

Illa tried to defend himself by arguing that the state opened the door for talking about relationships when Eakes, in her opening statements, brought up Kim's relationship with David—how it started as a crush, evolved into dating, and then became a maternalistic relationship. The nature of the relationship was also the topic of a previous court ruling in which the judge ordered the attorneys not to mention any romantic involvement between David and Kim; that was because David denied being romantically involved with her, and to suggest so would be misstating the facts. While the defense might have overstepped court boundaries by asking Gauntlett about Kim's relationship with Sarah Lamp, it was quick to point out Eakes was equally guilty for implying a romance between David and Kim during her opening statements.

Judge Ramsdell was not impressed with the defense's rationale behind baiting Gauntlett to disclose Kim's sexual orientation.

"This is a violation of *motion eliminée*, end of story," Ramsdell said. "This is a little disconcerting. I'm disinclined to decide whether sanctions are appropriate at this point. I don't want to make a rash judgment, but the issue is on the table and I think we're all on notice, and I won't tolerate it anymore."

As in David's first trial, the first two days and half-dozen witnesses out of the gate were essentially the same—Jeff Gomes, and five witnesses who testified to either spending time with Kim Wilson on the night of the murders or finding her body. In the last trial, the state presented its case with an early focus on the Wilson family, and then on the young man it believed killed them, starting with his boastful remarks to his girlfriends and building up to his invitation to one young man—Mike Dickinson—to join in the murder plot.

The presentation of this trial was slightly different. Baird and Eakes knew they had to somehow build a stronger case against David Anderson, with a more narrow and more immediate focus on the evidence against him.

As in the last trial, they would provide witness testimony to prove David planned to kill the Wilsons. But three years is a long time to remember dates, times, conversations. It is enough time for witnesses to forget certain things and recall others. If David's new trial proved anything, it would be that nobody's memory is perfect, that some pieces of memory come back to us later in our lives, and that some people intentionally change their minds, for any number of reasons, about what they saw, heard, or felt in years prior.

The state's first witness to prove this point was Marisa Cats, now seventeen years old, the Wilsons' next-door neighbor who, in the first trial, testified to hearing loud arguing coming from the Wilson home at around 11 P.M. the night of the murders. Cats' testimony remained the same as when she had last sat in the witness chair: she heard arguing the night of the murders and then noticed her neighbors' trash bins were still at the curbside after the trash collectors had already emptied the others. But apparently, in the past three years, something else from that night came back to the soft-spoken, petite young woman, something that continued to haunt her.

"When was the last time you saw David Anderson in or around the Wilson home?" Baird asked.

"I saw him a couple of days after the murders," Cats said.

"Where was he a couple of days after the murders?"

"He was standing outside of the Wilson house, um, like where the TV crews were. For about the first week, there were a lot of TV crews around, and I saw him standing out there one day," Cats said.

She told the jury how David, dressed in dark clothing, was standing about ten feet away from her in a crowd of people, watching the news crews tape their broadcasts.

"Did Mr. Anderson make eye contact with you?" Baird asked.

"Yes, he looked right at me," Cats said. "He kind of looked at me weird. It kind of creeped me out, so I ran inside."

"Did you tell anybody what you'd seen?"

"Yes, I did. One of the detectives was in our house and he was walking outside our house. He was just about to leave and my mom and my stepdad were there and I walked inside and I tugged on my mom's shirt and I was like, 'I think I know who did it.' "

Baird had no more questions. Cats' last statement was an obvious blow, and surprise, to the defense. If it were true, then it would be hard to believe anyone who just committed such a brutal crime would then decide to hang out at the crime scene. But David had always behaved as if he were in control, and that he was above the law. It was possible that he would be so brazen as to stand on a crowded street crawling with cops shortly after the murders. He had been known to tempt fate.

Connick believed Cats was lying. And he was outraged that she was allowed to testify as to her thoughts on who the killers might be. But during direct examination, he failed to object to Cats' remark, which would be pointed out by the judge a short while later. He tried to repair the damage at the start of his cross-examination.

"Isn't it true you never mentioned seeing David Anderson around the house [in a previous police statement]?" Connick asked.

"I didn't say it in that statement," Cats replied.

"Did you ever testify against David Anderson that you saw David Anderson outside the Wilson home after January 3, 1997?"

"I just did," Cats said defiantly.

"Have you ever before?"

"No."

After completing a brief cross-examination, Connick promptly moved for a mistrial.

"We were sandbagged," he insisted, appearing frustrated as he glanced at the prosecutors.

Connick raised legitimate concerns. Cats' statement about seeing David Anderson in front of the Wilson home the Monday after the murders and running to her mother to suggest who did it was never covered in the previous trial, nor was it mentioned in any interviews Cats had had with the investigators and attorneys.

Baird insisted that Cats made mention of seeing David in front of the Wilson home shortly after the murders, but could not remember when she made that statement. Cats' suspicions that David killed the Wilsons, which she vocalized during direct examination, was sufficient to raise the ire of any defense attorney, but was it enough to warrant a mistrial?

Judge Ramsdell later denied the motion for mistrial, as he believed that Baird did not intentionally elicit testimony of guilt from Cats. However, he did agree that it potentially could be prejudicial to the jury. As a compromise, Ramsdell would ask the jury to disregard and strike Cats' statement.

For nearly three years, Leslie Anderson had gone on with her life without being able to physically touch David, and the distance was wearing on her. The closest she could get to him was a couple of feet away at a visitor's booth at the King County Jail, twice a week. But even then they were separated by a glass partition and had to speak into a telephone. She had a mother's natural instinct when her child was in danger or in a bad situation—she was desperate to hold him. On the third day of the retrial, Leslie Anderson could no longer hold back her emotion.

David's guardsmen, who had escorted him into the courtroom, were standing near her one morning before court officially began. "I just want a hug," she moaned to one of the officers. Jurors were streaming out of the jury room just as she said it.

The comment would have gone largely unnoticed—even some in the press row didn't hear—if it hadn't been for Jeff Baird, who brought it to the court's attention. He asked that the judge request all family members to restrain from making such remarks in the presence of the jury because of its obvious prejudicial nature. It was likely that none of the jurors heard the comment. But Judge Ramsdell nonetheless asked that all spectators refrain from such outbursts, or face the prospect of being fined or barred from the courtroom for the remainder of the trial. Leslie said nothing, but kept her head down and focused on her stitching.

By the third day of trial, the obvious friction between David's defense lawyers and the prosecutors became evident. Judge Ramsdell had the unfortunate task of playing referee in one of the most contentious and complicated legal games ever held at the King County Courthouse. The testimony of Amryn Decker, David's ex-girlfriend, prompted Connick to request a second mistrial in as many days.

In the course of Baird's testimony, Decker suggested she might know who killed the Wilsons, but Baird staved off a response before it left Decker's lips. Decker explained to the jury how she was in her first-period gym class when she learned of the murders. She grabbed her friend Danielle Berry and they raced to the counselor's office between 9 and 10 A.M. That afternoon, Detective John McBride and Officer Molly McBride arrived to interview Decker.

"Did you talk to the detectives?" Baird asked.

"Yes, sir, for two hours," Decker said.

"Did you give a name to the Bellevue detectives?" Baird asked.

"Of whom I believed had committed these murders?"

Baird suddenly realized where Decker was going. Worried that she might blurt out David's name, he answered: "No, never mind, strike that question."

Even though she never said David's name, the exchange still angered the defense. Attorneys are banned from eliciting opinions of guilt or innocence from witnesses, and Baird nearly crossed that line in his direct examination. At the end of the day, Connick again requested a mistrial.

In his plea to the judge, Connick noted that Baird asked Decker about her reactions to various events leading up to her hearing about news of the murders and what she thought afterward. Connick insisted that Baird's style of questioning was such that a witness would naturally respond with an opinion.

"We move for a mistrial," Connick said evenly.

Judge Ramsdell gave Baird a stern look and allowed him to defend himself before ruling on the matter. Instead, Baird personally attacked Connick in his cunning way.

"One of the reasons I hope for a conviction in this case is that someday someone will review this record and observe that Mr. Connick seems to have an almost pathological inability to recite testimony clearly and accurately," Baird said. That comment drew a sharp glare from Connick, and criticism from Judge Ramsdell, who asked all of the attorneys to refrain from personal attacks.

"I know there's frustrations on both sides," Ramsdell said.

"I beg the court's pardon, but I did not ask her emotional reactions to anything. The question that precipitated at another sidebar, another interruption of this trial, was when she was asked a question, she heard about the murders and didn't understand it until the following day . . . She interpreted it completely gratuitously as some kind of question concerning whether she believed Mr. Anderson was guilty or not. I didn't let her answer it. I asked that the question be stricken. I didn't pursue it."

Already nerves were beginning to fray on both sides of the attorneys' tables, and even the judge was beginning to get frustrated at this early stage in the trial. Ramsdell denied the motion for mistrial, but urged the prosecutors to inform their witnesses what they were allowed to say. He said he trusted the lawyers to act professionally, because he was at a disadvantage in not knowing every detail of testimony in the previous trial.

"To be honest with you, Counsel, you all have been through this trial several times," Ramsdell said. "I'm playing catch-up, and what's happening here is difficult to control."

It was just the beginning.

On Thursday, the state began direct examination of what would become one of the key testimonies in David's new trial.

As with Marisa Cats, three years of retrospection brought back a few compelling memories to Marsha Rash.

When she testified in David's first trial, Rash offered a rather detailed testimony of where she was and what she was doing, and where David was on January 3, 1997: She was at work at RadioShack at Factoria Mall until 9:30 or 10 P.M.; David had come by earlier in the day to borrow her stepfather's pickup truck; David picked her up when she got off work and drove her home to the rental house; he then asked to borrow the car again so he could hang out with Alex. Rash was awakened at 2:30 A.M. by Michael Anderson, and agreed to accompany him to Denny's. Michael Anderson and Rash got back to the rental house at around 5:30 A.M., and David was dead asleep. Rash had been interviewed at least five times by police and had testified in two trials, and her story remained essentially the same.

Yet in this new trial, Rash, now unmarried at age twenty-two with an infant son, became more detailed about what she saw after getting home from Denny's at 5:30 A.M. Wearing a red, flower-patterned dress with white canvas shoes, she could easily have passed as a grade school teacher.

"Miss Rash, when you got home at five-thirty A.M. and saw the defendant sleeping in bed, how was he dressed?" Eakes asked.

"In the clothes he left in," Marsha responded.

"I'm sorry, he had clothes on?"

"Yes."

"And other than his clothes, did he have anything else on?"

"His shoes."

David leaned over to whisper something to his attorneys, then looked up and glowered at Rash. The testimony as to David falling asleep with his shoes on was something new that the defense should have been warned about, but Eakes continued anyway, without any objections from the defense.

"Do you recall what shoes he had on?"

"The ones he always wore," Rash said.

"Which were . . . ?"

"They were like a boot."

"Have you seen those boots again since January 3, 1997?"

Before she could answer, Connick finally objected. Eakes immediately withdrew the question.

He was fully dressed and wearing his boots to bed? It was incredibly damning evidence against David and a significant detail that should have been brought up earlier. It was hard to imagine why anyone would wait three years to disclose that kind of critical information.

Rash's testimony regarding David's boots drew yet another motion for mistrial from Connick. He offered a compelling argument that that statement had never been made in police statements or prior testimony.

But the prosecutors insisted Rash had given investigators that information on at least one occasion. If the prosecutors were to be believed, one would have to wonder why they failed to mention that crucial piece of information in David's first trial. Eakes and Baird later argued that there were so many interviews and so many pieces of information that even they had forgotten some details.

The defense, however, didn't buy it.

"The state again has engaged in sandbagging practices," Connick said to the judge. "You can see in my recross that caught me by surprise."

Eakes tried to explain by saying she was simply asking Rash whether there was anything unusual about finding David asleep when she returned to the house at 5:30 A.M.

Judge Ramsdell said that he, too, was surprised at Rash's comment. Offering to clear things up, Eakes volunteered to review previous statements Rash had made to police or attorneys to prove that she had made the comment previously. The judge granted Eakes the time to look over her notes and transcripts to see where Rash's statement came from.

Connick was not satisfied. He reiterated his plea for a mistrial, or for Rash's testimony to be stricken. "That testimony is absolutely crucial," he told the judge. But no one would ever have imagined just how crucial.

Following the lunch break, Eakes produced notes made by Jeff Baird, purportedly of an interview Rash had with the prosecutors, Gomes, and Rash's mother, Tammy Deacy, on September 17, 1997. But it was unclear whether the defense would have had access to those notes.

"My notes are clear that the defense did know about this," Eakes said. "I did not consider this new information."

Connick was becoming irritated with the state's response to the mistake.

"There are no interviews," Connick said outright. He told the judge he'd consulted with Michael Kolker and his defense investigator, Larry Walsh, and they both agreed no such statements were ever made by Rash. "We want a mistrial. I think Ms. Eakes is dishonest at best." Connick also asked for Baird's original notes, which he planned to have examined for authenticity. Although Connick didn't say it, the suggestion was that Baird had doctored his notes.

Judge Ramsdell was faced with a hard decision, one of many he would make throughout the trial. The prosecutors clearly had notes to prove Rash had made the comment, but the defense had no such notes from its own investigator. Seeing no easy solution, the judge once again denied the defense's motion for mistrial, but allowed the defense extra time to reinterview Rash, if it wished to do so. Ramsdell ordered Baird to hand over his notes, and he also warned the state to be more careful in its direct examination.

"Counsel needs to exercise caution from here on out," Ramsdell said, looking at Baird and Eakes. "We need to be a lot more careful as to what transpires in this trial."

The following morning, on October 19, the attorneys spent the better part of it arguing about the previous day's snafu. Connick, still upset at what happened, asked the court to impose a stiffer penalty on the prosecution.

"If I don't say something, the Court of Appeals says I'm weak," Connick said. "I'm alleging deliberate misconduct. I'd also ask for sanctions."

"For what?" Ramsdell asked.

"For her eliciting the testimony she did from Marsha Rash."

The judge looked somewhat perturbed. "To what end does that foster fairness of the procceedings?"

"We're on our third motion for mistrial," Connick said, pacing up and down the courtroom. "Whether it's improper delving into opinion or discovery violation, this is the third time. A sanction might get it through to Ms. Eakes that she shouldn't be conducting herself the way she is."

Judge Ramsdell was swift to point out that the defense transgressed its bounds at least twice already. He indicated that he preferred not to impose sanctions, monetary or otherwise, but if the lawyers continued to misbehave, he would do so at the end of the trial.

The allegations of prosecutorial misconduct raised by the defense were excessive, and, arguably, unfounded. Baird and Eakes were walking on eggshells in this new trial. It would make no sense for them to intentionally break any court rules that might cause another mistrial. But Connick persisted with his accusations. For him, it was a way of laying the groundwork for a potential appeal.

The defense team nitpicked on such a minute level that even members of the press could not avoid their indictments of wrongdoing. After the lawyers spent hours arguing the same issue from the day before, Illa rose to take up an entirely separate issue that seemed to symbolize just how hypersensitive David's new defense team felt it had to be. As Illa had been packing his briefcase at the end of the previous day, he overheard a reporter for the *Eastside Journal*, Noel Brady, ask the court clerk to clarify the issue of double jeopardy.

"We'd like the court to let the press know that's not proper. We're not accusing the court of misconduct. Because we overheard this, we wanted to put it on the record."

The judge obliged and put the press on notice not to have contact with court staff. He then remarked: "I think I'm the only one in the courtroom right now who hasn't been accused of some kind of misconduct." The comment drew laughter from the attorneys and court spectators. However, it would not hold true for the entire trial.

That afternoon, the state put on a new witness, twenty-one-year-old Nanda Prabhakar, a friend of Kim's who now lived in Philadelphia, where she was a social worker. Prabhakar testified that she met Kim while attending Bellevue High School. When she left BHS to attend the Seattle Art Institute, Prabhakar remained in close contact with Kim, spending time with her during holiday breaks. Wearing black slacks and a cropped blazer, Prabhakar appeared professional. She was well spoken and confident. While most witnesses leaned away from defense attorneys during cross-examination, she remained calm and poised. Prabhakar testified that on the day of the murders, she and Kim went to see the movie *One Fine Day*, a love story starring George

Clooney and Michelle Pfeiffer, at a cinema near the Factoria Mall in the late afternoon after Kim had visited Bellevue High School. When they walked into the mall to use a pay phone to call Kim's parents after the movie, they bumped into someone they knew.

"What, if anything, happened after you went to the mall?" Eakes asked.

"After walking into the mall, we encountered David Anderson and Sarah Lamp walking out of the mall."

"What, if anything, was said between Kim Wilson and David Anderson that day?"

"They exchanged greetings, and Kim made a mention of a sum of money that David had owed her and had not yet paid."

"What did Kim say?" Eakes asked.

"It was something along the lines of, 'You still haven't paid me back the money you owed me,' or, 'You owe me money,' something like that."

"What was Kim Wilson's demeanor?"

"I would say she was not angry or confrontational, but at the same time she was not happy that David still owed her a sum of money."

"What did the defendant say in response to Kim?"

"To the best of my knowledge, it was something along the lines of, 'Yeah, yeah, I know I owe you money. I'll pay you when I pay you.' "

"What was the defendant's demeanor?"

"He seemed rather indifferent. Not confrontational, just acknowledging that this was in fact true."

"What did you do after they had this conversation?"

"We walked away to find a pay phone to call Kim's parents. I believe they exited the mall."

Prabhakar's testimony set the defense back. Her statements corroborated Marsha Rash's testimony in which Rash explained how she was working at Factoria Mall the day of the murders when David came to borrow the truck. It was also a new opportunity for the state to prove David lied to detectives when questioned about the murders; on the Wednesday following the murders, he told the McBrides the last time he saw Kim was right around Christmas of 1996. Here was a witness who confidently said Kim bumped into David the very day she was killed. What's more, Prabhakar recalled Kim bringing up the debt David owed her, which the state hoped to prove as part of the motive for the crime.

The defense raised few objections and conducted only a brief cross-examination.

But by the next morning, Connick came to court with something new to quibble about. Barely ending the second week of witness testimony, David's retrial was becoming more fiction than nonfiction. Allegations of misconduct, mostly by the defense, were growing ostensibly outlandish.

Since David's trial ran only Mondays through Thursdays, most of the attorneys, and even Judge Ramsdell, juggled other trial obligations on Fridays. During David's retrial, Patty Eakes was prosecuting a murder-for-hire case in King County Superior Court on her days off. The defendant in that murder case was housed in the King County Jail, where David Anderson was incarcerated. Connick believed that Eakes was using the inmate to draw a confession out of David.

"I understand the state's in the habit of planting informants in jail," Connick told Judge Ramsdell. But the allegation appeared to have no premise.

Eakes said the accusation was preposterous, and Ramsdell thought so, too. He promptly disregarded Connick's claim and proceeded with other court matters.

30 Even though the Wilsons had been dead for nearly three years by the time David's second trial got under way, new evidence was continuing to surface. In the fourth week of the trial, Gail Harris, Bill Wilson's sister and the executor of the Wilsons' estate, came across something that she knew Gomes and the prosecutors would be interested in: the Wilsons' MCI phone bill, which included calls made early on the morning of Saturday, January 4, 1997.

On Tuesday, November 2, Harris brought it to court and gave it to Gomes. According to the phone bill, a half-hour call was placed from the Wilson home to West Germany just before 2 A.M. on Saturday, January 4, 1997. After receiving the phone bill, Gomes followed up and called the number. He discovered that the call was made by Julia to a friend of hers who had temporarily lived with the Wilsons during a recent student-exchange visit. That meant that Julia had to have been attacked after 2:30 A.M., when she got off the phone, and before 3:30 A.M., when Ron Boyd reported seeing David and Alex come home. The information narrowed the time frame in which the Wilsons were killed and helped prove the point that it was more than likely two people had committed the murders. It would be hard to imagine one person, in that short of a time period, could overcome three people inside a home and kill them all without a hitch.

There was more evidence. Jeff Gomes had been in contact

with a young woman named Megan Varner, said to be a close friend of David's. The state wanted to put Varner on the stand to testify about statements David had made to her prior to the Wilson murders. Her testimony was expected to echo that of Danielle Berry and Amryn Decker.

In a preemptive and arguably overzealous move, Connick requested a mistrial. As one might expect, the judge refused to entertain the motion because it was premature—*the witness had not even testified.* But Judge Ramsdell acknowledged Connick's frustrations with the prosecutors for bringing in new evidence and testimony at the last minute.

"If there's continuing discovery, it changes the trial process as the trial is going," Ramsdell said. "It seems to me there has to be some point where discovery is too late. The frustrating part for me is that something always keeps coming up and we have to do it on the fly." Ramsdell was making reference to the previous three weeks' worth of testimony seeded with surprises from witnesses who blurted out opinions of guilt, to testimony that included new information to which the defense claimed it was not privy.

Baird acknowledged the late discovery, but insisted that there was no way he could have known new witnesses relevant to the case would be coming out of the woodwork.

"It is the nature of trials to expect the unexpected," Baird said emphatically.

And the unexpected came again the next day. That's when forensic expert Kirsten Gleim took the stand to testify about the bloodstains found on David's boots. Her testimony was a defining point for the defense, because it opened the door to a new—albeit far-fetched—theory on who besides David could have been wearing his boots during the murders.

It had already been established that a pair of black shoelaces, which tested positive for the blood of Bill Wilson, were found in Alex's bedroom. The defense's newly evolved theory was that Alex's laces were in David's boots, and that

Alex was wearing the boots when he killed the Wilsons. But in order for this to be true, the defense was banking on Gleim to testify that no blood at all was found on the leather shoelaces currently in David's boots.

It was as far-fetched a theory as anyone could imagine. The evidence of David's boots was damning in and of itself, and there was very little the defense could do with it up until this point. Finally, they had an explanation, and a new chance to take the focus off David and place it back onto Alex. But would it be enough to raise doubts in the minds of the jury, and if so, would those doubts be reasonable enough to acquit him?

Using a blowup of Gleim's examination notes, Eakes asked the Washington State Patrol Crime Lab forensic expert to tell the jury where she found evidence of Bill and Julia Wilson's blood. In her original notes, Gleim used a red marker to place dots on the shoes, signifying blood drops.

After detailed testimony regarding blood spatter and smears on both boots, Illa began his cross-examination. He asked, pointedly, whether Gleim found any blood drops on the shoelaces.

Much to Illa's surprise, Gleim said she did—one small speck on the left lace. He fully expected her to say there was no blood on David's laces, according to her written report.

Illa didn't know what to do with Gleim's response, so he asked her whether she had testified to blood being on David's shoelaces in previous proceedings. She had not. Gleim, a middle-aged, bespectacled woman with silvery hair, found herself with her back against the wall because no mention of that drop of blood was in her original written report. The only note of it that was ever made was on her diagram: a single dot on the left lace amid dozens of other dots all over the shoe.

The seemingly innocuous testimony of Kirsten Gleim

was a turning point for the defense. They took their new theory of Alex's shoelaces in David's boots and ran with it.

At the end of the fourth week of witness testimony, the defense made their seventh motion for mistrial. In a wordy plea to the judge, Stephan Illa argued that Gleim had never before testified to blood being found on David's shoelaces. That she did so in David's retrial meant that it was new information, and it had not been properly disclosed to the defense team prior to her testimony.

"I note that in her August report, the only report that was disclosed to us, she described reddish deposits on the boots," Illa said. "It says nothing at all about the shoelaces."

But Baird rose to give a persuasive counterargument to Illa's claim that the state deliberately withheld evidence. He told the judge that the state was also surprised by Gleim's testimony of blood on the shoelaces. They had no idea she was going to make that claim, as she'd failed to bring it up before.

"If there was blood on those shoelaces, I would have elicited it in the first trial, second trial, and in direct examination," Baird said.

Illa pressed on in his request for a mistrial, and if the judge was unwilling to grant one, he wanted a continuance. He also requested that Gleim not be recalled as a witness.

The situation left Ramsdell in a quandary. The seemingly minor revelation of a small speck of blood on David's laces would prove crucial for the defense in finding a focus for its case. After calling for a recess and consulting case law, Ramsdell denied the motion for mistrial and also denied the defense's request for a continuance.

However, the defense would not accept Judge Ramsdell's ruling. They insisted that other expert witnesses who examined the boots never found any blood on the shoelaces and argued again that that information had not surfaced in any prior proceeding.

That wasn't true. When Terry McAdam, another forensic expert with the Washington State Patrol Crime Lab, testified in David's first trial, he indicated that there was, in fact, blood on the laces. Eakes had asked him then, on direct examination, "Looking at the left boot, the stains are under the laces, is that right?" McAdam responded: "Yes. It's just a little bit forward of the laces and some on the lace itself."

Some on the lace itself. There it was. Ramsdell reiterated his prior ruling and indicated that Baird would be allowed to recall Gleim and to question her fully and completely about blood on the boots.

The issue would become a lingering question in the minds of the jurors, who would later debate behind closed doors whether to believe the expert testimonies of Gleim and McAdam, or whether it was remotely possible that Alex's shoelaces had been in David's boots.

As the Thanksgiving holiday approached, it became clear that David's retrial would last longer than the court's original estimate of six to eight weeks. David's defense team had a large role to play in that. Delays and interruptions continued to unfold on a daily basis. For starters, the lawyers inevitably had issues to take up with the judge and often spent the better part of each morning arguing motions and taking up other issues outside the jury's presence. During the testimony, a plethora of objections and requests for sidebars was made, all using up valuable time. The trial's slow pace was further exacerbated by Connick's style. His general habit was to take the same amount of time to cross-examine witnesses as the prosecutors took during direct examination. As he questioned witnesses, he often paused between questions and wasted time searching through dozens of exhibits to find the one he wanted to use—organization that he should have completed before the jury entered each morning. He even moved slowly.

Conversely, the movements of the other three attorneys were much quicker and more energetic. Jeff Baird, especially, seemed to zip from one end of the courtroom to the other. His questions were short, snappy, and direct. But no matter how fast Baird moved, the trial would face several more delays that no one could predict or control.

In the fifth week of testimony, the court closed for Veterans Day, eliminating one day of the trial. Then, the following week, Judge Ramsdell caught the flu and canceled court for two days. The seventh week of testimony ended early, with two days off for Thanksgiving. And finally, in the eighth week, Ramsdell called for a recess during the World Trade Organization meetings in downtown Seattle.

As it happened, Ramsdell made a sound decision. Downtown Seattle turned into a battleground when several hundred protesters, of the estimated 40,000 protesters who descended on Seattle, clashed with police. Bus service came to a complete stop in the downtown core, and that would have prevented some of the jurors in the Anderson case from getting to court.

When the trial resumed the following week, the state recalled Marsha Rash to talk about the next time she saw David Anderson after the murders, the writings she found among David's possessions when she moved out, and the knives he was known to carry.

A new twist in the case surfaced during cross-examination.

Pete Connick took his time in cross-examining this witness. He tried to undermine Rash's credibility by asking whether or not she had lied or changed her story in certain matters regarding the case. Rash admitted she lied to her mother when she said no one but herself was driving the truck the night of the murders, worried she would get into trouble if she admitted she loaned it to David, and Connick drew that out.

But then Connick changed course. He wanted to know about a particular incident that had not been brought up in the previous trials.

"Do you recall destroying anything you thought was evidence in this case?" Connick asked pointedly.

"No," Rash said.

"You have a good friend named Jeannie Kern."

"Correct."

"Do you recall being with Jeannie Kern roughly three weeks after you found out about the murders and finding a glove, taking a glove and disposing of it in a slough near Shari's restaurant?"

"I have to think about it," Rash said quietly.

While Rash thought about it, Connick went on to a new line of questioning. He had previously noted in court that Rash's testimony was crucial, and it was. She was the last person to see David just before the murders occurred, and at the time of the murders, she was the closest person to him.

In Connick's deliberate attempt to destroy her credibility, he ended up putting Rash on trial. Connick tried to suggest not only that Rash lied to her mother and changed her story in various interviews with investigators, but that she was unfaithful to David. Connick coaxed Rash into saying that she had dated Michael Anderson before becoming David Anderson's girlfriend. Up to two weeks prior to the murders, David had suspected that she was cheating on him with Michael. Connick attempted to show how Rash's alleged infidelities struck at the heart of her credibility.

He began to question Marsha about the nature of her relationship with Michael just days before the murders.

"Did you have sexual relations—" Connick started to ask.

But Eakes shouted: "Objection!"

Judge Ramsdell sustained. Clearly, Connick was crossing the line. The defense attorney tried to explain that he was asking Rash about her relations with Mike Anderson to show the jury she was dishonest, but Ramsdell barred him from continuing with that line of questioning since it was improper and irrelevant in proving David's guilt or innocence.

But Connick wasn't done. He tried to trip Rash up by pointing out the inconsistencies in her previous testimony and statements to police. At one point, she told police she and Mike Anderson were having coffee and talking at Denny's on the night of the murders, and at another point, she had said she and Mike were at Snoqualmie Falls. And then he tried to show that Marsha might have had a motive for lying and changing her story so many times.

"After David's arrest, did you find out David cheated on you with a person named Sunshine Crane?" Connick asked.

"Yes, I did," Marsha said, her voice barely audible.

"Did that anger you?"

"I wasn't particularly happy about it."

In a matter of a few hours, Rash had suddenly become a completely unreliable witness. In redirect, Eakes tried to show that the young mother was merely confused. It had been a long time since the murders. Anyone's memory was bound to fail. But the fact that Rash had changed her story so many times made her appear suspect.

Not only did the defense lawyers try to ruin Marsha Rash's credibility, they also tried to point the finger at Bob Boyd as Alex's accomplice. In cross-examination of several witnesses, the defense wanted to know where Bob was, what he was doing, and who was with him on the night of the murders. They tried to show he smoked marijuana and led a dead-end life, and that he, too, was involved in discussions of crime in which David was present.

To counter that argument, the state had to switch gears and try to prove Bob's alibi. In doing so, the prosecutors put someone on the stand who ended up being one of the most disagreeable witnesses in the entire case.

David James Bly was another member of the Denny's crowd. He had long, naturally curly blond hair and a beard, and he wore baggy pants and a T-shirt that read: "Rage Against The Machine"—the name of a punk-rock band. Bly, who lived with his parents in Bellevue and worked part-time at a bowling alley, was one of several young men who was with Bob Boyd on the night of January 3 and in the early morning of January 4, 1997. He had been called by the state to help prove Bob's alibi, that he was bowling with a friend until 2 A.M. and that he subsequently spent the night with another friend, Andy Tonoko. Bellevue Police detectives interviewed Bly at his home two weeks before he was called to testify in David's second trial, and at that time he told them that yes, in fact, another friend, Ian Macdougal, offered him $10 to drive him and Bob to the bowling alley.

But when the twenty-year-old took to the witness stand, he was uncooperative, unwilling to admit that those events happened on the night of the murders, as he previously had indicated to police. No matter how much coaxing Baird tried, Bly would say simply, "I don't really remember." Frustrated at how the direct examination was progressing, Baird destroyed his own witness and made him look like a selfish jerk.

"Do you remember being asked why it was that you didn't tell the police after the Wilson homicide, after Mr. Baranyi and Mr. Anderson were arrested, why you didn't tell them you saw the two of them that night?"

"Yes, I remember being asked that," Bly said flatly.

"What was your answer?"

"I believe it was something along the lines of, 'Because it's not my business.' Because the events that took place were completely beyond my control and I was completely ignorant of the circumstances surrounding them, so I didn't take it upon myself to make a judgment," Bly said.

Baird expounded. "You told the police something like this. You said, 'I didn't like the police very much, still don't. The murders had nothing to do with me whatsoever and if you guys want to go through the little media circus and court process, then you're more than welcome to do it, but it's not my responsibility to take my time to, you know, help beyond reason. I'll help out when I can, you know, I'll sit down and record this crap, but you know, I'm not going to come forward. I'm not like that good of a Samaritan.' "

It was clear that this witness had nothing to offer. He even admitted, in his earlier interview with Bellevue Police officers, that his level of cooperation would get progressively worse.

"You're not too happy to be here, are you?" Baird finally asked.

"Not very."

"Wasn't the first thing you told me this morning was that you had to get up at eleven A.M.?"

"That's usually my sleep time, since I work nights," Bly said woodenly.

"Thank you," Baird finally said. "Nothing further."

Four people were brutally murdered, and this young man, who had information that would have clearly helped the investigation, could care less. It became increasingly evident with testimony from several members of the Denny's crowd that this was more than David Anderson's trial, it was their trial, too, the trial of a vastly apathetic generation who lived in a "me, me, me" world.

As the state began to wind up its case, the defense was gearing up to begin its own. Connick and Illa still believed there was no blood on either of the laces of David's boots. To that end, on December 2—at the end of the eighth week of court testimony—defense counsel requested Terry McAdam of the Washington State crime lab to reexamine them for any traces of blood. What McAdam discovered proved problematic for the state. He found no blood on the laces.

The state would argue that there was, in fact, blood on one of the laces—Kirsten Gleim saw it and diagrammed it, and McAdam himself remembered seeing it the first time he examined the blood. The state believed that the blood might have flaked off over the course of almost three years and two previous trials in which dozens of people, from attorneys to lay witnesses to expert witnesses, had handled them. The laces also had been subjected to several testings by labs, including a lab in Canada where the defense had sent the boots to conduct its own expert examination.

On December 8, McAdam became the catalyst for a showdown between the prosecutors and the defense over what was or was not found on David's boots.

In about two hours of direct examination by Eakes, McAdam told the jury that he analyzed some fifty to seventy-five stains on David's left boot—stains which were very small and consistent with expired blood that had sprayed onto the boot. McAdam determined the angle of the blood was such that it had to have been sprayed from a source that was two inches off the ground, like the blood Julia had expired onto the lower part of her bedroom door. On the right boot, McAdam saw six areas of stains with larger drops of blood, indicating blood had projected or impacted onto that boot. Then Eakes asked about the laces on the left boot.

The defense was suggesting to the jury that it was Alex's bloodstained shoelaces that were in David's boots at the time of the crimes. But in direct examination of McAdam, Eakes was trying to prove that David's shoelaces also had blood on them, so it would make no sense for Alex's laces to be in David's shoes.

"Were the stains on the left boot confined to any area?"

"The majority of the blood drops were very small . . . extending up to the laces," McAdam said.

"Did the bloodstains on the left boot actually go up to the laces?" Eakes asked.

"Yes, they were down in the lower places."

"The stains on the left boot, were they visible to the naked eye?"

"No," McAdam said. "They were very small, a fiftieth of an inch."

As Eakes continued her direct examination, the long hand on the courtroom clock pushed closer to 4 P.M. McAdam would have to come back the next day.

On Thursday, after giving more direct testimony to Eakes, McAdam was finally subjected to cross-examination by Pete Connick. Connick was using McAdam to show the jury that the state's own witnesses were incomplete in their examination and documentation of bloodstains on David's boots. He was trying to strike at their credibility by showing lapses in their documentation. He pointed out there were no *written* notes by either Kirsten Gleim or McAdam indicating the presence of blood on the laces.

Using a blowup of Gleim's written notes, Connick wasted no time in making his point.

"So there's no notation by Kirsten Gleim as to shoelaces, correct?"

"With the exception of her diagrammatically association—"

Connick interrupted him: "My question is—"

But then Eakes interrupted with an objection: "Your Honor, the witness should be permitted to finish his answers."

"Were there any notations on this exhibit related to shoelaces?" Connick continued.

"No, there was not."

"In your March 2, 1998, report, you make no mention of blood on the shoelaces."

"That is correct."

"Do you recall testifying in a prior proceeding that there was no drops on the shoelaces?"

"I don't recall that, no."

But Connick asked McAdam to read a portion of his previous testimony in which he indicated there was blood on the right-hand side of the left shoe, on the inner lace hole area, in between the lace holes, but "not on the laces but on the leather itself."

Connick emphasized McAdam's statement. "Not on the laces . . ."

The prosecutors were cornered. McAdam had contradicted himself, and now, as with that of Gleim, his credibility was being called into question.

But in redirect, Eakes clarified McAdam's response by asking him to read a larger portion of the trial transcript.

"Defense counsel showed you testimony of February 8, 1999. Were you asked any questions by any of the lawyers directly about the absence of blood on the laces?"

"No."

"What were you referring to in that specific answer that was asked of you by counsel? . . . Tell us what the answer was and what you were referring to."

" 'I am locating what you see in close-up,' " McAdam said.

In a different part of David's first trial, McAdam noted that he did, in fact, see stains on the laces.

"Yes, it's just a little bit forward of the laces and on the lace areas themselves."

Although Eakes saved McAdam's testimony from being a total loss, his contradictions would linger in the minds of the jurors, who ultimately had the difficult task of deciding just whom and what to believe.

By Monday, December 13, the jury had heard nine weeks of witness testimony. Signs of the holiday season were fast approaching as decorative lights strung along downtown Seattle streets made the city glow. Stop-sign poles were painted red and white, like candy canes, and wreaths hung from doors. That day, the state presented its last witness, Dr. Richard Harruff, to testify regarding the injuries to Julia Wilson.

As the medical examiner did so, David remained as stoic as ever. His expressionless face didn't help him. Every now and then, jurors, especially the female jurors, scanned his face for any show of emotion, expecting to see something in light of the fact that a close friend of his and her family were murdered. But it was not to be. As he had done during Harruff's previous testimony, David glanced at the grotesque autopsy photos and made notes, as if he were some sort of medical examiner's assistant. He didn't so much as flinch at the disturbing pictures.

What the jury might not have noticed from their seats was a change in David's physical appearance. By now, he had started to look gaunt, his high cheekbones more pronounced than ever before. His black Levi's Dockers were loose around the waist and they would have drooped more had he not had a shirt to tuck into them. Perhaps the stress of the situation was finally wearing on him.

That afternoon, the defense put its first witness on the stand. Joseph Robert Kern was a tall, dark-haired young man who wore blue jeans and cowboy boots and spoke with a faint Southern drawl. He said, "Yes, ma'am," and "No, sir," when addressing the lawyers, and answered questions promptly. He was one of only a few young witnesses who showed good manners. Kern, who moved to Little Rock, Arkansas, a year after the murders, testified that he had an affinity for knives and swords and that he'd seen David and Alex at Denny's on Saturday after the murders occurred. He told the jury he hadn't sensed anything strange or unusual about David's and Alex's behavior.

Jacob Brock, the twenty-one-year-old former boyfriend of Jeannie Kern (Joseph Kern's sister, who testified in the previous two trials), also got on the stand to testify that he, too, liked and collected knives and swords. Brock marched into the courtroom wearing ripped blue jeans, combat boots, and a T-shirt. His orange-tinted hair, cut in a Mohawk, caught everyone's attention.

The point the defense tried to make to the jurors was simple: just because David liked knives and swords didn't mean he was a killer.

The defense also called Marek Kasprzyk, its investigator, to put an extra dent in Marsha Rash's credibility. What Rash told him during a few separate interviews didn't jibe with what she testified to in court. But on cross-examination, Baird destroyed Kasprzyk's credibility by showing he focused his questions on Alex during his interviews, rather than on David and his alibi.

On Wednesday, the defense put on its last witnesses. Amber Ballard, who claimed she had had a relationship with David for fifteen months following his arrest, described him as a good person, a peacemaker in the Denny's crowd, not a killer. Even while he sat behind bars, David managed to keep a following of girls who idolized him. The jury also heard from Jeff Gomes and Bob Thompson, and listened to the testimony from Sarah Lamp without her being in the courtroom. Lamp was nine months pregnant at the time, and her doctor indicated she could not travel for health reasons, so the judge allowed her to testify by phone. But even by phone, Lamp, who since had married and changed her last name to Holland, proved to be an unreliable witness. She contradicted herself several times during both direct and cross-examination and she, too, changed her story from the previous two times she testified in court.

She was the last person to testify for the defense, and it might have been the wrong impression to leave with the jurors. The defense had tried to break the credibility of one of the state's key witnesses, Marsha Rash, yet if anyone in the case was not to be believed, it was Sarah, who from the beginning clearly knew more than she was willing to admit in court.

After an arduous nine weeks of witness testimony in the retrial of David Anderson, the attorneys prepared to deliver their closing arguments just as Christmas—only a week away—began to loom ominously close. Judge Ramsdell urged the prosecution and defense attorneys to hand the case over to the jury by the end of the week, fearing jurors would get distracted and annoyed if they were forced to change holiday plans.

The defense wrapped up its case in exactly two and a half days, but not without a battle. Ramsdell refused to allow the defense to put on two witnesses because of their anticipated vague testimony on matters the defense appeared unwilling to fully disclose. Connick then accused the judge of pressuring the defense to rush through its case so Ramsdell would not have to cancel his own vacation plans. For the first time since the trial began, the defense was now accusing the judge of misconduct. Ramsdell vehemently denied the accusation, indicating he planned to be in court Christmas week. His main goal was to get the case to the jury as soon as possible. He then berated the defense for making such an allegation.

Both sides officially rested their case the following day. For the jurors, who remained remarkably attentive and patient throughout the trial, the end was finally in sight.

On an unseasonably dry and warm December 16, 1999, relatives of both the Wilsons and the defendant, several members of the Bellevue Police Department, and court watchers streamed into Judge Ramsdell's courtroom to hear attorneys on both sides give their final words either accusing or defending the twenty-year-old young man who had sat poker-faced through often disturbing testimony. For the occasion, David wore a cotton sweater with multicolored pinstripes over a white dress shirt, and the same black slacks and shoes he had worn through most of the trial. Leslie Anderson wore a cherry-red cotton dress with a white blouse. When the court clerk commented on her holiday attire, she replied: "I'm trying to be festive for David."

Jeff Baird, who would deliver closing arguments for the state, wore his hallmark pinstriped black suit with a white button-down shirt and one of his usual conservative ties. Patty Eakes, who would give a rebuttal, donned the same suit she wore during opening statements.

In the back row, more than a dozen young attorneys from the Prosecutor's Office squeezed in to hear Baird's closing arguments. But conspicuously absent was the media frenzy present in Alex Baranyi's trial and David Anderson's first trial. It was not that the media hadn't been informed of the proceeding; a KIRO news cameraman arrived by noon to set up a camera in the courtroom and a microphone for its radio-station partner, and a couple of reporters from other news agencies arrived. Elaine Porterfield with the *Seattle Post-Intelligencer*, Ian Ith of the *Seattle Times*, and Noel Brady of the *Eastside Journal*—the only newspaper reporter to attend the entire trial—were also present. The murders of the Wilson family had occurred three years ago, and by now, it was old news that captured the interest of only a few media outlets.

The lack of media attention did not discourage Jeff Baird and Stephan Illa from delivering dramatic speeches. But before they could begin, Pete Connick, as was his practice, rose to make one last motion regarding closing arguments. He asked the judge to ban several Bellevue Police officers and detectives from sitting in the front row, reserved for the press, fearing the police "show of force" would prejudice the jurors. However, Ramsdell was not inclined to keep anyone from hearing the arguments. The judge said he expected a packed courtroom and any police officers who might attend would have to get in line with the press.

The goal of the day, somewhat atypical from the rest of the trial, was efficiency. In order to allow both sides enough time to deliver closing arguments, Judge Ramsdell gave a brief obligatory reading of jury instructions just after noon, finishing at 12:30 P.M. Then he released the jurors for a half-hour lunch break. He reminded them that they each would get a copy of the instructions when they began deliberations.

In addition to cutting short the lunch break, Ramsdell imposed a three-hour time limit for each side to give its arguments; both sides would have an opportunity to speak, no matter how late it got. With or without time limits, this would prove to be the longest day of the trial.

Just after lunch, at 1:18 P.M., Jeff Baird, poised and relaxed, opened up a folder of notes and began what he hoped would be the last time he and the jurors would have to reenter the horrible scene inside the Wilson home.

Baird first provided verbal snapshots of the murders: Kim being lured to the park by someone she thought was a friend; a couple attacked in their bed; and a young woman who emerged from her bedroom and saw two young men she might have recognized as her schoolmates coming toward her with knives.

As he had done in closing arguments in David's first trial, Baird graciously thanked the jury for its patience and attention, acknowledging the trial had lasted much longer than anyone expected. "This case has been ours long enough. It's about time to give it to you," he said.

Because the state has the burden of proof, it also has the added burden of explaining the law to the jurors, which Baird did as quickly and succinctly as possible. And after doing that, his strategy in closing arguments became clear. He would present the jury first with the defense's flawed theories on David's innocence before reiterating to the jury the state's theories on his guilt.

Baird reminded the jurors of the two defense theories, one of which he whimsically called the AAA theory: Alex acted alone. The second was that some other suspect acted with Alex.

"The defense tried to have it both ways," Baird said. "The truth is, you can't have it both ways." The reason why is because the evidence, both testimonial and physical, would contradict both theories.

To show that, Baird began a lengthy discussion of the evidence presented in court. Two black shoelace bows, one of which tested positive for William Wilson's blood, were retrieved from Alex Baranyi's trash can during a search. Baird told the jury the defense tried to argue those shoelaces were in David's boots at the time of the murders, but there were several problems with that theory. "The first is that big old bloody shoeprint stain on the back of William Wilson's shirt"—a stain that was not made by David's bloodstained boots. Another problem was that, even though the defense tried to prove there were no bloodstains found on David's pair of boot laces, expert testimony in David's previous trial already indicated blood had, in fact, spattered on them.

Baird went on to suggest that if the defense would have the jury believe another suspect acted with Alex, who was that suspect? David Anderson had the motive and the opportunity to kill Kim Wilson and her family.

Baird suggested that no one would kill over a debt of some $300.

"Let me suggest a different motive to you: he killed Kim Wilson because he had to," Baird said. "Mr. Anderson was a person who wanted to kill. He talked about it to all of his friends." Baird went on to suggest that David killed Kim Wilson because she was the only one who confronted him, the only one who said no to his criminal intentions.

Baird acknowledged that the state had very few pieces of physical evidence to prove David killed the Wilsons, but what evidence it did have was powerful. "There isn't very much. Look at how little we have: a rope, a truck, a cigarette butt. That's basically it."

He reminded the jury that the rope found around Kim's neck matched a piece of rope found in the black pickup truck, and in Neil Deacy's garage (which Deacy kept for his job as a power utilities repairman), and David had borrowed the truck from Marsha Rash, who had parked it in a lot at Factoria Mall, where she worked. In addition, Nanda Prabhakar testified that she and Kim saw David at the mall the day of the murders. David had also admitted to police he was driving the truck the night of the murders. Hair from both David and Alex also was found in the truck, which meant David was not distancing himself from Alex at the time of the murders, as the defense tried to prove. Finally, a Woodridge resident had seen the truck at the park at around midnight the night of the murders.

Less compelling evidence was a swipe of blood found on the floor mat on the passenger side of the truck—a sample that the defense would argue was not blood, but some sort of human biological material which the state's own experts testified could be something other than blood, such as saliva or mucus.

But the cigarette butt seemed to be the most compelling

evidence. The Marlboro butt found by Detective Jerry Johnson near Kim's body tested positive for her DNA. She
smoked a cigarette that night—her last. That could only
mean she was comfortable with whomever she was with.
Kim was scared of Alex Baranyi. Because the jury in this
trial knew that Alex Baranyi was already convicted of the
murders, Baird urged them to consider that Kim would
never have gone to Water Tower Park alone with Alex; she
had to have gone with someone she trusted. "Who do they
have in common, Alex and Kim?" Baird asked.

David got caught up in a web of lies that Baird was now
untangling strand by strand in front of the jurors. He lied to
police when he told them the last time he saw Kim Wilson
was a few days before the murders. "He lied when he said he
stayed at Alex Baranyi's house the entire night. We all know
Mr. Baranyi took time out that night to kill four people."

And then there was David's demeanor, Baird said.
Through truths and lies, David's demeanor remained the
same. "The person who chuckled and yawned through police interrogation is the true David Anderson." As Baird
spoke, David remained poker-faced, but the back of his neck
turned red. Several jurors looked at him, hoping to see
changes in his facial expression. He remained stoic.

Baird had made a strong case of guilt against David Anderson regarding Kim. Now he wanted to move on to the rest
of the Wilsons.

"If Mr. Anderson had stopped with Kim, there would have
been no blood at all," Baird said.

But David Anderson chose to enter the Wilson home and
execute the rest of Kim's family, Baird said. And so it was
that the prosecutor once again took the jurors on a journey
through the nightmare in the home. The motive was not to
acquire the Wilsons' property, Baird suggested to the jury.
The true motive was written all over the bruised and battered
bodies of the Wilsons. The attack was excessive and gratu-

itous. The motive was "murder as an experience." Rose, Bill, and Julia Wilson were each beaten and stabbed to death, and then beaten and stabbed some more, Baird said.

After an hour and a half, Baird called for a break on behalf of the court reporter. Baird was just warming up, like an actor on stage giving a soliloquy. The jurors did not take their eyes off him. When he reapproached them at 3 P.M., he hit his stride, injecting even more energy into his delivery.

Baird came back to the defense's theory that Alex Baranyi's black shoelaces were in David Anderson's boots. In order for anyone to accept that theory, then Alex would have to have taken David's shoes, switched his laces with David's, killed four people, cut the shoelace bows off, put David's laces back in, and returned the boots to David's bedroom. This wasn't reasonable, Baird said. "Why would anyone go through the trouble of trying to sell a theory like this?" he asked, then answered, "It's because of the boots, isn't it? The boots are overwhelming evidence."

Baird acknowledged that no one's memory is perfect, and that can make lay witness testimony unreliable. But there was one witness that, no matter how many years passed, would never lie.

"These are the best witnesses, folks," he said, holding up David's boots. "These boots. This boot was right in the thick of it, Mr. Anderson's right boot." Baird reminded the jury that blood had spattered, sprayed, and smeared all over the boot. The left boot was "sprayed with a fine, almost invisible chorus of blood," Baird said. It was Julia's blood, as she took her last gasps of air. "And you have to lean in close to hear the testimony."

At 3:29 P.M., Baird thanked the jury again for its patience and unyielding attention. As he took his seat, three female jurors wiped tears from their faces as others let out deep, long breaths.

The tide of the afternoon shifted once Stephan Illa ap-

proached the jury with a fistful of index cards. Illa staved off
any further flow of emotions from the jury box by quickly
jumping into his closing arguments, beginning with an analogy of the state's case. He took a much lighter approach to
closing arguments than Baird's more serious, emotionally
charged approach. The switch was abrupt for jurors, some of
whom literally went from crying to laughing.

Illa asked the jurors to pretend they were food critics in a
restaurant called "Chez Baird's." Patty Eakes was to be the
waitress, and Jeff Gomes the cook's help. As Illa set the
stage for the restaurant staff, he contorted his body into a little teapot pose and slightly lifted up a leg in a bad imitation
of Eakes as a waitress. The jurors then were to imagine they
were there to sample Baird's beef stew—what several press
members commented as a creative, albeit poor, analogy for
this particular case, in which the attack on three of the
Wilsons had been described by numerous witnesses and attorneys in terms such as "slicing" and "chopping"—cooking
vocabulary.

Some of the jurors laughed, while others rolled their eyes
and seemed to glare with looks of incredulity etched on their
faces. Four people had been viciously murdered, and a defense attorney was making light of the situation by compar-
ing it to beef stew? Illa was trying to take the emotional sting
out of Baird's closing arguments, but clearly, he was offend-
ing not only the relatives of the Wilsons but members of the
jury as well.

Whether he noticed the expressions on people's faces or
not, Illa went on with his analogy, starting with the expert
witnesses in the case. He likened them to guest chefs who
merely boiled the water to cook elements of the stew. Dr.
Ranajit Chakravorti, a DNA expert, and Ross Gardner, the
crime-scene-reconstruction expert, specifically were flown
in from out of state with their extensive résumés and unblemished reputations to merely impress the jurors, Illa sug-

gested. They added nothing to the case—or to the "stew"—besides their good name.

Illa suggested that Baird indiscriminately tossed any piece of evidence he could—"ingredients"—into the case simply because investigators had found it. "When you get back to the jury room, it's going to be crowded because they put in every piece of evidence," whether it related to the case or not, Illa said. For instance, an empty pack of "Dave's" brand of cigarettes and a Rainier beer bottle cap found at the park were placed into evidence, as were a cut braid of Marsha Rash's hair found in the Boyds' storage room, Julia Wilson's chemistry book found in her bedroom, and knives and swords taken from Alex's and David's bedrooms, as well as a knife owned by one of the witnesses, and one which Detective Gomes ordered through *Excaliber* magazine. He described the knives and swords as "red herring" in the beef stew, thrown into the mix to distract the jurors from the fact that investigators never found any of the murder weapons.

"It shows you what they didn't have, and what they wish they had," Illa said.

As the defense had done throughout the trial in cross-examination, Illa tried to use the state's own witnesses to prove his client's innocence. Illa reminded the jury that Ross Gardner testified that if a bat had been used in the attack on Bill and Rose Wilson, divets would have appeared in the low ceiling. There were no divets. However, he failed to mention that divets consistent with a bat were found in the frame of Julia Wilson's bedroom door. Dr. Harruff suggested it would take a stout blade, stronger than an ordinary kitchen knife, to do that sort of damage on Rose, Bill, and Julia, disproving a theory of the prosecution that David used kitchen knives he had stashed underneath his bed for the attack.

At 4:30 P.M.—a half hour past the usual time the jury was released—the air-conditioning system in the courtroom abruptly shut off. Illa's closing arguments were slipping past closing time for the King County Courthouse. Several spectators began to undo buttons and pull off their jackets and sweaters. Outside the courtroom, the temperature hovered just above forty degrees, but inside, the body heat generated from so many people pressed together filled the air with an uncomfortable stuffiness. During a later break, the court clerk would open both doors of the courtroom and bring in a large, square fan to try to circulate cool air into the room.

Now Illa wanted to talk about the blood.

"There was blood everywhere," he said, letting the word "everywhere" hang in the crowded air before continuing. Police investigators, hoping to link David to the crime, searched the truck he was driving and took four bags of clothes from his home and knives and bats from in or around his bedroom. "They didn't find any blood at all," Illa said. That wasn't entirely true. Illa conveniently failed to mention the blood found on David's boots. He also didn't say that perhaps the reason that police didn't find any bloody clothes or murder weapons was because David and Alex already got rid of them.

Then, out of the blue, Illa suggested a surprising new theory: that there were two other attackers besides Alex in the Wilson home at the time of the murders.

Forensic experts who tested the black shoelace bows found in Alex's room discovered a passive blood drop with mixed DNA; the blood was determined to have come from two separate sources. However, David Anderson, Alex Baranyi, and all four members of the Wilson family were ruled out as sources of that blood.

"There's two other people's blood on those laces . . . There had to have been two other people" at the crime scene, Illa said.

To believe that, jurors would have to accept that two suspects had to have been cut and bleeding at the Wilson home and had to have stood directly above Alex's shoes sometime during the murders for the blood to drop onto the laces. It was clear the defense lawyer at this point was reaching for whatever theory he could manufacture.

After trying to dismantle the state's physical evidence, or lack thereof, Illa then took jabs at the state's witnesses.

"If there's anything we've seen in this trial it's that human memory is frail," Illa said. He started with Marsha Rash, a crucial witness to both the state and the defense. "There's only one person who says David Anderson was wearing these boots on the night of the murders, and that's Marsha Rash. She has told a story. Her story has changed like a weather vane. What Marsha Rash did was as she became more and more angry, her story got more and more detailed about David Anderson. What you have to ask yourself is, 'Is Marsha Rash credible?' Some of the reasons for her bias are evident. Shortly after he was arrested, she learned he was cheating on her with a woman named Sunshine Crane . . . Can you believe Marsha Rash?"

The obvious answer to anyone sitting in on her testimony was, "No." But can anyone believe David Anderson, who lied to police on numerous occasions?

Credibility is the only leg that lay witnesses have to stand on, and Illa did a fine job at knocking each of them down, especially Marsha Rash.

Just after 5 P.M., the jurors began to shift in their seats, and some looked at the clock on the wall behind them. They had been listening intently to closing arguments for four hours now and appeared to be growing weary. And Illa was barely halfway finished.

Then, in a bizarre moment in his closing arguments, Illa talked about a piece of evidence that didn't come to light until midway through the trial: the phone bill which indicated a call to Germany from about 2 A.M. to 2:30 A.M. on Saturday, January 4. Illa tried to make Gomes' investigation

look shoddy by telling jurors that he never followed up on
that call. Yet it was not true; Gomes followed up shortly after receiving the phone bill from Bill Wilson's sister. "Don't
you think he would have wanted to reach out and touch
someone in *Deutschland*?" The gratuitous comment
sparked guffaws from a few jurors and several from court
spectators. Were they laughing because it was funny, or
were they laughing at Illa's outlandish behavior and ges-
tures?

The heat was finally getting to Illa, too, and he wiped his
forehead with the sleeve of his blazer. The pressure was also
on to get through his closing quickly, because the jury was
obviously growing impatient and starting to lose focus.

At around 5:30 P.M., Illa could sense he was losing the jurors' interest. He told them he was about to wrap up and finally, just after 6 P.M., he did.

"These were senseless, brutal crimes, committed by a
senseless, brutal person: Alex Baranyi," Illa said. "He committed those crimes with the help from someone, and that is
not David Anderson."

At 6:15 P.M., Eakes began her rebuttal. She pointed out
several areas in Illa's closing arguments where she claimed
that he outright lied or misstated the evidence. She reiterated
various points Baird made in his arguments, with a focus on
the damaging evidence of David's boots. Then Eakes tried to
give David a chance to testify, since he had never taken the
stand in his own defense. She read the last part of a journal
entry that, as she said, offered a rare glimpse into the mind
of David Anderson.

Eakes read: " 'I see myself walking my own path of darkness and light. I see people fall to my touch of extacy [sic],
and I see people fall to my charming smile of friendship.
And I wonder which of those smiles I have feigned and
which ones are true.'

"Mr. Anderson was many things to many people," Eakes said. "The fact that he told some people about his intention to kill the Wilsons and didn't tell others doesn't mean anything about whether he abandoned his plan."

In the end, Eakes made a full circle and brought her discussion back to the victims.

"I would ask maybe one thing sometime during your deliberations, at some moment just take a moment and think about the Wilsons, not for who you got to know them to be in this trial with evidence of their broken bodies, but think about who they were." She held up the photographs of each member of the Wilson family, as she had done in her opening remarks. "What this case is about is what happened to them on January 3, 1997. Those four people, how they were viciously attacked and murdered by David Anderson. They waited three years for justice, and that decision is now in your hands."

At 7:30 P.M., when Eakes finished her rebuttal, Connick managed to get one last word in.

"Objection," he said. He urged the judge to strike Eakes' last comment, which clearly was aimed at stirring emotions among the jurors. Judge Ramsdell sustained the objection, and asked that the jurors not rely on sympathy when they begin deliberations.

Now it was the judge's turn to deliver some final words.

"Ladies and gentlemen, this has been a very long day for all of you," Ramsdell said. "At this point in time, the various lawyers have done their job, I've done mine. Now the case is in your hands for what is the most important part of the entire process, which is deliberations."

By now, there were only fifteen jurors, as one had been excused earlier in the trial for health reasons. After Judge Ramsdell excused three alternates, he dismissed the remaining jurors so they could go home and begin the decision-making process the next day. Shortly afterward, Connick made his fourteenth motion for mistrial after Eakes made what he believed to be potentially prejudicial remarks during rebuttal, which were sustained by the judge. However, after hearing arguments from both sides, Judge Ramsdell believed that the comments would not be sufficient grounds for a mistrial and once again denied the defense's motion. The case was nearing its home stretch, much to the relief of everyone involved, especially Ramsdell. Despite all the skirmishes he had to quell, he appreciated the passion and persistence shown by all four attorneys.

"If there ever was a well-fought battle, this was it," Ramsdell would later say.

At 9 A.M. on Friday morning, December 17, the hallways outside Judge Jeffrey Ramsdell's courtroom were empty for the first time in two months. But behind locked doors in the jury room, twelve jurors—seven men and five women—were discussing the fate of twenty-year-old David Carpenter Anderson. The only activity inside the courtroom came from other defendants standing before the judge in red jail suits for hearings on other matters. Three years ago around this time, Kim Wilson was home for the holidays, spending time with her family in what would be the last Christmas for all of them.

In David's first trial, members of the press made bets on how long it would take for the jury to deliberate. Some guessed a few hours, others estimated a few days. But no one imagined it would take eight days for any decision to come down. That decision—a hung jury—was devastating to the prosecutors and to relatives of the Wilsons.

This time, every one guessed the jury would deliberate through the end of the day and then return with a verdict in the early part of the following week—Christmas week. So by midafternoon, almost everyone but David's parents and the Wilsons' relatives had left the courthouse. Nobody knew the jurors had already taken their first votes that day.

When members of the media were paged by the court bailiff at 3:55 P.M. that Friday afternoon, they knew something was up.

Bruce and Leslie Anderson held hands, and bent their heads in prayer at the far end of the hallway, while a few friends and members of the Wilson family huddled about twenty feet from Judge Ramsdell's courtroom. It was a week before Christmas, and all the Andersons wanted was for David to come home.

The court reporter was one of the first to arrive back at the courtroom. Patty Eakes, who had been sitting in a steam room on the Eastside, rushed back to the courthouse and consulted with the Wilson relatives. Everyone who showed up at court braved the wet and blustery weather. Television news crews began arriving in force to set up their equipment outside the newsroom, and the last remaining prosecutors interested in the case once again found their way to the courtroom.

Jeff Gomes and Bob Thompson, who were also paged, maneuvered through the Friday-afternoon commute to get to downtown Seattle from Bellevue. Stephan Illa and Pete Connick were also notified.

At 4:10 P.M., one person—in addition to the defendant—was still missing: Jeff Baird. Baird had left early that afternoon, like Eakes, and was relaxing into a professional massage when he was paged by the court bailiff. Baird pulled on his court clothes, donned black-rimmed glasses (which he never wore to court), and rushed to the courthouse, his hair still glistening with rubbing oil.

The hallway outside Courtroom 932 quickly filled up with people and commotion. At 4:30 P.M., David Anderson was led into the courtroom once again, his attorneys walking together in front of him to prevent members of the media from getting too close. He made no comment to reporters and walked with his head held high. He had the same confident stride as in the first trial, and as he had throughout his life.

The press row was more crowded than the day before, with TV reporters jamming in next to newspaper reporters. Jerry Mahoney, Rose Wilson's brother, and his wife, Jacquie, sat in the second row with a few friends who also attended the entire trial. In the third row, an alternate juror who came to hear the verdict sat next to Bruce Anderson, who clutched his wife's hand. An unidentified couple—reportedly David's aunt and uncle—sat next to Leslie Anderson.

At 4:35 P.M., the jurors quietly filed back into their seats. Their expressionless faces gave no hint of their decision. However, the press and experienced courtroom watchers knew a speedy return often indicated a guilty verdict.

Even though it didn't look good for David, he laughed and bantered with Pete Connick, which was unusual. He usually spoke with Stephan Illa, rarely to Connick.

The judge asked the jury foreperson to stand up and identify him or herself, at which time Rodney White rose to hand over the jury's verdict sheets to court bailiff Donna Beatty, who in turn passed the verdict sheets to Judge Ramsdell. The judge quietly skimmed the pages without saying a word, then handed them to the court clerk.

David, who was sitting poised in his chair as he always did, looked squarely at the nervous clerk, Richard Crumley, who was about to announce his fate.

"We, the jury, find the defendant, David C. Anderson"— Richard paused for an unbearably brief moment—"guilty of the crime of premeditated murders."

There was shuffling amid the press row as reporters hastily noted the verdict and glanced over their shoulders to see the reactions of David's family and the Wilsons' relatives.

As David heard the verdict, his shoulders suddenly slackened. He lowered his face, and, in a rare moment, his stone-cold mask finally crumbled. For the first time in over nine weeks, he finally showed some emotion—the same emotion he probably expressed when he slaughtered the four members of the Wilson family on the night of January 3, 1997, and that emotion was rage. Pure, wholesale, unequivocal rage.

Leslie Anderson dropped her head and sobbed as Bruce Anderson, his face and neck bright red, tried to comfort her. The muscles in his face tensed, as if he were trying to hold back tears of his own. Relatives and friends of the Wilsons wept quietly as well. Finally, after three years, there was justice.

The judge then suggested the attorneys set a time in January for David's sentencing. But it would only be a formality. The conviction of aggravated murder automatically carries a life sentence without the possibility of parole. Similar to his best friend, Alex Baranyi, David would receive four life sentences for the four innocent lives he took. Under the accomplice liability rule, David was as guilty as Alex for being present at the time of the crime, no matter what specific role he played in the murders.

As Eakes and Baird left the courtroom, Eakes was overcome with emotion and began to cry. Baird trailed quietly behind her. They were met at the coat rack by relatives of the Wilsons, who hugged Eakes and shook Baird's and Gomes' hands. They thanked the prosecutors and the detective for finally giving them closure.

The two security guards who stood blocking the door once again placed handcuffs on David and led him out of the courtroom. The Andersons quickly exited right behind their son, who was now a convicted multiple murderer.

Bruce shepherded Leslie and their youngest son, Stephen, into an elevator while the prosecutors, who were cornered at the end of the hall, spoke with reporters. The elevator doors slowly pushed together, shutting out the sound of a mother's long, loud wail.

Epilogue

For the first time in more than a decade, according to FBI statistics, violent crime rates across the country are going down, but at the same time, a disturbing phenomenon is emerging: violent crime among youths is surging. To give one example, the number of murderers age ten to seventeen has tripled between 1984 and 1994 alone.

More and more youths like David Anderson and Alex Baranyi are getting swept into the current of crime. Their deviant behavior is sending an alarming message to society about how we are raising, or failing to raise, our children.

"Sociopathic teenagers are the new breed of criminals," according to Michael Rustigan, a criminologist at San Francisco State University who specializes in juvenile crime.

Many of the crimes being committed are senseless, self-indulgent acts fused with youthful innocence. These children lack the capacity for any sympathy for their victims. Their violent behavior "suggests a certain moral numbness," Rustigan said. He believes what these kids often don't understand is that their actions have consequences: to take the life of another often results in sacrificing their own by spending the rest of their lives behind bars.

More alarming than the rise in violent crime among kids is that so many are killing just for kicks.

Thrill kills are rapidly gaining attention across the country as more of them occur. One of the most notable cases took place over seventy-five years ago in Chicago, far removed from the rain-swept landscape of the Puget Sound region. The crime bears striking similarities to David and Alex's story.

Nathan Leopold, eighteen, was a young graduate of the University of Chicago. His friend, Richard Loeb, seventeen, had already graduated from the University of Michigan. Like David and Alex, Nathan and Richard were inseparable friends. Their lives entangled together in emotional and social knots that were impossible to untie.

Products of wealthy Chicago families, Nathan and Richard had discussed the idea of committing murder for years before they finally did it in 1924. They signed a pact, and drew up a hit list of potential victims. They selected a fourteen-year-old boy named Bob Franks, whom they abducted one afternoon as the boy left his exclusive private school.

As Leopold drove, Loeb dangled a rope in front of the frightened boy's face. Instead of using it, Loeb suddenly grabbed a chisel, which he plunged four times into his victim.

Leopold and Loeb left the boy bleeding to death in the backseat of the car as they ate an elaborate dinner at a Chicago restaurant. They then took the body to a remote, swampy area where they stuffed it into a culvert drainpipe, which was where they left a ransom note, and accidentally left Leopold's eyeglasses, which ultimately linked them to the murder.

More recently, the thrill kill of two pizza deliverymen captured the headlines, just a few months after the Wilson family slayings.

The victims, Georgio Gallara, twenty-four, and Jeremy

Giordano, twenty-two, were lured by Thomas Koskovich, eighteen, and Jayson Vreeland, seventeen, to an abandoned house on a desolate road in Franklin, New Jersey. When they arrived, the deliverymen were met with a barrage of gunshots. Giordano's car rolled into a small marsh, where they were found the following morning. They died from multiple gunshot wounds. Slices of pizza lay scattered about the crime scene as if the killers were making a mockery of their crime and their victims. One of the first medical workers at the scene later told a reporter: "I know in my heart that they did it just for kicks. They wanted to see what it was like to kill someone and see what it felt like inside."

Just what drives teenagers to kill for the thrill is unclear. Society casts the blame on the usual spectrum of social ills—high divorce rates, the never-ending war on drugs, teenage pregnancy, and the accessibility of weapons. But the answers could lie in something far more innocuous—the games kids play.

On April 20, 1999, teenagers Eric Harris and Dylan Klebold armed themselves with a shockingly large arsenal of guns and bombs and stormed their Littleton, Colorado, high school, killing thirteen people and injuring dozens more. The two were part of a marginalized group known as the Trenchcoat Mafia and, much like David and Alex, were known to be a part of the Gothic subculture, wearing black clothing and listening to the funereal rock music of Marilyn Manson. They were also obsessed with the violent, interactive video game Doom, in which players rack up points by killing people.

That was the same game favored by a Pearl, Mississippi, boy and a Springfield, Oregon, teenager, both of whom stalked into their schools and began firing at classmates and teachers.

While David and Alex didn't play the particular game of Doom, they reveled in equally violent and massacre-oriented video and fantasy games. Just two days after murdering the Wilsons, the two spent several hours playing Dungeons and Dragons on their Nintendo. They also regularly participated in an extension of fantasy video games through live-action role-playing games in which a group of people gather to act out a story line in a make-believe setting constructed by one of the participants. Gamers, as participants are called, take on the persona of a character, anything from a dwarf to a magician to a fallen angel, and must navigate their way through the fantasy world, earning experience points by "killing" other participants.

In *Shared Fantasy*, a book about role-playing games, author Gary Alan Fine writes: "These games are centered on killing and death—the struggle between 'good' and 'evil,' in which evil must be wiped out without mercy or pity . . . Within the context of the game, players are oriented toward murder and death without consideration of any moral niceties."

Many people, among them a renowned psychologist who evaluated Alex, believe that David and Alex perhaps blurred the lines between fantasy and reality. While it would be a stretch to say the boys' participation in these games led them to kill, it's likely that playing them enhanced the boys' propensity for violence.

We may never know why David Anderson and Alex Baranyi killed the four innocent people, but perhaps tangled somewhere in the strands of this story, there are clues that will emerge to help us understand why this happened, and how we can prevent a crime like this from recurring.

Compelling True Crime Thrillers

PERFECT MURDER, PERFECT TOWN
THE UNCENSORED STORY OF THE JONBENET MURDER AND THE GRAND JURY'S SEARCH FOR THE TRUTH
by Lawrence Schiller
0-06-109696-2/ $7.99 US/ $10.99 Can

A CALL FOR JUSTICE
A NEW ENGLAND TOWN'S FIGHT TO KEEP A STONE COLD KILLER IN JAIL
by Denise Lang
0-380-78077-1/ $6.50 US/ $8.99 Can

SECRETS NEVER LIE
THE DEATH OF SARA TOKARS— A SOUTHERN TRAGEDY OF MONEY, MURDER, AND INNOCENCE BETRAYED
by Robin McDonald
0-380-77752-5/ $6.99 US/ $8.99 Can

THE GOODFELLA TAPES
by George Anastasia
0-380-79637-6/ $5.99 US/ $7.99 Can

THE SUMMER WIND
THOMAS CAPANO AND THE MURDER OF ANNE MARIE FAHEY
by George Anastasia
0-06-103100-3/ $6.99 US/ $9.99 Can

A WARRANT TO KILL
A TRUE STORY OF OBSESSION, LIES AND A KILLER COP
by Kathryn Casey
0-380-78041-0/ $6.99 US/ $9.99 Can

Available wherever books are sold or please call 1-800-331-3761 to order.

CRM 0700

The Best in Biographies

HAVE A NICE DAY!
A Tale of Blood and Sweatsocks
by Mankind

0-06-103101-1/$7.99 US/$10.99 Can

THE ROCK SAYS
by The Rock

0-06-103116-X/$7.99 US/$10.99 Can

JACK AND JACKIE:
Portrait of an American Marriage
by Christopher Andersen

0-380-73031-6/$6.99 US/$8.99 Can

WALK THIS WAY:
The Autobiography of Aerosmith
by Aerosmith, with Stephen Davis

0-380-79531-0/ $7.99 US/ $9.99 Can

EINSTEIN: THE LIVES AND TIMES
by Ronald W. Clark

0-380-01159-X/$7.99 US/$10.99 Can

IT'S ALWAYS SOMETHING
by Gilda Radner

0-380-81322-X/ $13.00 US/ $19.95 Can

I, TINA *by Tina Turner and Kurt Loder*

0-380-70097-2/ $6.99 US/ $9.99 Can

....